1936

PARODIES
AND
IMITATIONS

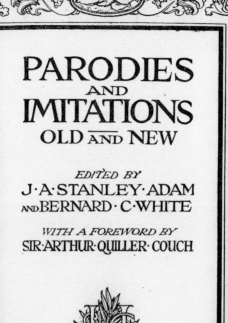

PARODIES
AND
IMITATIONS
OLD AND NEW

EDITED BY
J·A·STANLEY·ADAM
AND BERNARD·C·WHITE

WITH A FOREWORD BY
SIR·ARTHUR·QUILLER·COUCH

LONDON
HUTCHINSON & CO.
PATERNOSTER ROW

First published in 1912

FOREWORD

ON THE GENTLE ART

SAYS Ruskin, in his lecture on *The Mystery of Life and its Arts*—"The moment a man can really do his work he becomes speechless about it. All words become idle to him—all theories." With a rhetorical flourish he goes on to ask, "Does a bird need to theorise about building its nest, or boast of it when built?"

Well, as to the bird, I don't know, and (with all respect) I very much doubt if Ruskin knew; though by the noise the sparrows were making, a few weeks ago, in the ivies outside this window of mine, I should judge that—as they say in Parliament —"the answer to the second part of the question is in the affirmative." But if Ruskin be right in his general proposition, that a man straightway falls silent about any work he can really do, it would seem that the editors of this anthology in asking me to write a Preface have paid a left-handed compliment, the blow of which is sharpened rather than softened by their gracefully including two or three parodies of my own!

Well, well—*en los nidos de antaño no hai pájaros*

hogaño ! I may theorise a little, perhaps, about last year's nests.

Now, the first thing to be said about Parody is that it plays with the gods : its fun is taken with Poetry, which all good men admit to be a beautiful and adorable thing, and some would have to be a holy thing.[1] It follows then that Parody must be delicate ground, off which the profane and vulgar should be carefully warned. A deeply religious man may indulge a smile at this or that in his religion ; as a truly devout lover may rally his mistress on her foibles, since for him they make her the more enchanting. Without being conscious of it, he knows unerringly "how far to go," as they say ; he cannot offend, because his true reverence does not so much control as permeate him :

> Thou art my life, my love, my heart,
> The very eyes of me :

and the tone of the laugh tells of that sweet understanding. So, or almost so, it should be with the parodist. He must be friends with the gods, and worthy of their company, before taking these pleasant liberties with them. Nor, if we keep a

[1] There are, of course, false gods in Poetry. But parodies of these directly expose their falsity, while parodies of true poetry subtly pay homage to its truth. Moreover, we may say generally that in parody, as elsewhere, exposure of the false (though useful and necessary) ranks below illustration of the true.

mind at once fearless and modest in approaching them, shall we fail of that friendship, thanks to their magnificent condescension. As Emerson has noted:

> " It is remarkable that involuntarily we always read as superior beings. Universal history, the poets, the romancers, do not in their stateliest picture—in the sacerdotal, the imperial palaces, in the triumphs of will or of genius anywhere lose our ear, anywhere make us feel that we intrude, that this is for our betters; but rather it is true that, in their grandest strokes, there we feel most at home. All that Shakespeare says of the King, yonder slip of a boy that reads in the corner feels to be true of himself. . . . "

If this be true—and I think no one will dispute it—then the more shame must we feel when an outsider comes along and takes advantage of their noble condescension to call hail-fellow with Milton, for example, or to slap Wordsworth on the back. A David may dance before the ark, to which an Uzzah may not put forth a hand : and even David must lay his account with Michal's shocked protestantism.

The material, then, on which Parody works is Poetry, and preferably great Poetry. Its method consists in a nice apposition of the incongruous, catching as nearly as possible the authentic speech of the bard and applying it unexpectedly, even absurdly, to things beneath his notice; thereby reminding him that he is mortal without denying —rather, insisting—that he is divine. In its easiest form Parody will take his actual words, and turn them to some new and ridiculous connotation. It is a trick not far removed from punning; yet, when well executed, it gives pleasure, I think, to anyone not born a prig. For an instance, I choose a few lines of Mr. Hartley Carrick's, one of our younger parodists. He takes Wordsworth's "She was a Phantom of delight," and applies the actual words, or some of them, which in our minds carry their own associations, to—a motor-omnibus.

> *It was a phantom of delight*
> *When first it gleam'd upon my sight,*
> And seem'd to hint a time of bliss
> In store for the metropolis . . .
> A *perfect* motor, *nobly plann'd*
> To traverse Holborn and the Strand. . . .
>
> But now from early morn till e'en
> I hear *the pulse of the machine*
> That clatters past my humble door
> In one unending shriek and roar;
> With aching head and deafen'd ear
> I note with apprehensive fear
> *The traveller 'twixt life and death*
> Endeavour to regain his breath,
> As once again it skids away
> To haunt, to startle, and waylay.

FOREWORD

At the risk of being numbered among the friends of Mr. Peter Magnus, I confess that these absurdities amuse me. But now let us compare the above with a specimen of parody carried almost, if not quite, to its fullest powers, and for this purpose let us choose another "imitation" of Wordsworth, this time by J. K. Stephen (genius untimely lost):

POETIC LAMENTATION ON THE INSUFFICIENCY OF STEAM LOCOMOTION IN THE LAKE DISTRICT

Bright Summer spreads his various hue
　　O'er nestling vales and mountains steep,
Glad birds are singing in the blue,
　　In joyous chorus bleat the sheep.
But men are walking to and fro,
　　Are riding, driving, far and near,
And nobody as yet can go
　　By train to Buttermere.

Wake, England, wake! 'tis now the hour
　　To sweep away this black disgrace—
The want of locomotion proves
　　In so enjoyable a place.
Nature has done her part, and why
　　Is mightier Man in his to fail?
I want to hear the porters cry,
　　"Change here for Ennerdale!"

　　.　　　.　　　.　　　.　　　.

Presumptuous Nature! do not rate
　　Unduly high thy humble lot,

> Nor vainly strive to emulate
>   The fame of Stephenson and Watt.
> The beauties which thy lavish pride
>   Has scatter'd through the smiling land
> Are little worth till sanctified
>   By Man's completing hand.

The form is here true Wordsworth, from the verbose title to the last exquisite quatrain, with scarcely a lapse. "Enjoyable" in stanza 2 is not quite Wordsworth, but a little more than Wordsworth, and "the fame of Stephenson and Watt" occupies Stephen for a moment with his own cleverness. On the other hand, what, for example, could be more exquisitely Wordsworthian in operation of mind and in actual cadence of speech than—

> But men are walking to and fro,
> Are riding, driving, far and near . . . ?

There is more than this, with almost diabolical cunning Stephen has seized on the subject that of all others would have engaged Wordsworth; has turned it upside down; and has presented the poet uttering to us in his own authentic words precisely the last sentiments his admirers would expect him to utter. And yet again (so clever it is), we are left with a frolic doubt (remembering Wordsworth's ineradicable streak of the prosaic and his actual return upon himself in his later years) that somehow, had it been possible to fill the great man up with laughing gas, in the moments preceding unconsciousness he might not improbably have uttered these very sentiments as he would assuredly have cast them in similar words. I call this the perfection of Parody.

But if the parodist can do so much as this, it follows further that Parody must be a form of Criticism, and may be enlightening as it is vivacious. Again I turn for the simplest illustration to the work of a young practitioner. Some years ago, in his last Oxford lectures, Mr. Froude lamented that no poet in this country had arisen to undertake a national epic of the great Elizabethan seamen; a hint which has since been acted on by Mr. Alfred Noyes in his fine *Drake*, an epic poem in twelve books. Now in any long poem of the sea there inheres the difficulty that while the action of Epic has to be rapid and the verse correspondingly rapid (as Matthew Arnold noted in his Lectures *On Translating Homer*), actually the business of seafaring is full of patience and *longueurs*. You cannot upon the wide Atlantic hustle action and reaction to and fro as upon the fields of windy Troy. Homer, when he came to the *Odyssey*, dodged a part of this difficulty by casting a whole mass of his hero's adventures into the form of reported speech—a traveller's yarn at the court of Alcinous; and another part he could dodge because he was dealing with the purely fictitious, and could introduce a shipwreck or a miracle whenever things were getting slow. But in these days you cannot play tricks like this with Drake, whose voyages are matters of history. This difficulty, then, was inherent in Mr. Noyes' subject, and it seems to me very shrewdly detected and hit off in Mr. Wilfrid Blair's parody:

THE NOYES OF BATTLE [1]

Meanwhile the wind had changed, and Francis Drake
Put down the helm, and drove against the seas.
Once more the wind changed, and the simple seaman,
Full-fraught with weather-wisdom, once again
Put down the helm, and so drove on, until
The everlasting and omnipotent
Dawn, through the splendid gloom and golden clouds
Broke: and a great, golden, gilded galleon
In raggy piles of gloom and shaggy splendour
Rose up against them, clouded with the dawn.

Plushed, plumed, and purpled on the imperious poop,
Crusty with cramoisie the Spaniards stood.
They quite refused surrender, till Drake cried
"I am El Draque!"—At once they recognised
The name, tho' spoken with a Devon burr.
Down came their flag at once upon the deck,
As when a fragment of the ceiling falls.

Brief and delicious simile!

So with instructions to the wheel
Drake went below, and had a glass of grog.

[1] *Poets on the Isis.* Oxford: B. H. Blackwell, 1910.

For a second and more accomplished illustration, let us take James Smith's famous parody of Crabbe in *Rejected Addresses*. Crabbe is a very considerable poet : for a certain power of poignancy, hard yet human, and (its best quality) stark clear of sentiment, you will hardly find his match. But he exhibited this power in versified stories, and in the art of introducing and laying out a story he was incurably clumsy and could be bald, unpoetical to the last degree. Those of us who love him best must have smiled oftenest over such passages as—

> Peter had heard there were in London then—
> Still have they being !—workhouse-clearing men,
> Who, undisturbed by feelings just or kind,
> Would parish-boys to needy tradesmen bind . . .

The difficulty here is somewhat cognate with that of logging Drake's voyages : and perhaps among narrative poets Homer stands alone in his handling of flat intervals, his skill in poetising such operations as cooking a dinner or hauling up a boat so that while never aspiring above their due level in the narrative they never fall below the grand manner. Crabbe ("a Pope in worsted stockings") avoided, to be sure, the Charybdis of Pope and his compeers. He seldom or never clothed triviality in fine and banal writing such as—

> The Heavens illumed by Sol's bright ray

or

> Inoculation ! heavenly maid, descend.

which was the approved way to talk of the weather or of Dr. Jenner's vaccine. On the other hand, at the beginning of a tale he would bump for twenty or thirty lines together upon a Scylla commonplace so bald and awkward that James Smith's famous lines contain more of criticism than of exaggeration:

> John Richard William Alexander Dwyer
> Was footman to Justinian Stubbs, Esquire;
> But when John Dwyer 'listed in the Blues,
> Emanuel Jennings polish'd Stubbs's shoes.
> Emanuel Jennings brought his youngest boy
> Up as a corn-cutter—a safe employ, etc.

This is fun and criticism together; and as criticism it indicates at once Crabbe's "worsted stockings" and his frequent, almost habitual clumsiness in starting them out for a walk.

Again, could the fatuity of the ordinary Prize Poem be better rationalised in twenty pages of prose than it was by the parodist who summarised all the Oxford Newdigates in one line?—

> What though no cenotaph enshrine thy bones!

Or, again, has the banality of poetic diction ever received a shrewder knock than it did from the parodies of the *Anti-Jacobin*?—

> The feather'd tribes on pinions cleave the air;
> Not so the mackerel, and, still less, the bear, etc.

Or yet, again, could the musical flagrancies of
our latest and greatest Strauss, and the affabilities
of all the eighteenth-century Odes to Saint Cecilia,
be more neatly touched than they are by Mr.
Charles L. Graves simply opposing them in an

ODE TO DISCORD

Hence, loathéd Melody, whose name recalls
The mellow fluting of the nightingale
    In some sequester'd vale,
    The Murmur of the stream
    Heard in a dream,
Or drowsy plash of distant waterfalls.
But thou, divine Cacophony, assume
The rightful overlordship in her room,
And with Percussion's stimulating aid
Expel the heavenly but no longer youthful maid.

The mischief with Parody is that while no
neater or swifter vehicle of criticism has ever been
invented, the most of men practise it in youth, as a
way of breaking their teeth upon literature, and
abandon it as middle age brings the critical judgment which it would seem designed to convey.
There once was an Aristophanes to whom years
but brought fresh gusto in the gentle art : and our
own times have in England, in Mr. Owen Seaman, a
parodist who has steadily followed up the art to
something as near perfection as our language is
likely to achieve—for his first living rival, Mr. A.

G. Godley, is an Horatian rather than a parodist, and indeed his line has lain in that direction from the first. Calverley, Hilton of *The Light Green*, J. K. Stephen, all died young. Perhaps the gods loved them. For, as I said at the start, Parody plays with the gods; and, as George Meredith says in his *Essay on Comedy*—and we may reverently apply it to the gods—"You may estimate your capacity for Comic perception by being able to detect the ridicule of them you love, without loving them less: and more by being able to see yourself somewhat ridiculous in dear eyes, and accepting the correction their image of you proposes."

ARTHUR QUILLER-COUCH.

CONTENTS

b

CONTENTS

CONTENTS

MODERN PARODISTS

CONTENTS

CONTENTS

CONTENTS

xxii

CONTENTS

CONTEMPORARY PARODISTS

CONTENTS

CONTENTS

APPENDIX—LIST OF AUTHORS PARODIED

CONTENTS

CONTENTS

CONTENTS

CONTENTS

EDITORIAL PREFACE

AN anthology, perhaps more than any other book, requires some slight explanation as regards its *raison d'être*, for an apparently indiscriminate collection of miscellaneous poems avails nothing either to the editors' credit or the reader's appreciation.

But the compilers of this little volume can plead that a definite aim has guided them in the selection of material for their anthology. It was desired to show the whole range of English Parody, and this by the best specimens to be found in verse. Only the early and archaic forms of English burlesque have been excepted, and these because not only are they of little interest to other than students, but also because the authors were in all probability entirely unconscious that they were the forerunners of a new art. With the Elizabethan period, however, Parody became a recognised branch of verse, and from that time onward a succession of able writers has enlivened English literature with quips and cranks and wanton wiles. None of these writers are of malice prepense unrepresented in the book, although in some cases the historical interest of the verse and not its wit or humour has gained its inclusion here, and the editors justify their attention to such historical detail by the argument that while Humour varies with the age and the individual, historical interest is a standard quality stamped with the hall-mark of Time.

The book is composed of three sections which form the natural divisions of Parody; they are entitled—

Early Parodists,

Modern Parodists, and

Contemporary Parodists.

The Early Parodists include all that attempted anything in the nature of Parody up to the death of Horace Smith in 1845. Horace and James Smith were the princes of the early parodists, and brought the period of tentative effort to a brilliant close. A period of quiescence, lasting roughly a score of years, intervened, and then Parody broke out into a riot of delicious fun and cultured satire. It became a popular art. This dignity could hardly be claimed for Parody in the days of Horace and James Smith, for at that time the brothers were *the* only exponents of this new fashion in comedy. Later, many master-minds were content to make use of Parody to point a moral and adorn a tale; they refined it and tempered it till it became a delicate weapon for criticism and satire in the hand of the humorist. This second era of Parody has been styled that of the Modern Parodists. In this group are included all writers whose work appeared later than 1845, except that, following the custom of French anthologists, the work of all living writers has been brought together into a separate section—Contemporary Parodists. This was thought advisable in order to avoid all unnecessary detail and any comparisons which might be construed as invidious; for although it is permitted to an editor to make comments and annotations in introducing the work of a dead author, such procedure would be unbecoming in respect to a writer of to-day, because the living is able, if he wish, to make his own appeal to the public.

The editors have been liberally assisted by many authors and publishers in the compilation of their book, and to these it is their pleasant duty to offer their grateful thanks. In certain cases, indeed, difficulties of copyright have necessitated the omission of a few desirable parodies from the book, but such cases have been the exceptions and not the rule.

Permissions to republish poems are gratefully acknowledged to the following authors and trustees :

Mr. E. B. V. Christian, for poems included in " At the Sign of the Wicket " and "Lays of a Limb of the Law"; Mr. Wilfrid Blair, for a poem from "Poets on the Isis"; Mr. S. D. Charles, for "The Everlasting Plumber"; the Rev. Anthony C. Deane, for several poems from "New Rhymes for Old"; Mr. M. J. C. Meiklejohn, for permission to include several poems by the late R. F. Murray; Mr. Mostyn T. Pigott, for several of his poems; Mr. E. G. V. Knox, for poems included in "The Brazen Lyre"; Mr. Cholmondeley Pennell, for permission to include two of his poems; Mr. Horatio Smith, for several poems; Mr. W. M. Rossetti, for permission to include "MacCracken," by D. G. Rossetti; Sir Frederick Pollock, for permission to include two of his poems from "Leading Cases done into English, and other Diversions"; Sir Herbert Stephen, for permission to republish several poems by the late J. K. Stephen; Mr. Theodore Watts-Dunton, for permission to republish "Nephelidia," by the late A. C. Swinburne; the late Mr. Andrew Lang, for two poems from "Jubilee Odes by Bards that were Silent"; Mr. Owen Seaman, for several of his poems, and Sir Arthur Quiller-Couch, for several poems; also to Miss Mary Kendall, for permission to republish "Education's Martyr"; to Miss Harriet Jay, for permission to republish "The Session of Poets," by the late Robert Buchanan; and to Mr. Ambrose G. Potter, for allowing the selection of a parody on Omar Khayyám from his splendid collection of Omar Khayyám literature.   Also to the following publishers for extracts from the respective books published by them:

Mr. J. W. Arrowsmith, of Bristol, "At the Sign of the Wicket"; "From a Cornish Window"; Mr. John Lane, "New Rhymes for Old"; Mr. Richard Ellis, "MacCracken"; Messrs. Vincent, "The Shotover Papers"; Messrs. Macmillan & Co., "Leading Cases done into English, and other Diversions"; Messrs. Bradbury, Agnew & Co., extracts from *Punch*; Messrs. Longmans, Green & Co., "Old Friends"; *The Westminster Gazette* for extract, "The Everlasting Plumber"; Messrs. Metcalfe & Co., "The Light Green"; Messrs. Smith, Elder & Co., "The Brazen Lyre"; Messrs. Chatto & Windus, "Heptalogia"; B. H. Blackwell, "Poets on the Isis"; Messrs. George Bell & Sons, Calverley's Poems.

But the editors' thanks are especially due to Sir Arthur Quiller-Couch for his consent to write a foreword to the book and for allowing certain of his poems to be included, and to Mr. Roger Ingpen and M. de V. Payen-Payne for their unfailing interest and advice, and their kind co-operation with the editors in seeing the book through the press.

BERNARD C. WHITE.

Early Parodists

ISAAC HAWKINS BROWNE

1705–1760

ISAAC HAWKINS BROWNE is chiefly remembered by his "Pipe of Tobacco," a very slender volume of humorous verse which appeared in 1768. Six parodies are included in the series, and all bear witness to the critical faculty of their author, and to a genuine sense of humour which is too cultivated to become boisterous. The parody on Pope is the most obvious, but the distinctive style of the author of "The Essay on Man" may account for this; as lesser wits, by more nearly approaching the average diction of their age, contrive to elude individual burlesque. The imitation of Thomson was first written by a Dr. Hoadley, who sent it to Browne, but the latter so improved it that the published version may fairly be credited to his skill.

Dr. Johnson is reported by Boswell to have regarded Browne as "one of the first wits of this country"; and Byron, when he wishes to laud the "Rejected Addresses," declares that they are "not at all inferior to the famous ones of Hawkins Browne."[1]

[1] Lord Byron to Mr. Murray, October 19th, 1812.

ISAAC HAWKINS BROWNE

IMITATION V
[Imitation—Pope]

BLEST Leaf! whose aromatic Gales dispense
To Templars Modesty, to Parsons sense :
So raptur'd Priests, at fam'd Dodona's Shrine
Drank Inspiration from the stream divine.
Poison that cures, a Vapour that affords
Content, more solid than the Smile of Lords :
Rest to the Weary, to the Hungry food,
The Last Kind refuge of the Wise and Good :
Inspir'd by Thee, dull Cits adjust the Scale
Of *Europe's* peace, when other Statesmen fail.
By Thee protected, and thy Sister, Beer,
Poets rejoice nor think the Bailiff near.
Nor less, the Critic owns thy genial Aid,
While supperless he plies the piddling trade.
What tho' to Love and soft Delights a Foe,
By Ladies hated, hated by the Beau,
Yet social Freedom, long to Courts unknown,
Fair Health, fair Truth and Virtue are thy own.
Come to thy Poet, come with healing Wings
And let me taste Thee, unexcis'd by Kings.

A Pipe of Tobacco

IMITATION III
[Imitation—J. Thomson]

O THOU, matur'd by glad Hesperian suns
Tobacco, fountain pure of *limpid truth,*
That looks the very soul; whence pouring thought

4

ISAAC HAWKINS BROWNE

Swarms all the mind; absorpt is yellow care,
And at each puff imagination burns.
Flash on thy bard, and with exalting fires
Touch the mysterious lip that chaunts thy praise,
In strains to mortal sons of earth unknown.
Behold an engine, wrought from tawny mines
Of ductile clay, with *plastic virtue* form'd,
And glaz'd magnifick o'er, I grasp, I fill,
From *Poetotheke* [1] with pungent pow'rs perfum'd,
Itself one tortoise all, where shines imbib'd
Each parent ray; then rudely ramm'd illume,
With the red touch of zeal enkindling sheet,
Mark'd with Gibsonian lore; [2] forth issue clouds,
Thought-thrilling, thirst-inciting clouds around,
And many-mining fires; I all the while,
Lolling at ease, *inhale* the breezy balm;
But chief, when *Bacchus waits with thee to join,*
In genial strife and orthodoxal ale,
Stream life and joy into the Muse's bowl.
Oh! be thou still my great inspirer, thou
My Muse; oh! fan me with thy zephyrs boon,
While I, in clouded tabernacle shrin'd
Burst for all oracle and mystick song.

[1] Defined as a poetical word for a Tobacco-Box.
[2] Edmund Gibson (1669–1748), Bishop successively of Lincoln
and of London, was both a learned divine and able Saxon scholar.
His great work was *Codex Juris Eccl. Anglicanae.*

ISAAC HAWKINS BROWNE

IMITATION IV

[Imitation—Edward Young]

CRITICS Avaunt! Tobacco is my theme;
  Tremble like Hornets at the Blasting steam.
And you, Court-insects, flutter not too near
Its Light, nor buzz within the scorching sphere.
Polles,[1] with Flame like thine, my Verse inspire,
So shall the Muse from smoke elicit Fire.
Coxcombs prefer the tickling sting of Snuff;
Yet all their claim to wisdom is—a puff:
Lord *Foplin* smokes not—for his teeth afraid:
Sir *Tawdry* smokes not—for he wears Brocade.
Ladies, when pipes are brought affect to swoon;
They love no *smoke* except the *smoke* of Town:
But Courtiers hate the puffing Tribe,—no matter,
Strange if they love the Breath that cannot *flatter!*
Its foes but show their Ignorance, can He
Who scorns the *Leaf* of Knowledge, love the Tree?
The tainted Templar (more prodigious yet)
Rails at Tobacco, tho' it makes him—*spit.*
Citronia vows it has an odious Stink.
She will not smoke (ye Gods!) but she will drink:
And chaste *Prudella* (blame her if you can)
Says, Pipes are used by that vile creature, Man:
Yet crowds remain, who still its worth proclaim,
While some for Pleasure smoke, and some for *Fame*—
Fame, of our actions, universal Spring,
For which we drink, eat, sleep, smoke—ev'ry thing.

[1] A celebrated writer on divination, mentioned by Suidas.

GEORGE GORDON, LORD BYRON

1788–1824

LORD BYRON was by nature too impetuous to observe the requisite conditions or content himself with the quiet satire and gentle raillery of Parody. Yet his imitation of the metre of Abel Whistlecraft in "Beppo" and its glorification in "Don Juan" show that he could, if he desired, turn the inventions of others to his own advantage. So it is in the following verses which were written during one of his brighter moods to his publisher Murray. The metre and the main argument are parodied from Cowper's song—To Mary—but after that the author's attention is fixed entirely on the discomfiture of his correspondent. It is an interesting *jeu d'esprit* from a great man.

To Mr. Murray

[*Parody—William Cowper*]

STRAHAN,[1] Tonson,[2] Lintot [3] of the times,
   Patron and publisher of rhymes,
For thee the bard up Pindus climbs,
      My Murray.

[1] William Strahan (1715–1785) published Johnson's "Dictionary" and Gibbon's "Decline and Fall."

[2] Jacob Tonson (1656?–1736) published for Otway, Dryden, and Addison; and from 1712 published *The Spectator*. He was secretary of the Kit-Cat Club.

[3] Barnaby Bernard Lintot (1675–1736) was at one time partner with Tonson. He published Pope's translations of the Iliad and Odyssey.

To thee, with hope and terror dumb,
The unfledged MS. authors come ;
Thou printest all—and sellest some—
　　　　　My Murray.

Upon the table's baize so green
The last new Quarterly is seen,—
But where is thy new Magazine,[1]
　　　　　My Murray ?

Along the sprucest bookshelves shine
The works thou deemest most divine—
The "Art of Cookery"[2] and mine,
　　　　　My Murray.

Tours, Travels, Essays, too, I wist
And Sermons, to thy mill bring grist ;
And then thou hast the "Navy List,"
　　　　　My Murray.

And Heaven forbid I should conclude
Without "the Board of Longitude,"[3]
Although this narrow paper would,
　　　　　My Murray.

---

[1] Murray bought a half-share in *Blackwood's Magazine* in 1818, but in 1819 the proprietorship became the sole property of William Blackwood.

[2] The "Art of Cookery" was one of Murray's greatest successes, the copyright of which he purchased from the author, Mrs. Rundell, for £2000.

[3] The sixth edition of "Childe Harold's Pilgrimage" (1813) was "printed by T. Davison, Whitefriars ; for John Murray, Bookseller to the Admiralty, and the Board of Longitude."

HENRY CAREY

1693(?)–1743

No particulars of the life-history of Henry Carey, the author of the famous song "Sally in our Alley," are forthcoming. Nothing is certain about him save that he wrote some popular burlesques and that he was the author of "Namby-Pamby," for we have that in his own words. The date of his birth is unknown; he died in 1743, but whether by his own hand or not is uncertain. There is no exact information as to his parentage, though he was possibly an illegitimate son of George Savile, Marquis of Halifax, and probability is given to the supposition by the fact that he is said to have received a pension from the family. Let us turn, however, to his epistle of Stage Tyrants, dedicated to Philip, Earl of Chesterfield, for there we have very certain news of "Sally in our Alley" and "Namby-Pamby" :—

> So when, long since, in simple sonnet lays,
> I made the 'Prentice sing his Sally's praise
> Tho' rude the Numbers, yet the subject mov'd,
> Immortal *Addison* the song approved ;
> Then Prejudice with Envy did combine,
> Because 'twas good, 'twas thought too good for mine.
> So common Jane did various authors chuse
> To Namby-Pamby, offspring of my Muse ;
> Till Pope who ever proved to Truth a Friend
> With gen'rous ardour did my cause defend ;
> Trac'd me obscure and in detractious spite
> Display'd me in a more conspicuous light.

Succeeding generations have approved of the judgment of Addison and his age. "Namby-Pamby" is one of the cleverest parodies in the English language.

HENRY CAREY
Namby-Pamby

A Panegyric on the New Versification addressed to A(MBROSE)
P(HILLIPS), Esqre.

[Parody—A. Phillips]

ALL ye poets of the age,
    All ye witlings of the stage,
Learn your jingles to reform :
Cross your numbers and conform,
Let the little verses flow
Gently, sweetly, row by row.
Let the verse the subject fit,
Little subject, little wit.
Namby Pamby is your guide,
Albion's joy, Hibernia's pride.

.   .   .   .

He no longer writes of mammy
Andromache and her lammy
Hanging panging at the breast
Of a matron most distrest.
Now the venal poet sings
Baby clouts and baby things,
Baby dolls and baby houses,
Little misses, little spouses ;
Little playthings, little toys,
Little girls and little boys.
As an actor does his part
So the nurses get by heart

HENRY CAREY

Namby Pamby's little rhymes,
Little jingles, little chimes.
Namby Pamby ne'er will die
While the nurse sings lullaby.
Namby Pamby's doubly mild,
Once a man, and twice a child;
To his hanging sleeves restored
Now he foots it like a lord;
Now he pumps his little wits,
All by little tiny bits.
Now, methinks I hear him say
Boys and girls come out to play,
Moon does shine as bright as day.
Now my Namby Pamby's found
Sitting on the Friar's ground,
Picking silver, picking gold,
Namby Pamby's never old.
Bally-cally they begin,
Namby Pamby still keeps in.
Namby Pamby is no clown,
London Bridge is broken down:
Now he courts the gay Ladee
Dancing o'er the Lady-lee:
Now he sings of lick-spit liar
Burning in the brimstone fire;
Liar, liar, lick-spit, lick,
Turn about the candle-stick.
Now he sings of Jacky Horner
Sitting in the chimney corner
Eating of a Christmas pie,
Putting in his thumb, oh, fie!

Putting in, oh, fie! his thumb!
Pulling out, oh, strange! a plum.

.   .   .   .

Guard him, ye poetic powers,
Watch his minutes, watch his hours :
Let your tuneful Nine inspire him,
Let poetic fury fire him :
Let the poets one and all
To his genius victims fall.

GEORGE CANNING

1770–1827

To George Canning belongs the double fame of politician and man of letters. As a boy he showed early signs of his great intellectual powers, and when, with Hookham Frere and others, he brought out a school magazine called *The Microcosm* he created a record by selling the copyright to a publisher for £50. His juvenile literary success was repeated on a larger scale in the triumph of the *Anti-Jacobin*, in which he associated again with Frere in contributing some of his cleverest parodies. The intention of the paper was to bring ridicule on the Revolutionary or more advanced Whig party, in order to counteract the strong feeling of discontent aroused in this country by the French Revolution of 1796; and its efforts were amply rewarded, for the paper became so prosperous that it was continued until 1821 as *The Anti-Jacobin Review*, a monthly magazine.

Canning never acknowledged his own contributions to the paper, but the Sonnet to Mrs. Brownrigg is usually attributed to him, while "The Needy Knife-Grinder" was chiefly his work, although he received some help from Frere. Both are exceedingly humorous parodies of Southey, who by his early republican views laid himself open to attacks in such a paper, for it was not till later that the poet became so violently a Tory.

GEORGE CANNING

The Elderly Gentleman

[*Parody—Nicholas Rowe*]

BY the side of a murmuring stream, an elderly gentleman sat ;
On the top of his head was his wig, and a-top of his wig
was his hat.

The wind it blew high and blew strong, as the elderly
gentleman sat,
And bore from his head in a trice, and plunged in the
river his hat.

The gentleman then took his cane, which lay by his side
as he sat ;
And he dropped in the river his wig, in attempting to get
out his hat.

His breast it grew cold with despair, and full in his eye
madness sat ;
So he flung in the river his cane to swim with his wig
and his hat.

Cool reflection at last came across, while this elderly
gentleman sat ;
So he thought he would follow the stream, and look for
his cane, wig, and hat.

His head being thicker than common, o'erbalanced the
rest of his fat ;
And in plumpt this son of a woman, to follow his wig,
cane, and hat.

GEORGE CANNING

The Friend of Humanity & the Knife-Grinder

[*Parody—Robert Southey*]

FRIEND OF HUMANITY

"NEEDY knife-grinder! whither are you going?
  Rough is the road, your wheel is out of order—
Bleak blows the blast;—your hat has got a hole in't,
    So have your breeches!

"Weary knife-grinder! little think the proud ones
Who in their coaches roll along the turnpike-
Road, what hard work 'tis crying all day, 'Knives and
    Scissors to grind O!'

"Tell me, knife-grinder, how came you to grind knives?
Did some rich man tyrannically use you?
Was it the squire? or parson of the parish?
    Or the attorney?

"Was it the squire, for killing of his game? or
Covetous parson, for his tithes distraining?
Or roguish lawyer, made you lose your little
    All in a lawsuit?

"(Have you not read the Rights of Man, by Tom Paine?),
Drops of compassion tremble on my eyelids,
Ready to fall as soon as you have told your
    Pitiful story."

GEORGE CANNING

KNIFE-GRINDER

"Story! God bless you! I have none to tell, sir,
Only last night a-drinking at the Chequers
This poor old hat and breeches, as you see, were
        Torn in a scuffle.

"Constables came up for to take me into
Custody; they took me before the justice;
Justice Oldmixon put me in the parish-
        stocks for a vagrant.

"I should be glad to drink your Honour's health in
A pot of beer, if you will give me sixpence;
But for my part, I never love to meddle
        With politics, sir."

FRIEND OF HUMANITY

"*I* give thee sixpence! I will see thee damn'd first—
Wretch! whom no sense of wrongs can rouse to ven-
    geance—
Sordid, unfeeling, reprobate, degraded,
        Spiritless outcast!"

[*Kicks the Knife-grinder, overturns his wheel, and exit in
   a transport of republican enthusiasm and universal philan-
   thropy.*]

GEORGE CANNING

Inscription

For the Door of the Cell in Newgate, where Mrs. Brownrigg, the Prenticecide was confined previous to her execution [1]

[Parody—Robert Southey]

FOR one long term, or e'er her trial came,
Here Brownrigg linger'd.   Often have these cells
Echoed her blasphemies, as with shrill voice
She scream'd for fresh Geneva.   Not to her
Did the blithe fields of Tothill, or thy street,
St. Giles, its fair varieties expand ;
Till at the last, in slow-drawn cart, she went
To execution.   Dost thou ask her crime ?
SHE WHIPP'D TWO FEMALE PRENTICES TO DEATH,
AND HID THEM IN THE COAL-HOLE.   For her mind
Shaped strictest plans of discipline.   Sage schemes !
Such as Lycurgus taught, when at the shrine
Of the Orthyan Goddess [2] he bade flog
The little Spartans : such as erst chastised
Our Milton, when at college.   For this act
Did Brownrigg swing. Harsh laws ! But time shall come,
When France shall reign, and laws be all repeal'd !

[1] Elizabeth Brownrigg (d. 1767) was the wife of a house-painter who lived in Fleur de Luce Court, Fetter Lane. She practised the most inhuman cruelties on her apprentices, one of whom she actually killed. She was hanged at Tyburn, and her skeleton was exposed at Surgeons' Hall in the Old Bailey "that the heinousness of her cruelty might make the more lasting impression on the minds of the spectators."

[2] Artemis or Diana.

GEORGE CANNING

The Soldier's Wife

[*Parody—Southey*]

WEARISOME Sonnetteer, feeble and querulous,
　　Painfully dragging out thy demo-cratic lays—
Moon-stricken Sonnetteer, "ah! for thy heavy chance!"

Sorely thy Dactylics lag on uneven feet :
Slow is the syllable which thou wouldst urge to speed,
Lame and o'erburthened, and screaming its wretchedness!"

.　　　　.　　　　.　　　　.

Ne'er talk of ears again! look at thy spelling book ;
Dilworth and Dyche are both mad at thy quantities—
Dactylics, call'st thou 'em?—"God help thee, silly one!"

SAMUEL TAYLOR COLERIDGE

1772-1834

THE gloomy metaphysician of the Lake Poets, "the archangel a little damaged" as he was described by Lamb, could sometimes wake from the perplexed imaginings that possessed his soul. As evidence we have the "Sonnets attempted in the Manner of Contemporary Writers." These form a scholarly addition to the ranks of parody, for "Coleridge alone among English writers is in the front rank at once as poet, as critic, as philosopher." About the time that he sent these sonnets to the *Monthly Magazine* he penned a letter (Cottle, E.R. i. 288 ; Rem. 160) in which he made reference to them :—

> "I sent to the *Monthly Magazine* three mock sonnets in ridicule of my own poems, and Charles Lloyd's, and Charles Lamb's, etc. etc., exposing that affectation of unaffectedness, of jumping and misplaced accent, in commonplace epithets, flat lines forced into poetry by italics (signifying how well and mouthishly the author would read them), puny pathos, etc. etc. The instances were all taken from myself and Lloyd and Lamb. I signed them 'Nehemiah Higginbottom.' I think they may do good to our young Bards." [1]

The second poem on Charles Lloyd has been omitted, as its subject is not of sufficient interest to present-day readers.

[1] Coleridge's Works by Dykes Campbell.

SAMUEL TAYLOR COLERIDGE

I

Sonnets Attempted in the Manner of Contemporary Writers

[*Imitation—S. T. Coleridge*]

PENSIVE at eve on the hard world I mus'd,
  And my poor heart was sad : so at the moon
I gaz'd—and sigh'd, and sigh'd !—for, ah ! how soon
Eve darkens into night.   Mine eyes perus'd
With tearful vacancy the *dampy* grass
Which wept and glitter'd in the paly ray ;
And I did pause me on my lonely way,
And mused me on those wretched ones who pass
O'er the black heath of Sorrow.   But, alas !
Most of Myself I thought : when it befell
That the sooth Spirit of the breezy wood
Breath'd in mine ear—" All this is very well ;
But much of *one* thing is for *no* thing good."
Ah ! my poor heart's inexplicable swell !

SAMUEL TAYLOR COLERIDGE

III

On a Ruined House in a Romantic Country

[Imitation—Chas. Lamb]

AND this reft house is that the which he built.
    Lamented Jack!   And here his malt he pil'd,
Cautious in vain! These rats that squeak so wild,
Squeak, not unconscious of their fathers' guilt.
Did ye not see her gleaming thro' the glade?
Belike, 'twas she, the maiden all forlorn.
What though she milk no cow with crumpled horn,
Yet *aye* she haunts the dale where *erst* she stray'd;
And *aye* beside her stalks her amorous knight!
Still on his thighs their wonted brogues are worn,
And thro' those brogues, still tatter'd and betorn,
His hindward charms gleam an unearthly white;
As when thro' broken clouds at night's high noon
Peeps in fair fragments forth the full-orb'd harvest-moon!

CATHERINE MARIA FANSHAWE

1765–1834

MISS FANSHAWE was born at Chipstead in Surrey; but on the death of her father came with her sisters to London and lived for some years at 15 Berkeley Square, and also at Richmond. Lockhart mentions that Sir Walter Scott held Miss Fanshawe in great admiration, though the formal manners of herself and her sisters narrowed their circle of friends. The most notable poem of Miss Fanshawe is "The Enigma on the Letter H"—"'Twas whispered in Heaven, 'twas muttered in Hell," so often attributed to Lord Byron—while the parody included in this volume received the highest praise from William Wordsworth that a poet could pay to his imitator.

Fragments in Imitation of Wordsworth

[*Imitation—W. Wordsworth*]

THERE is a river clear and fair,
  'Tis neither broad nor narrow;
It winds a little here and there—
It winds about like any hare;
And then it holds as straight a course
As, on the turnpike road, a horse,
Or, through the air, an arrow.

The trees that grow upon the shore
Have grown a hundred years or more;
So long there is no knowing:
Old Daniel Dobson does not know

When first those trees began to grow ;
But still they grew, and grew, and grew,
As if they'd nothing else to do,
But ever must be growing.

The impulses of air and sky
Have reared their stately heads so high,
And clothed their boughs with green ;
Their leaves the dews of evening quaff,—
And when the wind blows loud and keen,
I've seen the jolly timbers laugh,
And shake their sides with merry glee—
Wagging their heads in mockery.

Fixed are their feet in solid earth
Where winds can never blow ;
But visitings of deeper birth
Have reached their roots below.
For they have gained the river's brink,
And of the living waters drink.

There's little Will, a five years' child—
He is my youngest boy ;
To look on eyes so fair and wild,
It is a very joy.
He hath conversed with sun and shower,
And dwelt with every idle flower,
As fresh and gay as them.
He loiters with the briar-rose,—
The blue-bells are his play-fellows,
That dance upon their slender stem.

And I have said, my little Will,
Why should he not continue still
A thing of Nature's rearing?
A thing beyond the world's control—
A living vegetable soul—
No human sorrow fearing.

It were a blessed sight to see
That child become a willow-tree,
His brother trees among
He'd be four times as tall as me,
And live three times as long.

JOHN HOOKHAM FRERE

1769–1846

AMONGST the writers of humorous verse the name of John Hookham Frere must always occupy a prominent position. With Canning, his life-long friend, he contributed largely to *The Anti-Jacobin*, or Weekly Examiner, and amongst their joint contributions is the famous poem on "The Friend of Humanity and the Knife-Grinder" (see Canning).

Robert Pollok, who is parodied in a few terse lines, was a Scotch poet who lived in the early nineteenth century and based his style of verse on that of Young and Cowper. His "Course of Time" was a philosophic treatise on the destiny of man, a work conceived beyond the limitations of the poet. Frere's criticism, however, supplies the reader with all that it is necessary to know about the original.

"The Loves of the Triangles" is a very exact parody of Dr. Darwin's "Loves of the Plants," and although appearing under the joint authorship of Canning and Frere, it is chiefly the work of the latter writer. Erasmus Darwin was grandfather of the famous scientist Charles Darwin.

JOHN HOOKHAM FRERE
The Loves of the Triangles

[*Imitation—Dr. Erasmus Darwin*]

STAY your rude steps, or e'er your feet invade
  The Muses' haunts, ye Sons of War and Trade!
Nor you, ye Legion Fiends of Church and Law,
Pollute these pages with unhallow'd paw!

Debased, corrupted, grovelling, and confined,
No DEFINITIONS touch *your* senseless mind;
To *you* no POSTULATES prefer their claim,
No ardent AXIOMS *your* dull soul inflame;
For *you* no TANGENTS touch, no ANGLES meet,
No CIRCLES join in osculation sweet!

For *me*, ye CISSOIDS, round my temples bend
Your wandering CURVES; ye CONCHOIDS extend;
Let playful PENDULES quick vibration feel,
While silent CYCLOIDS rests upon her wheel;
Let HYDROSTATICS, simpering as they go,
Lead the light Naiads on fantastic toe;
Let shrill ACOUSTICS tune the tiny lyre;
With EUCLID sage fair ALGEBRA conspire;
The obedient pulley strong MECHANICS ply,
And wanton OPTICS roll the melting eye!

26

JOHN HOOKHAM FRERE

I see the fair fantastic forms appear,
The flaunting drapery and the languid leer;
Fair sylphish forms—who, tall, erect, and slim,
Dart the keen glance, and stretch the length of limb;
To viewless harpings weave the meanless dance,
Wave the gay wreath, and titter as they prance.

Such rich confusion charms the ravish'd sight,
When vernal Sabbaths to the Park invite,
Mounts the thick dust, the coaches crowd along,
Presses round Grosvenor Gate the impatient throng;
White muslin'd misses and mammas are seen,
Link'd with gay Cockneys glittering o'er the green:
The rising breeze unnumber'd charms displays,
And the tight ankle strikes the astonish'd gaze.

But chief, thou Nurse of the Didactic Muse,
Divine NONSENSIA, all thy sense infuse;
The charms of SECANTS and of TANGENTS tell,
How LOVES and GRACES in an ANGLE dwell;
How slow progressive *Points* protract the *Line*,
As pendant spiders spin the filmy twine;
How, lengthen'd *Lines*, impetuous sweeping round,
Spread the wide *Plane*, and mark its circling bound;
How *Planes*, their substance with their motion grown,
Form the huge *Cube*, the *Cylinder*, the *Cone*.

Lo! where the chimney's sooty tube ascends,
The fair TROCHAIS from the corner bends!
Her coal-black eyes upturn'd, incessant mark
The eddying smoke, quick flame, and volant spark;

JOHN HOOKHAM FRERE

Mark with quick ken, where flashing in between
Her much-loved *Smoke-Jack* glimmers thro' the scene;
Mark, how his various parts together tend,
Point to one purpose,—in one object end:
The spiral *grooves* in smooth meanders flow,
Drags the long *chain*, the polish'd axles glow,
While slowly circumvolves the piece of beef below:
The conscious fire with bickering radiance burns,
Eyes the rich joint, and roasts it as it turns.
So youthful Horner roll'd the roguish eye,
Cull'd the dark plum from out his Christmas pye,
And cried in self-applause—" How good a boy am I."

So she, sad victim of domestic spite,
Fair Cinderella, past the wintry night,
In the lone chimney's darksome nook immured,
Her form disfigured and her charms obscured.
Sudden her God-mother appears in sight,
Lifts the charm'd rod, and chants the mystic rite.
The chanted rite the maid attentive hears;
And feels new ear-rings deck her listening ears;
While 'midst her towering tresses, aptly set,
Shines bright with quivering glance, the smart aigrette;
Brocaded silks the splendid dress complete,
And the Glass Slipper grasps her fairy feet.
Six cock-tail'd mice transport her to the ball,
And liveried lizards wait upon her call.

Alas! that partial Science should approve
The sly RECTANGLE's too licentious love!
For three bright nymphs, &c. &c.

JOHN HOOKHAM FRERE

The Course of Time

[*Imitation—Robert Pollok*]

ROBERT POLLOK, A.M.! this work of yours
   Is meant, I do not doubt, extremely well,
And the design I deem most laudable,
But since I find the book laid on my table,
I shall presume (with the fair owner's leave)
To note a single slight deficiency :
I mean, in short (since it is called a poem)
That in the course of ten successive books
If something in the shape of poetry
Were to be met with, we should like it better ;
But nothing of the kind is to be found,
Nothing, alas ! but words of the olden time,
Quaint and uncouth, contorted phrase and queer,
With the familiar language that befits
Tea-drinking parties most unmeetly matched.

JOHN HOOKHAM FRERE

Isabelle

[*Imitation—S. T. Coleridge*]

CAN there be a moon in heaven to-night,
    That the hill and the grey cloud seem so light?
The air is whitened by some spell,
For there is no moon, I know it well:
On this third day, the sages say,
('Tis wonderful how well they know),
The moon is journeying far away,
Bright somewhere in a heaven below.

    It is a strange and lovely night,
A greyish pale, but not white!
Is it rain, or is it dew,
That falls so thick I see its hue?
In rays it follows, one, two, three,
Down the air so merrily,
Said Isabelle, so let it be!

    Why does the Lady Isabelle
Sit in the damp and dewy dell
Counting the racks of drizzly rain,
And how often the Rail cries over again?
For she's harping, harping in the brake,
Craik, craik—Craik, craik.—
Ten times nine, and thrice eleven;—
That last call was an hundred and seven.

JOHN HOOKHAM FRERE

Craik, craik—the hour is near—
Let it come, I have no fear !
Yet it is a dreadful work, I wis,
Such doings in a night like this !

Sounds the river harsh and loud ?
The stream sounds harsh, but not loud.
There is a cloud that seems to hover,
By western hill the churchyard over,
What is it like ?—'Tis like a whale ;
'Tis like a shark with half the tail,
Not half, but third and more ;
Now 'tis a wolf, and now a boar ;
Its face is raised—it cometh here ;
Let it come—there is no fear.
There's two for heaven, and ten for hell,
Let it come—'tis well—'tis well
Said the Lady Isabelle.

What ails that little cut-tailed whelp,
That it continues to yelp, yelp ?
Yelp, yelp, and it turns its eye
Up to the tree and half to the sky,
Half to the sky and full to the cloud,
And still it whines and barks aloud.
Why I should dread I cannot tell ;
There is a spirit ; I know it well !
I see it in yon falling beam—
Is it a vision or a dream ?
It is no dream, full well I know,
I have a woful deed to do !
Hush, hush, thou little murmurer ;
I tell thee hush—the dead are near !

JOHN HOOKHAM FRERE

If thou knewest all, poor tailless whelp,
Well mightest thou tremble, growl, and yelp ;
But thou knowest nothing, hast no part,
(Simple and stupid as thou art)
Save gratitude and truth of heart.
But they are coming by this way
That have been dead for a year and a day ;
Without challenge, without change,
They shall have their full revenge !
They have been sent to wander in woe
In the lands of flame, and the lands of snow ;
But those that are dead
Shall the greensward tread,
And those that are living
Shall soon be dead !
None to pity them, none to help !
Thou mayest quake, my cut-tailed whelp !

There are two from the grave
That I fain would save ;
Full hard is the weird
For the young and the brave !
Perchance they are rapt in vision sweet,
While the passing breezes kiss their feet ;
And they are dreaming of joy and love !
Well, let them go—there's room above.

There are three times three, and three to these,
Count as you will, by twos or threes !
Three for the gallows, and three for the wave,
Three to roast behind the stone,

And three that shall never see the grave
Until the day and the hour are gone !
For retribution is mine alone !
The cloud is redder in its hue,
The hour is near, and vengeance due ;
It cannot, and it will not fail,—
'Tis but a step to Borrowdale !
Why shouldest thou love and follow me ?
Poor faithful thing !   I pity thee !

Up rose the Lady Isabelle,
I may not of her motion tell,
Yet thou mayest look upon her frame ;
Look on it with a passing eye,
But think not thou upon the same,
Turn away and ask not why ;
But if thou darest look again,
Mad of heart and seared of brain,
Thou shalt never look again !

What can ail that short-tailed whelp ?
'Tis either behind or far before,
And it hath changed its whining yelp
To a shortened yuff—its little core
Seems bursting with terror and dismay,
Yuff, yuff—hear how it speeds away.
Hold thy peace, thou yemering thing,
The very night-wind's slumbering,
And thou wilt wake to woe and pain
Those that must never wake again.

Meet is its terror and its flight,
There's one on the left and two on the right!
But save the paleness of the face,
All is beauty and all is grace!
The earth and air are tinged with blue;
There are no footsteps in the dew;
Is this to wandering spirits given,
Such stillness on the face of heaven?
The fleecy clouds that sleep above
Are like the wing of beauteous dove,
And the leaf of the elm tree does not move!
Yet they are coming! and they are three!
Jesu! Maria! can it be!

THE CONCLUSION

Sleep on, fair maiden of Borrowdale!
Sleep! O sleep! and do not wake!
Dream of the dance, till the foot so pale,
And the beauteous ankle shiver and shake;
Till thou shalt press, with feeling bland,
Thine own fair breast with lover's hand.
Thy heart is light as summer breeze,
Thy heart is joyous as the day;
Man never form of angel sees,
But thou art fair as they!
So lovers weep, and so they say,
So thine shall weep for many a day!
The hour's at hand, O woe is me!
For they are coming, and they are three!

JOHN HOOKHAM FRERE

The Curse of the Laureate

[*Parody—Robert Southey*]

THEN pointing with my sceptre to the sky,
    With vehemence that might not be restrained
I gave the awful curse of destiny !
I was asleep, but sore with passion pained.
It was a dreadful curse ; and to this day,
Even from my waking dreams it is not worn away.

THE CURSE

May heaven and earth,
And hell underneath,
Unite to ensting thee
In horrible wrath.
May scorning surround thee,
And conscience astound thee,
High genius o'erpower,
And the devil confound thee.
The curse be upon thee
In pen and in pocket,
Thy ink turn to puddle,
And gorge in the socket ;
Thy study let rats destroy,
Vermin and cats annoy,
Thy base lucubrations
To tear and to gnaw,

JOHN HOOKHAM FRERE

Thy false calculations
In Empire and Law.
The printers shall harass,
The devil shall dun thee,
The trade shall despise thee,
And C—t—e shun thee.
The judge shall not hear thee,
But frown and pass by thee,
And clients shall fear thee,
And know thee, and fly thee!
I'll hunt thee, I'll chase thee,
To scorn and deride thee,
The cloud shall not cover,
The cave shall not hide thee;
The scorching of wrath
And of shame shall abide thee,
Till the herbs of the desert
Shall wither beside thee.
Thou shalt thirst for revenge
And misrule, as for wine,
But genius shall flourish!
And royalty shine!
And thou shalt remain
While the Laureate doth reign,
With a fire in thy heart,
And a fire in thy brain,
And Fame shall disown thee
And visit thee never,
And the curse shall be on thee
For ever and ever!

OLIVER GOLDSMITH

1728–1764

OLIVER GOLDSMITH was master of every branch of the profession of letters : comedy, novel, critique, heroic poem, lyric, or parody ; all were made the richer by some contribution from his pen. The following parody first appeared in *The Busy-Body*, 1759, where it was pronounced to be the production of Swift, and so excellent is the imitation that Sir Walter Scott included it in his editions of that poet's works.

The Logicians Refuted

[*Imitation—J. Swift*]

LOGICIANS have but ill defin'd,
　　As rational the human mind ;
Reason, they say, belongs to man,
But let them prove it if they can.
Wise Aristotle and Suinglesius,
By ratiocinations specious,
Have strove to prove with great precision,
With definition and division,
Homo est ratione preditum ; [1]
But for my soul I cannot credit 'em,
And must in spite of them maintain
That man and all his ways are vain ;

---

[1] Man is marked out by his ability to reason.

37

And that this boasted lord of nature
Is both a weak and erring creature ;
That instinct is a surer guide
Than reason, boasting mortal's pride ;
And that brute beasts are far before 'em,
Deus est anima brutorum.[1]
Who ever knew an honest brute
At law his neighbour prosecute,
Bring action for assault and battery,
Or friend beguile with lies and flattery ?
O'er plains they ramble unconfin'd,
No politics disturb the mind ;
They eat their meals, and take their sport,
Nor know who's in or out at court ;
They never to the levée go
To treat as dearest friend, a foe ;
They never importune his Grace,
Nor ever cringe to men in place ;
Nor undertake a dirty job,
Nor draw the quill to write for Bob ; [2]
Fraught with invective they ne'er go
To folks at Pater-Noster Row :
No judges, fiddlers, dancing masters,
No pickpockets, or poetasters,
Are known to honest quadrupeds,
No single brute his fellows leads.
Brutes never meet in bloody fray,
Nor cut each other's throats for pay.

[1] God alone is the mind of the beasts.
[2] Sir Robert Walpole.

OLIVER GOLDSMITH

Of beasts, it is confess'd, the ape
Comes nearest us in human shape ;
Like man he imitates each fashion,
And malice is his ruling passion ;
But both in malice and grimaces
A courtier any ape surpasses.
Behold him humbly cringing wait
Upon the minister of state ;
View him soon after to inferiors
Aping the conduct of superiors :
He promises with equal air,
And to perform takes equal care.
He in his turn finds imitators ;
At court, the porters, lacqueys, waiters,
Their master's manners still contract,
And footmen, lords, and dukes can act,
Thus at the court both great and small,
Behave alike, for all ape all.

JAMES HOGG

1770–1835

WHILE Scott and Byron, Wordsworth and Coleridge are names familiar to "every schoolboy," that of the Ettrick Shepherd is remembered only by the students of English literature, or, taken at the most liberal estimate, it only survives as the source of some beautiful lyrics, lyrics as full of the genius of Scotch poetry as those of Burns, the poet whom James Hogg took for his model. Hogg did, indeed, start at Ettrick, in Selkirkshire, as a shepherd. According to his own account he received little enough schooling, yet he managed to read, and later on learn the violin, while fortune assisted him when in 1790 he became shepherd to Mr. Laidlaw, and was soon on intimate terms with the son, William Laidlaw, the future friend of Sir Walter Scott. His first song, "Donald M'Donald," was printed in 1800, and ten years later he commenced a literary career in real earnest. In 1816 he suggested the publication of a volume of poems by living authors, but the persons selected by himself for the undertaking were very averse to the plan, and Scott voiced the prevailing opinion in the pithy remark : "Every herring should hing by its ain head." Hogg, however, was not to be put off so easily ; he produced a book on his own initiative parodying these principal authors, and entitled "The Poetic Mirror" or the "Living Bards of Great Britain." Perhaps the best parody in the volume is that on himself, "The Gude Greye Katte," but it is unfortunately too long for insertion here. His other parodies, however, are themselves very clever examples of their kind, especially "Isabelle," in imitation of Coleridge ; while there are few keener criticisms of Wordsworth's "The Excursion" than the parody of "James Rigg," from which an excerpt is given. From this date to the time of his death, 21st November, 1835, Hogg was constantly engaged in literary work.

JAMES HOGG

JAMES HOGG

James Rigg

[*Imitation—William Wordsworth*]

ON Tuesday morn at half-past six o'clock,
    I rose and dressed myself, and having shut
The door o' the bedroom still and leisurely,
I walk'd downstairs.   When at the outer-door
I firmly grasped the key that 'ere night-fall
Had turned the lock into its wonted niche
Within the brazen implement, that shone
With no unseemly splendour,—mellow'd light,
Elicited by touch of careful hand
On the brown lintel; and the obedient door,
As at a potent necromancer's touch,
Into the air receded suddenly,
And gave wide prospect of the sparkling lake,
Just then emerging from the snow-white mist
Like angel's veil slow-folded up to heaven.
And lo! a vision bright and beautiful
Sheds a refulgent glory o'er the sand,
The sand and gravel of my avenue!
For standing silent by the kitchen-door,
Tinged by the morning sun, and in its own
Brown natural hide most lovely, two long ears
Upstretching perpendicularly, then

41

With the horizon levelled—to my gaze
Superb as horn of fabled Unicorn,
Each in its own proportions grander far
Than the frontal glory of that wandering beast,
Child of the Desert! Lo! a beauteous Ass,
With paniers hanging silent at each side!
Silent as cage of bird whose song is mute,
Though silent yet not empty, fill'd with bread
The staff of life, the means by which the soul
By fate obedient to the powers of sense,
Renews its faded vigour, and keeps up
A proud communion with the eternal heavens.
Fasten'd to a ring it stood, while at its head
A boy of six years old, as angel bright,
Patted its neck and to its mouth applied
The harmless thistle that his hand had pluck'd
From the wild common, melancholy crop.

THOMAS HOOD (THE ELDER)

1799–1845

THOMAS HOOD was born in London at No. 31 Poultry, where his father was partner in a publishing business. Young Hood was prepared to gain his livelihood as an engraver, when a post as sub-editor of the *London Magazine* was offered and accepted by him in the summer of 1821. He came into touch with many notable men of his day, including Lamb, Hazlitt, John Hamilton Reynolds, and others. With the last-named writer he brought out anonymously a little volume of " Odes and Addresses to Great People." This was instantly made welcome by the public, and even Coleridge took it for the work of his friend Lamb. From this book is taken the " Ode to Mr. Graham," a production of the joint authorship which Coleridge thought a most excellent parody of " Peter Bell." But besides being a humorous writer, Hood had undoubtedly genuine poetic gifts, which have never received the recognition they deserved, although certain poems, such as the " Bridge of Sighs " and " The Song of the Shirt," will make his name remembered as long as genuine pathos can awaken echoes in the human heart.

The " Ode on a Distant Prospect of Clapham Academy " does not accurately commemorate his own schooldays, for Hood was educated at " Wanostrocht's Academy for Young Gentlemen at Camberwell." After a busy life, in which he added much to the gaiety of nations, Hood died at the early age of forty-six.

THOMAS HOOD (THE ELDER)

Ode to Mr. Graham[1]

[*Parody—W. Wordsworth*]

I

DEAR Graham, whilst the busy crowd,
  The vain, the wealthy and the proud,
 Their meaner flights pursue,
Let us cast off the foolish ties
That bind us to the earth and rise
 And take a bird's-eye view !—

II

A few more whiffs of my segar
And then in Fancy's airy car,
 Have with thee for the skies :—
How oft this fragrant smoke upcurl'd,
Hath borne me from this little world,
 And all that in it lies !—

III

Away !—away !—the bubble fills—
Farewell to Earth and all its ills !—
 We seem to cut the wind !—
So high we mount, so swift we go,
The chimney-pots are far below,
 The Eagle's left behind !—

[1] Graham was a celebrated aeronaut who made a notable ascent
in 1823.

44

THOMAS HOOD (THE ELDER)

IV

Ah me! my brain begins to swim!
The world is growing rather dim;
  The steeples and the trees—
My wife is getting very small!
I cannot see my babe at all!—
  The Dollond,[1] if you please!—

V

Do, Graham, let me have a quiz.
Lord! what a Lilliput it is,
  That little world of Moggs,[2]—
Are those the London Docks,—that channel,
The mighty Thames?—a proper kennel
  For that small Isle of Dogs!—

VI

What is that seeming tea-urn there?
That fairy dome, St. Paul's!—I swear
  Wren must have been a wren!—
And that small stripe?—it cannot be
The City Road! Good lack! to see
  The little ways of men.

[1] A particular fine make of telescope named after the firm who placed it on the market.

[2] This little world of Moggs refers in all probability to the *Pocket Itinerary of the Roads of England and Wales*, edited by Edward Moggs.

45

THOMAS HOOD (THE ELDER)

XII

Think ! what a mob of little men
Are crawling just within our ken
   Like mites upon a cheese !
Pshaw !—how the foolish sight rebukes
Ambitious thoughts ! Can there be *Dukes*
   Of *Gloster* such as these ?

XV

The world recedes—it disappears !
Heaven opens on my eyes—my ears
   With buzzing noises ring !—
A fig for Southey's [1] laureate lore !—
What's Rogers [2] here ?—who cares for Moore
   That hears the Angels sing !—

XVI

A fig for earth and all its minions,
We are above the world's opinions,
   Graham ! we'll have our own !—
Look what a vantage height we've got.
Now—*do* you think Sir Walter Scott
   Is such a Great Unknown ?

---

[1] Southey was Poet Laureate from 1813 to 1843.

[2] Samuel Rogers was the author of "The Pleasures of Memory" and "Italy." He considered himself to be one of the Immortals, but posterity has not endorsed his opinion. Turner contributed many sketches to the illustration of his poem on Italy, of which it was commonly said, "that it would have been dish'd were it not for its plates."

THOMAS HOOD (THE ELDER)

XXVI

Campbell[1]—(you cannot see him here)—
Hath scorn'd my *lays :*—do his appear
    Such great *eggs* from the sky ?—
And Longman, and his lengthy Co.
Long, only, in a little Row,
    Have thrust my poems by !

XXVII

What else ?—I'm poor, and much beset
With damn'd small duns—that is—in debt
    Some grains of golden dust !
But only worth, above, is worth—
What's all the credit of the earth ?
    An inch of cloth on trust !

XXIX

What's all the ground rent of the globe ?—
Oh, Graham, it would worry Job
    To hear its landlords prate !
But after this survey I think
I'll ne'er be bullied more, nor shrink
    From men of large estate !

XXX

And less, still less, will I submit
To poor mean acres' worth of wit—
    I that have heaven's span—
I that like Shakespeare's self may dream
Beyond the very clouds, and seem
    An Universal Man !

[1] "Campbell" is Thomas Campbell the poet, who at this time
was editor of the *New Monthly Magazine.*

THOMAS HOOD (THE ELDER)

Ode on a Distant Prospect of Clapham Academy [1]

[Parody—T. Gray]

AH me! those old familiar bounds!
  That classic house, those classic grounds,
My pensive thought recalls!
What tender urchins now confine,
What little captives now repine,
  Within yon irksome walls?

Ay, that's the very house! I know
Its ugly windows, ten a-row!
  Its chimneys in the rear!
And there's the iron rod so high,
That drew the thunder from the sky,
  And turn'd our table-beer!

There I was birch'd! there I was bred!
There like a little Adam fed
  From Learning's woeful tree!
The weary tasks I used to con!—
The hopeless leaves I wept upon!—
  Most fruitless leaves to me!—

The summon'd class!—the awful bow!—
I wonder who is master now

[1] No connexion with any other ode.—Author's note.

THOMAS HOOD (THE ELDER)

And wholesome anguish sheds!
How many ushers now employs,
How many maids to see the boys
    Have nothing in their heads!

And Mrs. S*** ?—Doth she abet
(Like Pallas in the parlour) yet
    Some favour'd two or three,—
The little Crichtons of the hour,
Her muffin-medals that devour,
    And swill her prize—bohea?

Ay, there's the play-ground! there's the lime
Beneath whose shade in summer's prime
    So wildly I have read!—
Who sits there *now*, and skims the cream
Of young Romance, and weaves a dream
    Of Love and Cottage-bread?

Who struts the Randall of the walk?
Who models tiny heads in chalk?
    Who scoops the light canoe?
What early genius buds apace?
Where's Poynter? Harris? Bowers? Chase?
    Hal Baylis? blithe Carew?

Alack! they're gone—a thousand ways!
And some are serving in 'the Greys,'
    And some have perish'd young!—
Jack Harris weds his second wife;
Hal Baylis drives the *wane* of life;
    And blithe Carew—is hung!

THOMAS HOOD (THE ELDER)

Grave Bowers teaches A B C
To savages at Owhyee ; [1]
   Poor Chase is with the worms !—
All, all are gone—the olden breed !—
New crops of mushroom boys succeed,
   ' And push us from our *forms !* '

Lo ! where they scramble forth, and shout,
And leap, and skip, and mob about,
   At play where we have play'd !
Some hop, some run (some fall), some twine
Their crony arms ; some in the shine,
   And some are in the shade !

Lo ! there what mix'd conditions run !
The orphan lad ; the widow's son ;
   And Fortune's favour'd care—
The wealthy-born, for whom she hath
Mac-Adamized the future path—
   The Nabob's pamper'd heir !

Some brightly starr'd—some evil born,—
For honour some, and some for scorn,—
   For fair or foul renown !
Good, bad, indiff'rent—none may lack !
Look, here's a White, and there's a Black !
   And there's a Creole brown !

Some laugh and sing, some mope and weep,
And wish *their* frugal sires would keep
   Their only sons at home ;—

---

[1] The earlier form of Hawaii.

THOMAS HOOD (THE ELDER)

Some tease the future tense, and plan
The full-grown doings of the man,
   And pant for years to come !

A foolish wish !   There's one at hoop ;
And four at *fives !* and five who stoop
   The marble taw to speed !
And one that curvets in and out,
Reining his fellow Cob about,—
   Would I were in his *steed !*

Yet he would gladly halt and drop
That boyish harness off, to swop
   With this world's heavy van—
To toil, to tug.   O little fool !
Whilst thou canst be a horse at school
   To wish to be a man !

Perchance thou deem'st it were a thing
To wear a crown,—to be a king !
   And sleep on regal down !
Alas ! thou know'st not kingly cares ;
Far happier is thy head that wears
   That hat without a crown !

And dost thou think that years acquire
New added joys ? Dost think thy sire
   More happy than his son ?
That manhood's mirth ?—Oh, go thy ways
To Drury Lane when —— *plays,*
   And see how *forced* our fun !

THOMAS HOOD (THE ELDER)

Thy taws are brave !—thy tops are rare !—
Our tops are spun with coils of care,
　　Our *dumps* are no delight !—
The Elgin marbles are but tame,
And 'tis at best a sorry game
　　To fly the Muse's kite !

Our hearts are dough, our heels are lead,
Our topmost joys fall dull and dead
　　Like balls with no rebound !
And often with a faded eye
We look behind, and send a sigh
　　Towards that merry ground !

Then be contented.　Thou hast got
The most of heav'n in thy young lot,
　　There's sky-blue in thy cup !
Thou'lt find thy Manhood all too fast—
Soon come, soon gone ! and Age at last
　　A sorry *breaking-up !*

BEN JONSON

1573?–1637

THE brilliant wit, the wide knowledge, and the essentially dramatic qualities of Ben Jonson demand for him the serious consideration of his lighter verse. His critical faculty, too, was of the keenest; and it is in a spirit of criticism that he replies to Master Wither's song. This reply approaches nearer an imitation than a parody, except that the writer follows out the same train of thought as that supplied by the original, but dexterously changes the sentiment of the speaker to point a paradoxical moral.

Answer to Master Wither's Song, "Shall I, Wasting in Despair?"

[*Parody—G. Wither*]

SHALL I mine affections slack,
      'Cause I see a woman's black?
Or myself, with care cast down,
'Cause I see a woman brown?
Be she blacker than the night,
Or the blackest jet in sight!
            If she be not so to me,
            What care I how black she be?

Shall my foolish heart be burst,
'Cause I see a woman's curst?
Or a thwarting hoggish nature
Joinèd in as bad a feature?

53

Be she curst or fiercer than
Brutish beast, or savage man!
    If she be not so to me,
        What care I how curst she be?

Shall a woman's vices make
Me her vices quite forsake?
Or her faults to me made known,
Make me think that I have none?
Be she of the most accurst,
And deserve the name of worst!
    If she be not so to me,
        What care I how bad she be?

'Cause her fortunes seem too low,
Shall I therefore let her go?
He that bears an humble mind
And with riches can be kind,
Think how kind a heart she'd have,
If he were some servile slave!
    And if that same mind I see,
        What care I how poor she be?

Poor, or bad, or curst, or black,
I will ne'er the more be slack!
If she hate me (then believe)
She shall die ere I will grieve!
If she like me when I woo,
I can like and love her too!
    If that she be fit for me,
        What care I what others be?

JOHN KEATS

1795–1821

THE following stanzas are interesting, as showing the poet's power of parody. Charles Armitage Brown was a close friend of Keats, and for a while, after the death of the poet's brother in December, 1818, the two lived together. Lord Houghton included the first parody in his 1848 edition of Keats' poems, and prefaced it with the following words : —

"Brown this morning is writing some Spenserian stanzas against Mrs., Miss Brawne, and me ; so I shall amuse myself with him a little, in the manner of Spenser." At the end of the verses Keats adds a note : "This character would ensure him a situation in the establishment of patient Griselda."

The poem "On Oxford" was written at Oxford, and sent in a letter to Reynolds, with a note : "Wordsworth sometimes, though in a fine way, gives us sentences in the style of school exercises. For instance—

> ' The lake doth glitter,
> Small birds twitter,' etc.

Now, I think this is an excellent method of giving us a very clear description of an interesting place such as Oxford is."

The poem of Wordsworth here parodied is entitled in the two volumes of poems which appeared in 1807—

"Written in March while resting on the Bridge at the Foot of Brother's Water."

JOHN KEATS

A Portrait

[*Imitation—E. Spenser*]

HE is to meet a melancholy carle :
    Thin in the waist, with bushy head of hair,
As hath the seeded thistle, when a parle
It holds with Zephyr, ere it sendeth fair
Its light balloons into the summer air ;
Thereto his beard had not begun to bloom.
No brush had touched his cheek, or razor shear ;
No care had touched his cheek with mortal doom,
But new he was and bright, as scarf from Persian loom.

Ne carèd he for wine, or half and half ;
Ne carèd he for fish, or flesh, or fowl ;
And sauces held he worthless as the chaff ;
He 'sdeigned the swine-head at the wassail-bowl :
Ne with lewd ribbalds sat he cheek by jowl ;
Ne with sly lemans in the scorner's chair ;
But after water-brooks this pilgrim's soul
Panted and all his food was woodland air ;
Though he would oft-times feast on gilliflowers rare.

The slang of cities in no wise he knew,
Tipping the wink to him was heathen Greek ;
He sipped no " olden Tom," or " ruin blue,"
Or Nantz, or cherry-brandy, drank full meek
By many a damsel brave and rouge of cheek ;

Nor did he know each aged watchman's beat,—
Nor in obscurèd purlieus would he seek,
For curlèd Jewesses, with ankels neat,
Who, as they walk abroad, make twinkling with their feet.

On Oxford

[Imitation—W. Wordsworth]

THE Gothic looks solemn,
    The plain Doric column
Supports an old Bishop and Crozier ;
    The mouldering arch,
    Shrouded o'er by a larch,
Stands next door to Wilson the Hosier.

    Vicè—that is, by turns—
    O'er pale faces mourns
The black tassell'd trencher and common hat ;
    The Chantry boy sings,
    The steeple-bell rings,
And as for the Chancellor—*dominat*.

    There are plenty of trees
    And plenty of ease,
And plenty of fat deer for parsons ;
    And when it is venison,
    Short is the benison,—
Then each on a leg or thigh fastens.

CHARLES LAMB

1775–1834

THE gentle and kindly humour of Elia is evident in the two following examples of his lighter verse, which, moreover, are excellent parodies. The "Nonsense Verses" are a brilliant travesty of his own "Angel-Help," and it is well that the author parodied his own lines, for had another dared to point the finger of raillery at so perfect a poem, he would have deserved our censure rather than our praise. The second parody was first published under the name of "A Conceipt of Diabolical Possession." It is supposed to be extracted from a common-place book which belonged to Robert Burton, the famous author of "The Anatomy of Melancholy," and caricatures the style and mannerisms of that author rather than individual specimens of his verse.

Nonsense Verses

[*Parody—Chas. Lamb*]

LAZY-BONES, lazy-bones, wake up, and peep !
The cat's in the cupboard, your mother's asleep.
There you sit snoring, forgetting her ills ;
Who is to give her her bolus and pills ?
Twenty fine angels must come into town,
All for to help you to make your new gown ;
Dainty Aerial, Spinsters, and Singers ;
Aren't you ashamed to employ such white fingers ?
Delicate hands, unaccustom'd to reels,
To set 'em a working a poor body's wheels ?

Why they came down is to me all a riddle,
And left Hallelujah broke off in the middle;
Jones Court, and the Presence angelical, cut—
To eke out the work of a lazy young slut.
Angel-duck, angel-duck, wingéd and silly,
Pouring a watering-pot over a lily,
Gardener gratuitous, careless of pelf,
Leave her to water her lily herself,
Or to neglect it to death if she choose it:
Remember her love is her own, if she lose it.

Hypochondriacus

[*Imitatiou—Robert Burton*]

BY myself walking,
   To myself talking,
When as I ruminate
On my untoward fate,
Scarcely seem I
Alone sufficiently,
Black thoughts continually
Crowding my privacy;
They come unbidden,
Like foe at a wedding,
Thrusting their faces
In better guests' places,
Peevish and malcontent,
Clownish, impertinent,
Dashing the merriment:

So in like fashion
Dim cogitations
Follow and haunt me,
Striving to daunt me,
In my heart festering,
In my ears whispering,
"Thy friends are treacherous,
Thy foes are dangerous,
Thy dreams ominous."
Fierce Anthropophagi
Spectra, Diaboli,
What scared St. Anthony,
Hobgoblins, Lemures,
Dreams of Antipodes,
Night-riding Incubi,
Troubling the fantasy,
All dire illusions
Causing confusions ;
Figments heretical,
Scruples fantastical,
Doubts diabolical,
Abaddon vexeth me,
Malice perplexeth me,
Lucifer teareth me—

Jesu! Maria! liberate nos ab his diris tentationibus
Inimici.

JOHN LEYDEN, M.D.

1775–1811

LEYDEN was born in Roxburghshire, and studied medicine at
Edinburgh University, obtaining a wide repute as a man of remarkable attainments. He was known to Campbell and Heber, and
through them to Sir Walter Scott, whom he assisted considerably
in the compilation of "Border Minstrelsy." He was, therefore,
well qualified to imitate "An Early Metrical Romance," and the
result is eminently successful. The "Squyere" and his "Dame" are
George Ellis, the compiler of "Specimens of the Early English
Poets," and his wife, who had a beautiful voice. The dwarf is
Ritson, a writer who had attacked Ellis in print.

The Lay of the Ettercap

[Imitation of a Border Ballad]

NOW shal y tellen to ye, y wis,
    Of that Squyere hizt Ellis,
And his Dame so fre :
So hende he is by goddes mizt,
That he nis not ymake a knizt
It is the more pitè.

He knoweth better eche glewe,
Than y can to ye shewe
Oither bi plume or greffe :
To hunte or hawke, bi frith or folde,
Or play at boules in alles colde,
He is wel holden cheffe.

JOHN LEYDEN

His eyes graye as glas ben,
And his visage alto kene,
Loveliche to paramour :
Clere as amber beth his faxe,
His face beth thin as battle-axe
That deleth dintes doure.

His witte beth both kene and sharpe,
To knizt or dame that wel can carpe
Oither in halle or boure :
And had y not that Squyere yfonde,
Y hadde ben at the se gronde,
Which had ben gret doloure.

In him y finden none nother evil,
Save that his nostril moche doth snivel,
Al throgh that vilaine snuffe :
But then his speche beth so perquire,
That those who may his carpyng here,
They never may here ynough.

His Dame beth of so meikle price,
To holden hemselves in her service,
Fele folks faine wolde be :
Soft and swote in eche steven,
Like an angel com fro heven,
Singeth sothe that fre.

I wot her carpyng bin ful queynt,
And her corps bothe smale and gent,
Semeliche to be sene :

JOHN LEYDEN

Fete, hondes, and fingres smale,
Of perle beth eche fingre nail;
She mizt ben Fairi Quene.

That Ladi gent wolde given a scarfe
To hym wolde kille a wreche dwarfe
Of paynim brode:
That dwarfe is a fell Ettercap,
And liven aye on nettle-sap,
And hath none nother fode.

That dwarfe he beth berdles and bare,
And weazel-blowen beth all his hair,
Lyke an ympe elfe;
And in this middel erd all and haile
Ben no kyn thyng he loveth an dele,
Save his owen selfe.

And when the Dame ben come to toune,
That Ladi gent sall mak her boune
A selcouth feat to try,
To take a little silver knyfe,
And end that sely dwarfes life,
And bake hym in a pye.

WILLIAM MAGINN, LL.D.

1793–1842

THE literary career of William Maginn commenced under brilliant auspices ; he was patronised by Murray, to whose notice his masterly contributions in *Blackwood's Magazine* had brought him, and for a time he was on the staff of *The Representative*, but his intemperance estranged his benefactors, and brought him into pecuniary difficulties. His chief work was the establishment of *Fraser's Magazine* in 1830, in which appeared his "Gallery of Literary Characters," where "his humorous letterpress kept pace with Maclise's perfectly inimitable sketches." He was now in the prime of his literary activity, producing some of his finest work—"Story without a Tail," "Bob Burke's Duel with Ensign Brady," and Homeric Ballads. By 1839 his health had been impaired and his good faith compromised ; he was beset by creditors, and at last he was thrown into the debtors' prison, whence he emerged broken-hearted and consumptive, to die at Walton-on-Thames, August 21st, 1842.

"The Auncient Waggonere" is taken from the "Gallery of Literary Characters."

WILLIAM MAGINN, LL.D.

The Rime of the Auncient Waggonere

[*Parody—Coleridge*]

PART FIRST

IT is an auncient Waggonere,
   And hee stoppeth one of nine,
" Now wherefore dost thou grip me soe
   With that horny fist of thine ? "

An auncient waggonere stoppeth ane tailore going to a wedding, whereat he hath been appointed best manne, and to take a hand in the casting of the slippere.

" The bridegroom's doors are opened wide,
   And thither I must walke ;
Soe, by your leave, I must be gone,
   I have noe time for talke ! "

The waggonere in mood for chat, and admits of no excuse.

Hee holds him with his horny fist—
   " There was a wain," quothe hee—
" Hold offe, thou raggamouffine tykke."
   Eftsoones his fist dropped hee.

The tailore seized with the ague.

Hee satte him down upon a stone,
   With ruefulle looks of feare ;
And thus began this tippsye manne,
   The red-nosed waggonere.

He listeneth like a three years and a half child.

F

WILLIAM MAGINN

The appetite of the tailore whetted by the smell of cabbage.

"The waine is fulle, the horses pulle,
    Merrilye did we trotte
Alonge the bridge, alonge the road,
    A jolly crewe, I wotte."
And here the tailore smotte his breaste,
    He smelte the cabbage potte !

The waggonere in talking anent Boreas maketh bad orthographye.

"The night was darke, like Noe's arke,
    Our waggone moved alonge,
The hail poured faste, loude roared the
        blaste,
    Yet still we moved alonge ;
And sung in chorus, 'Cease, loud Borus,'
    A very charming songe.

"'Bravoe, bravissimoe,' I cried,
    The sounde was quite elatinge ;

Their mirth interrupted

But in a trice, upon the ice,
    We hearde the horses skatinge.

and the passengers exercise themselves in the pleasant art of swimminge, as doeth also their prog, to witte, great store of colde roasted beef, item ane beef-stake pye : item, viii choppines of usquebaugh.

"The ice was here, the ice was there,
    It was a dismale mattere
To see the cargoe, one by one,
    Flounderinge in the wattere !

"With rout and roare, we reached the
        shore,
    And never a soul did sinke ;
But in the rivere, gone for evere,
    Swum our meate and drinke.

WILLIAM MAGINN

"At lengthe we spied a good grey goose,
  Through the snow it came ;
And with the butte end of my whippe
  I hailed it in Goddhis name.

The waggonere hailethe ane goose with ane novel salutatione.

"It staggered as it had been drunke,
  So dexterous was it hitte ;
Of brokene boughs we made a fire,
  Thomme Loncheone roasted itte."—

"Be done, thou tipsye waggonere,
  To the feaste I must awaye."
The waggonere seized him by the coatte,
  And forced him there to staye,
Begginge, in gentlemanlie style,
  Butte halfe-ane-hour's delaye.

The tailore impatient to be gone, but is forcibly persuaded to remain.

PART SECOND

"The crimson sun was rising o'ere
  The verge of the horizon,
Upon my worde, as faire a sunne
  As ever I clapped eyes onne.

The waggonere's bowels yearn towards the sunne.

"'Twill bee ane comfortable thinge,"
  The mutinous crewe 'gan crye ;
"'Twill be ane comfortable thinge
  Within the jaile to lye ;
Ah! execrable wretche," said they,
  "That caused the goose to die !

The passengers throwe the blame of the goose massacre on the innocent waggonere.

WILLIAM MAGINN

The sunne suf-feres ane artificial eclipse, and horror follows, the same not being men-tioned in the Bel-faste Almanacke.

"The day was drawing near ittes close,
  The sunne was well nighe settinge;
When lo! it seemed as iffe his face
  Was veiled with fringe-warke-nettinge.

Various hypo-theses on the sub-ject frome which the passengers draw wrong conclusions.

"Somme saide itte was ane apple tree,
  Laden with goodlye fruite,
Somme swore itte was ane foreigne birde,
  Some said it was ane brute;
Alas! it was ane bumbailiffe
  Riding in pursuite!

Ane lovely sound ariseth; ittes ef-fects described.

"A hue and crye sterte uppe behind,
  Whilke smote our ears like thunder,
Within the waggone there was drede,
  Astonishmente and wonder.

The passengers throw somersets.

"One after one, the rascalls rann,
  And from the carre did jump;
One after one, one after one,
  They felle with heavy thump.

"Six miles ane houre theye offe did
    scoure,
  Like shippes on ane stormye ocean,
Their garments flappinge in the winde,
  With ane short uneasy motion.

"Their bodies with their legs did flye,
   Theye fled withe fears and glyffe;
Why star'st thou soe?—With one goode
    blow,
 I felled the bumbailiffe!"

*The waggonere
complimenteth the
bumbailiffe with
ane Mendoza.*

PART THIRD

"I feare thee, auncient waggonere,
   I feare thy hornye fiste,
For itte is stained with goose's gore,
   And bailiff's blood I wist.

*The tailore meet-
eth Corporal Feare.*

"I fear to gette ane fisticuffe
   From thy leathern knuckles brown";
With that the tailore strove to ryse—
   The waggonere thrusts him down.

"Thou craven, if thou mov'st a limye,
   I'll give thee cause for feare;"
And thus went on that tipsye man,
   The red-billed waggonere.

"The bumbailiffe so beautiful!
   Declared itte was no joke,
For, to his knowledge, both his legs
   And fifteen ribs were broke.

*The bailiffe com-
plaineth of con-
siderable derange-
ment of his animal
economye.*

WILLIAM MAGINN

Policemen with their lanthornes pursue the waggonere.

"The lighte was gone, the nighte came on,
  Ane hundrede lanthernes' sheen
Glimmerred on the kinge's highwaye—
  Ane lovelye sighte, I ween.

" ' Is it he,' quoth one, ' is this the manne ?
  I'll laye the rascalle stiffe ; '
With cruel stroke the beak he broke
  Of the harmless bumbailiffe.

Steppeth twenty feet in imitation of the Admirable Chrichtoun.

"The threatening of the saucye rogue
  No more I coulde abide ;
Advancing forthe my goode right legg
  Three paces and a stride,
I sent my left foot dexterously
  Seven inches through his side.

Complaineth of foule play and falleth down in ane trance.

"Up came the second from the vanne ;
  We had scarcely fought a round,
When someone smote me from behind,
  And I fell down in a swound :

One acteth the parte of Job's comfortere.

"And when my head began to clear,
  I heard the yemering crew—
Quoth one, ' This man hath penance done,
  And penance more shall do '."

70

WILLIAM MAGINN

PART FOURTH

" O Freedom is a glorious thing !
   And, tailore, by the by,
I'd rather in a halter swing
   Than in a dungeon lie.

The waggonere maketh ane shrewd observation.

" The jailere came to bring me foode,
   Forget it will I never,
How he turned up the white o' his eye
   When I stuck him in the liver.

The waggonere tickleth the spleen of the jailer, who daunces ane Fa-dango.

" His threade of life was snapt : once more
   I reached the open streete ;
The people sang out ' Gardyloo '
   As I ran down the streete.
Methought the blessed air of heaven
   Never smelte so sweete.

Rejoicethe in the fragrance of the aire.

" Once more upon the broad highwaye
   I walked with feare and drede ;
And every fifteen steppes I tooke
   I turned about my heade,
For feare the corporal of the guarde
   Might close behind me trede !

Dreadeth Shoan Dhu, the corporal of the garde.

71

WILLIAM MAGINN

" Behold, upon the western wave
    Setteth the broad bright sunne ;
So I must onward, as I have
    Full fifteen miles to runne.

" And should the bailiffes hither come
    To aske whilke way I've gone,
Tell them I took the othere road,
    Said hee, and trotted onne."

The waggonere taketh leave of the tailore

The tailore rushed into the roome
    O'erturning three or foure ;
Fractured his skulle against the walle,
    And worde spake never more ! !

to whome a small accident happeneth. Whereupon followeth the morale very proper to be hadde in minde by all members of the Dilettanti Society when they come over the bridge at these hours. Wherefore let them take heede and not lay blame where it lyeth nott.

MORALE

Such is the fate of foolish men.
    The danger all may see
Of those who list to waggonere,
    And keepe bad companye.

WILLIAM MAGINN

To a Bottle of Old Port

[*Parody—T. Moore*]

WHEN he who adores thee has left but the dregs
  Of such famous old Stingo behind,
Oh! say will he bluster and weep—no 'ifegs!
  He'll seek for some more of the kind.
He'll laugh and though doctors perhaps may condemn,
  Thy tede shall efface the decree,
For many can witness though, subject to phlegm,
  He has always been faithful to thee!

With thee were the dreams of his earliest love,
  Every rap in his pocket was thine,
And his very last prayer, ev'ry morning, by Jove!
  Was to finish the evening in wine.
How blest are the tipplers whose heads can outlive
  The effects of four bottles of thee;
But the next dearest blessing that Heaven can give,
  Is to stagger home muzzy from three!

JOHN PHILIPS

1676–1709

"The Splendid Shilling" was written by the son of the Vicar of Bampton for the instruction of a colleague in the art of taking care of the pence.

Philips knew his Virgil almost by heart, and delighted in the splendours of Milton's verse. His parody met with an immense success, and became in its turn the subject for vastly inferior imitations, such as "The Crooked Sixpence," "The Copper Farthing," etc.

Professor Henry Morley, in his note on this poem, concludes: "The Miltonic grandeur of tone John Philips happily caught from a long and loving study of the English poet whom he reverenced above others, and 'The Splendid Shilling' has a special charm as a burlesque in which nobody is ridiculed."

The Splendid Shilling

[Imitation—Milton]

HAPPY the Man, who void of Cares and Strife,
In silken, or in Leathern Purse retains
A *Splendid Shilling*: he nor hears with Pain
New Oysters cry'd, nor sighs for chearful Ale;
But with his friends, when Nightly Mists arise,
To *Juniper's-Magpye*, or *Town-Hall*[1] repairs:
Where, mindful of the Nymph, whose wanton eye

---

[1] Two noted alehouses in Oxford, 1700.

74

JOHN PHILIPS

Transfixed his Soul, and kindled Amorous Flames,
CHLOE, or PHILLIS; he each Circling Glass
Wisheth her Health, and Joy, and equal Love.
Mean while, he smoaks, and laughs at Merry Tale,
Or *pun* ambiguous, or *Conundrum* quaint.
But I, whom griping Penury surrounds,
And hunger, sure Attendant upon Want,
With scanty Offals, and small acid Tiff
(Wretched Repast!) my meagre Corps sustain:
Then solitary walk, or doze at home
In Garret vile, and with a warming Puff
Regale chill'd Fingers; or from Tube as black
As Winter-Chimney, or well-polish'd Jet,
Exhale *Mundungus*,[1] ill-perfuming Scent:
Not blacker Tube, nor of a shorter Size
Smoaks *Cambro-Britain* (vers'd in Pedigree,
Sprung from *Cadwalader*[2] and *Arthur*,[3] Kings
Full famous in Romantick Tale) when he
O'er many a craggy Hill and barren Cliff,
Upon a Cargo of fam'd *Cestrian*[4] Cheese,
High over-shadowing Rides, with a design
To vend his Wares, or at th' *Arvonian* Mart,
Or *Maridunum*,[5] or the Ancient Town
Yclip'd *Brechinia*,[6] or where *Vaga's* Stream

[1] A branch of particularly rank tobacco.
[2] Surnamed the Blessed. His heroic exploits hold an important
place in Welsh tradition.
[3] The Great Hero of Celtic Legend.
[4] Cheshire.
[5] Caermarthen.
[6] Brechin, a town in Forfarshire.

JOHN PHILIPS

Encircles *Ariconium*,[1] fruitful Soil!
Whence flow Nectareous Wines, that well may vie
With *Massic*, *Setin*, or renown'd *Falern*.[2]

Thus, while my joyless Minutes tedious flow,
With Looks demure, and silent Pace, a *Dun*
Horrible Monster! hated by Gods and Men,
To my Aerial Citadel ascends,
With Vocal Heel thrice thund'ring at my Gate,
With hideous Accent Thrice he calls; I know
The Voice ill-boding, and the solemn Sound.
What shou'd I do? or whither turn?   Amaz'd,
Confounded, to the dark Recess I fly
Of Woodhole; strait my bristling Hairs erect
Thro' sudden Fear; a chilly Sweat bedews
My shud'ring Limbs, and (wonderful to tell!)
My Tongue forgets her Faculty of Speech;
So horrible he seems! his faded Brow
Entrench'd with many a Frown, and Conic Beard,
And spreading Band, admir'd by Modern Saints,
Disastrous Acts forebode; in his Right Hand
Long Scrolls of Paper solemnly he waves,
With Characters, and Figures dire inscrib'd,
Grievous to Mortal Eyes; (ye Gods avert
Such Plagues from Righteous Men!) Behind him stalks
Another Monster, not unlike himself,
Sullen of aspect, by the Vulgar call'd

[1] Weston in Herefordshire.

[2] Three of the most renowned Roman wines. Of these *Massic*
was the coarsest, *Setinu* the Imperial wine, and *Falernum* the
choicest of the second-rate wines.

JOHN PHILIPS

A *Catchpole*, whose polluted Hands the Gods
With Force incredible, and Magick Charms
Erst have endu'd, if he his ample Palm
Should haply on ill-fated Shoulder lay
Of Debtor, strait his Body to the Touch
Obsequious, (as whilom Knights were wont)
To some Inchanted Castle is convey'd
Where Gates impregnable, and coercive Chains
In Durance strict detain him, till in form
Of Money, PALLAS sets the Captive free.

Beware, ye Debtors, when ye walk beware,
Be circumspect ; oft with insidious Ken
This Caitif eyes your Steps aloof, and oft
Lies perdue in a Nook, or gloomy Cave,
Prompt to inchant some inadvertent Wretch
With his unhallow'd Touch.   So (Poets sing)
Grimalkin [1] to Domestick Vermin sworn
An everlasting Foe, with watchful Eye
Lies Nightly brooding o'er a chinky Gap
Protending her fell Claws, to thoughtless Mice
Sure Ruin.   So her disembowell'd Web
Arachne [2] in a Hall, or Kitchin spreads,
Obvious to vagrant Flies : She secret stands
Within her woven Cell ; the Humming Prey,
Regardless of their Fate, rush on the Toils
Inextricable, nor will aught avail

[1] Gray-malkin, a cat, especially an old cat.   Grimalkin is often
supposed to accompany a witch on her broomstick.

[2] Arachne challenged Minerva to compete with her in weaving,
and for her presumption was changed into a spider.

Their Arts, or Arms, or Shapes of lovely Hue;
The Wasp insidious, and the buzzing Drone,
And Butterfly proud of expanded Wings
Distinct with Gold, entangled in her Snares,
Useless Resistance make : With eager Strides,
She tow'ring flies to her expected Spoils;
Then, with envenomed Jaws the vital Blood
Drinks of reluctant Foes, and to her Cave
Their bulky Carcasses triumphant drags.

So pass my Days.   But when Nocturnal Shades
This World invelop, and th' inclement Air
Persuades Men to repel benumming Frosts
With pleasant Wines, and crackling Blaze of Wood;
Me lonely sitting, nor the glimmering Light
Of Make-weight Candle, nor the joyous Talk
Of loving Friend delights; distress'd, forlorn,
Amidst the Horrors of the tedious Night,
Darkling I sigh, and feed with dismal Thoughts
My anxious Mind; or sometimes mournful Verse
Indite, and sing of Groves and Myrtle Shades,
Or desperate Lady near a purling Stream
Or Lover pendant on a Willow-Tree.
Mean while, I labour with eternal Drought,
And restless with, and rave; my parched Throat
Finds no Relief, nor heavy Eyes Repose :
But if a Slumber haply does invade
My weary Limbs, my Fancy's still awake,
Thoughtful of Drink, and eager, in a Dream,
Tipples imaginary Pots of Ale,
In vain; awake I find the settled thirst
Still gnawing, and the pleasant Phantom curse.

JOHN PHILIPS

Thus do I Live from Pleasure quite debarr'd,
Nor taste the Fruits that the Sun's genial Rays
Mature, *John-Apple*,[1] nor the downy *Peach*,
Nor *Walnut* in rough-furrow'd Coat secure,
Nor *Medlar*-Fruit, delicious in decay :
Afflictions great ! yet Greater still remain :
My *Galligaskins*[2] that have long withstood
The Winter's Fury, and incroaching Frosts,
By Time subdu'd, (what will not Time subdue !)
An horrid Chasm disclose, with Orifice
Wide, discontinuous ; at which the Winds
Eurus and *Auster*, and the dreadful Force
Of *Boreas*, that congeals the *Cronian* Waves,
Tumultuous enter with dire chilling Blasts,
Portending Agues. Thus a well-fraught Ship
Long sail'd secure, or thro' th' Aegean Deep,
Or the *Ionian*, till Cruising near
The *Lilybean* Shore, with hideous Crush
On *Scylla*, or *Charybdis* (dang'rous Rocks)
She strikes rebounding, whence the shatter'd Oak,
So fierce a Shock unable to withstand,
Admits the Sea ; in at the gaping Side
The crowding Waves gush with impetuous Rage,
Resistless, Overwhelming ; Horrors seize
The Mariners, Death in their Eyes appears.
They Stare, they Lave, they Pump, they Swear, they Pray :
(Vain Efforts !) still the battering Waves rush in,
Implacable, till delug'd by the Foam,
The Ship sinks found'ring in the vast Abyss.

[1] An apple that can be stored for winter use.
[2] A fashion of hose or slops worn in the sixteenth century ; also
called *grogs*, *venetians*, and *gaskins*.

ALEXANDER POPE

1688–1744

THE peculiar genius of Pope was a spirit of criticism which absorbed the manners and affections of other men, and which was endowed with a lynx-eye that could see into the very crevices of the brains of his fellows. "Of the brains" it is necessary to emphasise, for he never got as far as their hearts ; but with a fixity of purpose, that would only have been hindered by attention to the more hidden qualities of human nature, he seized on their foibles, he picked to pieces their intelligences, and served them up to the public as a *chef* serves up a "*ragoût*" spiced with his own wit.

Sometimes, however, he was willing to bind himself with the fetters that had bound other men, and such occasions are com- memorated by a thin section of "Imitations" among his numerous works. All these Imitations, as is to be expected, are excellent, but all are not seemly. The parody of Swift, however, is exact, and who shall decide whether the "Ode on a Fan" or "To Delia Weeping," be the finer ? so admirably are these imitations matched for pungent satire and exact parody.

ALEXANDER POPE

On a Fan of the Author's Design

(In which was painted the story of Cephalus and Procris,
with the motto " Aura Veni ")

[Imitation—Waller]

" COME, gentle Air ! " th' Æolian shepherd said,
While Procris [1] panted in the secret shade :
" Come, gentle Air," the fairer Delia cries,
While at her feet her swain expiring lies.
Lo ! the glad gales o'er all her beauties stray,
Breathe on her lips, and in her bosom play !
In Delia's hand this toy is fatal found,
Nor could that fabled dart more surely wound :
Both gifts destructive to the giver prove ;
Alike both lovers fall by those they love.
Yet guiltless, too, this bright destroyer lives,
At random wounds nor knows the wound she gives :
She views the story with attentive eyes,
And pities Procris, while her lover dies.

[1] Procris was deeply beloved of Cephalus, who became her hus-
band, and by whom she was fated to be killed.

ALEXANDER POPE

Weeping

[*Parody—Cowley*]

WHILE Celia's tears make sorrow bright,
    Proud Grief sits swelling in her eyes;
The Sun, next those the fairest light,
    Thus from the Ocean first did rise;
And thus through Mists we see the Sun,
Which else we durst not gaze upon.

These silver drops, like Morning dew,
    Foretell the fervour of the day:
So from one Cloud soft show'rs we view,
    And blasting lightnings burst away.
The Stars that fall from Celia's Eye
Declare our Doom is drawing nigh.

The Baby in that sunny sphere
    So like a Phaëthon [1] appears,
That Heaven, the threaten'd World to spare,
    Thought fit to drown him in her Tears:
Else might th' ambitious Nymph aspire,
To set, like him, Heav'n too on fire.

[1] Phaëthon persuaded his father Helios to allow him to drive the chariot of the sun across heaven, but he was too weak to check the mad career of the flaming steeds, so that the earth was nearly set on fire.

ALEXANDER POPE

The Happy Life of a Country Parson

[Imitation—Swift]

PARSON, these things in thy possessing
  Are better than the bishop's blessing :
A wife that makes conserves ; a steed
That carries double when there's need ;
October store, and best Virginia,
Tithe-pig, and mortuary guinea ;
Gazettes sent gratis down, and frank'd ;
For which thy patron's meekly thank'd ;
A large Concordance, bound long since ;
Sermons to Charles the First, when Prince ;
A chronicle of ancient standing ;
A Chrysostom [1] to smooth thy band in ;
The Polyglott [2]—three parts—my text :
Howbeit,—likewise—now to my next :
Lo here the Septuagint,[3]—and Paul,
To sum the whole,—and close of all.

[1] St. Chrysostom (the golden-mouthed) was born about the year A.D. 344, and was one of the most renowned of the Church Fathers. He was a great writer, and his works would form an essential part of a parson's library. As a folio volume they would no doubt make an excellent press for the worthy owner's linen band."

[2] The Polyglott—a Bible in various languages, usually Hebrew, Greek, and Latin.

[3] The Septuagint—the Alexandrine version of the Old Testament—is the most ancient translation of the Scriptures, and is in

He that has these, may pass his life,
Drink with the Squire, and kiss his wife ;
On Sundays preach, and eat his fill ;
And fast on Fridays—if he will ;
Toast Church and Queen, explain the news,
Talk with churchwardens about pews,
Pray heartily for some new gift,
And shake his head at Doctor Swift.

Greek.   There is an old story that the work was translated separately by seventy learned scholars, and that upon comparison all their translations were found to be alike.   It is either from this or from the acceptance of the translation by the seventy who formed the Sanhedrin that the title of Septuagint is derived.

THOMAS LOVE PEACOCK

1785–1866

Most of Peacock's worldly prosperity was derived from his connection with the India House, in which he became a clerk in 1819, but his fame rests upon his novels, of which the most notable are "Maid Marian," "Crotchet Castle," and "Headlong Hall and Nightmare Abbey." He was, besides, the friend of Shelley, whom he knew intimately for some seven years and of whom he wrote his recollections. In 1837 he brought out a volume of light verse entitled "Paper Money Lyrics and other Poems," which he says were written in 1825 and 1826 "during the prevalence of an influenza," and in it "The Wise Men of Gotham" is to be found. As the title of the poem shows, it attacks Coleridge on the charge of Mysticism, and there is some justice in the accusation, although the accuser fails to prove that he can beat his opponent in his own style, the *sine qua non* of the parodist proper. The poem is, nevertheless, an interesting travesty of the less successful part of Coleridge's work—his ill-finished themes and vague moralisings.

The Wise Men of Gotham

[*Imitation—S. T. Coleridge*]

IN a bowl to sea went wise men three,
  On a brilliant night of June :
They carried a net, and their hearts were set
  On fishing up the moon.

The sea was calm, the air was balm,
  Not a breath stirred low or high,
And the moon, I trow, lay as bright below,
  And as round as in the sky.

THOMAS LOVE PEACOCK

The wise men with the current went,
    Nor paddle nor oar had they,
And still as the grave they went on the wave,
    That they might not disturb their prey.

Far, far at sea, were the wise men three,
    When their fishing-net they threw ;
And at the throw, the moon below
    In a thousand fragments flew.

The sea was bright with a dancing light
    Of a million gleams,
Which the broken moon shot forth as soon
    As the net disturbed her beams.

They drew in their net : it was empty and wet,
    And they had lost their pain,
Soon ceased the play of each dancing ray,
    And the image was round again.

Three times they threw, three times they drew,
    And all the while were mute ;
And evermore their wonder grew,
    'Till they could not but dispute.

Their silence they broke, and each one spoke
    Full long, and loud, and clear ;
A man at sea their voices three
    Full three leagues off might hear.

The three wise men got home again
    To their children and their wives :
But, touching their trip, and their net's vain dip,
    They disputed all their lives.

The wise men three could never agree,
    Why they missed the promised boon ;
They agreed alone that their net they had thrown,
    And they had not caught the moon.

I have thought myself pale o'er this ancient tale,
    And its sense I could not ken ;
But now I see that the wise men three
    Were paper money men.

" Rub-a-dub-dub, three men in a tub "
    Is a mystic burthen old,
Which I've pondered about till my fire went out,
    And I could not sleep for cold.

I now divine each mystic sign,
    Which robbed me oft of sleep,
Three men in a bowl, who went to troll,
    For the moon in the midnight deep.

Three men were they who science drank
    From Scottish fountains free ;
The cash they sank in the Gotham bank,
    Was the moon beneath the sea.

The breaking of the imaged moon,
    At the fishing-net's first splash,
Was the breaking of the bank as soon
    As the wise men claimed their cash.

The dispute which lasted all their lives,
    Was the economic strife,
Which the son's son's son of every one
    Will maintain through all his life.

The son's son's sons will baffled be,
  As were their sires of old ;
But they only agree, like the wise men three,
  That they could not get their gold.

And they'll build systems dark and deep,
  And systems broad and high ;
But two of three will never agree
  About the reason why.

And he who at this day will seek
  The Economic Club,
Will find at least three sages there,
As ready as any that ever were,
  To go to sea in a tub.

WALTER RALEIGH

1552 (?)–1618

Despite his adventurous career, the affairs of letters claimed no small share of Sir Walter Raleigh's genius. His most important gift to literature is his "History of the World"—"one of the noblest literary enterprises." It was begun for the benefit of Princ Henry, the eldest son of James I, and was continued during his imprisonment ; but unfortunately it was never completed, for only the first volume was published, and that deals with subjects no lat than B.C. 103.

There are besides many beautiful poems from his pen, and amongst them is the following well-known "Answer" to Mr. Wither's song. It deserves comparison with the "Answer" to the same song of Ben Jonson, who, by the way, considered Raleigh his ather in literature.

Another Answer to Wither

[Parody—G. Wither]

SHALL I, like a hermit, dwell
    On a rock, or in a cell,
Calling home the smallest part
That is missing of my heart,
To bestow it where I may
Meet a rival every day ?
        If she undervalue me,
        What care I how fair she be ?

WALTER RALEIGH

Were her tresses angel-gold,
If a stranger may be bold
Unrebukèd, unafraid,
To convert them to a braid,
And, with little more ado,
Work them into bracelets too ;
 If the mine be grown so free,
 What care I how rich it be ?

Were her hand as rich a prize
As her hairs, or precious eyes,
If she lay them out to stake
Kisses for good manners' sake,
And let every lover skip
From her hand unto her lip ;
 If she seem not chaste to me,
 What care I how chaste she be ?

No ; she must be perfect snow,
In effect as well as show ;
Warming but as snowballs do,
Not, like fire, by burning too ;
But when she by change hath got
To her heart a second lot,
 Then, if others share with me,
 Farewell her, whate'er she be !

THE ROLLIAD

1784

THE purpose of the series of satires published under the name of the "Rolliad" was political rather than critical. The title was taken from the first satire, which humorously caricatured Mr. Rolle, the member for Devonshire, who was afterwards raised to the peerage. The following attacks, however, appear to be aimed at the unpopular Court party and the still more unpopular king, George III, who fretted at the limitations of the royal power, and was set upon obeying his mother's oft-repeated advice : "Be a king, George !" But the popular idea resented the creation of a "Back-stairway" (as promotion through the direct favour of the king was termed), and it was owing to the strong feeling aroused that John Wilkes obtained such notorious popularity on account of his spirited attacks on the Bute Ministry—a mere puppet-show, worked from behind the throne—which he conducted through the medium of the *North Briton*. This resentment is voiced in the following satire, which has for its basis Dryden's Ode for St. Cecilia's Day, "Alexander's Feast," and some passages follow the original very closely. It is a remarkable parody, both as regards literary and historical interest.

THE ROLLIAD

By the Reverend Doctor Prettyman

Irregular Ode for Music

[*Imitation—J. Dryden*]

RECITATIVE, BY DOUBLE VOICES

Hail to the Lyar ! whose all persuasive strain,
 Wak'd by the master touch of art,
And prompted by th' inventive brain,
 Winds its fly way into the easy heart.

SOLO

 Hark ! do I hear the golden tone ?—
 Responsive now, and now alone !
  —Or does my fancy rove ?
 Reason-born Conviction, hence !
 And frenzy wrapt by ev'ry sense
  With the untruth I love.
 Propitious fiction, aid the song,
 Poet and Priest to thee belong.

SEMI-CHORUS

By thee inspired, e'er yet the tongue was glib,
The cradled infant lisp'd the nurs'ry fib ;
 Thy votr'y in Maturer Youth
 Pleas'd, he renounc'd the name of Truth
And often dared the specious to defy,
Proud of th' expansive bold uncovered lie.

THE ROLLIAD

AIR

Propitious fiction, hear !
And smile as erst thy father smil'd
Upon his first-born child,
Thy sister dear ;
When from the nether shades among
Sin from his forehead sprung.

FULL CHORUS

Grand deluder !   Arch imposter !
Countervailing *Orde* [1] and *Foster* [2] !
Renowned Divine,
The Palm is Thine :
Be thy name or sung or trist,
Alone it stands, conspicuous fabulist !

RECITATIVE

for the celebrated female singer from Manchester. Symphony of Flutes,
pianissimo

Now in cotton robe arrayed
Poor Manufacture, tax-lamenting maid,
Thy story heard by her devoted wheel
Each busy-sounding spindle hush'd—

Fugue

Now, dreading Irish rape
Quick-shifting voice and shape—

[1] Thomas Orde, first Baron Bolton (1746–1807).   He was
Secretary to the Duke of Rutland when the latter was Lord-
Lieutenant of Ireland.   On the death of the Duke, in '87, Orde
retired on a handsome but not altogether just pension.

[2] John Foster, Baron Oriel (1740–1828), was the last Speaker of
the Irish House of Commons.   Was Chancellor of the Exchequer
in Ireland from 1804–1811.

THE ROLLIAD

DEEP BASS

from Birmingham

With visage hard, and furnace flush'd
And black-hair'd chest, and nerve of steel,
    The sex-changed listener stood
    In surly, pensive mood.

AIR

accompanied with double Bassoons, etc.

While the promise maker spoke,
The anvil missed the wonted stroke
In air suspended hammers hung
While *Pitt's* own frauds came mended from that
    tongue.

PART OF CHORUS REPEATED
Renown'd Divine, etc.

AIR

Soothed with the sound the priest grew vain,
And all his tales told o'er again,
    And added hundreds more ;
By turns, to this or that, or both
He gave the sanction of an oath,
And then the whole forswore.
" Truth," he sung, " was toil and trouble,
Honour but an empty bubble "—
Gloster's aged—*London* [1] dying—
Poor, too poor is simple lying !

---

[1] The Bishops of Gloucester and London respectively.

If the lawn is worth the wearing,
Win, oh win it by thy swearing!

FULL CHORUS REPEATED

Grand deluder, etc.

PART II

RECITATIVE

accompanyed

Enough, the parents' praise—see of Deceit
The fairer progeny ascends!
Evasion, nymph of agile feet,
    With half-veiled face;
Profession whispering accents sweet
And many a kindred fraud attends;
Mutely dealing courtly wiles
Fav'ring nods and hope-fraught smiles,
A fond, amusive, tutelary race,
That guard the home-pledg'd faith of Kings—
Or flitting, light, on paper wings;
Speed Eastern guile across this earthly ball,
And waft it back from *Windsor* to *Bengal*.
But chiefly thee, I woo, of changeful eye,
In courts yclept *Duplicity!*
Thy fond looks on mine imprinting,
Vulgar mortals call it squinting—
Baby, of Art and Int'rest bred
Whom, stealing to the back stairs head
In fondling arms—with cautious tread,

THE ROLLIAD

Wrinkle-twinkle Jenky [1] bore,
To the baize-lined closet-door.

AIR

Sweet nymph that liv'st unseen
   Within that lov'd recess
   Save when the Closet Council press
And Junto's [2] speak the thing they mean;
   Tell me by every busy power
Where shall I trace thee in the vacant hour?
Art thou content, in the sequester'd grove,
To play with hearts and vows of love?
Or emulous of prouder sway,
Dost thou to list'ning senates take thy way?
Thy presence let me still enjoy
With Rose and the lie-loving boy.

AIR

    No rogue that goes
    Is like that *Rose*
    Or scatters such deceit:
    Come to my breast—
    There ever rest
    Associate counterfiet.

[1] Charles Jenkinson, first Earl of Liverpool (1727–1808. Was Secretary of War under Lord North, and was also one of the " King's friends," as some of the Tory party called themselves.

[2] The Junto was a group of Whig politicians, very influential in the reigns of William III and Anne. After it any strong and secret political society was called a Junto.

THE ROLLIAD

PART III

LOUD SYMPHONY

But lo ! what throngs of rival bards !
More lofty themes ! more bright rewards !
See Sal'sbury a new Apollo sit
Pattern and Arbiter of wit
The laureate wreathe hangs graceful from his wand ;
Begin, he cries, and waves his whiter hand.
      'Tis *George's* natal day—
      Parnassian Pegasus away—
Grant me the more glorious steed
Of royal Brunswick breed—
I kneel, I kneel
And at his snowy heel,
Pindarick homage vow ;—
He neighs ; he bounds ; I mount, I fly—
The air-drawn crosier in my eye
The visionary mitre on my brow—
Spirit of hierarchy exalt thy rhyme,
And dedicate to George the lie sublime.

AIR

for a bishop

Hither, brethren, incense bring,
To the mitre-giving king ;
Praise him for his first donations ;
Praise him for his blest translations,
Benefices, Dispensations.

THE ROLLIAD

By the powers of a crown ;
By the many made for one ;
By a monarch's awful distance,
Rights divine and non-resistance,
Honour, triumph, glory give.—
Praise him in his might !
Praise him in his height !
The mighty mighty height of his prerogative !

RECITATIVE
by an Archbishop

Orchestras of thousands strong,
With Zadoc's zeal each note prolong
                    Prepare !
                    Prepare !
Bates [1] gives the animating nod—
Sudden they strike—unnumbered strings
Vibrate to the best of Kings—
Eunuchs, stentors, double-basses
Lab'ring lungs, inflated faces,
          Bellows working,
          Elbows jerking,
          Scraping, beating,
          Roaring, Sweating.
Thro' the old Gothic roofs be the chorus rebounded
'Till Echo is deafened and Thunder dumfounded :
And now another pause, and now another nod
—All proclaim a present God !

[1] Joah. Bates (1741–1799). A musician of no mean powers.
He was made Conductor to the Concerts of Ancient Music, and
was presented by the King with several lucrative offices under the
Crown.

THE ROLLIAD

Bishops and Lords of the Bedchamber

George submissive Britain sways
Heavy Hanover obeys
Proud Ierne's volunteers,
Abject commons, prostrate peers—
All proclaim a present God—
(On the necks of all he trod)
    A present God!
    A present God!
            Hallelujah!

JOHN HAMILTON REYNOLDS

1796–1852

REYNOLDS was a man of genius who wanted the devoted purpose and the sustaining power which are requisite to its development. He wrote fitfully. "He was one of the most brilliant men I have ever known, though in late years failing health and failing fortune somewhat soured his temper and sharpened his tongue"—such was the character sketch of a contemporary. He might have added that Reynolds was a particularly handsome man with a high, arched forehead, large dark eyes and a fine, sensitive mouth ; if we may judge from the portrait by Joseph Severn.

Certainly Reynolds's want of success in life was not due to want of opportunity, for Fate threw him into the company of many celebrated men. He was known to Leigh Hunt, and through him became the friend of Keats, and it was owing to this friendship that he received the liberal patronage of James Rice, who established him in the profession of the law. In 1824 Tom Hood married Reynolds's sister Jane, and the next year the two brothers-in-law brought out "Odes and Addresses to Great People," which contains another parody (not in metre, but in diction) of Wordsworth's poem.

The most curious fact concerning the following parody is that it appeared in print before the original. Keats, writing to a friend, remarks :—

"Wordsworth is going to publish a poem called 'Peter Bell.' What a perverse fellow it is ! Why will he talk about Peter Bells ? I was told not to tell—but to you it will not be telling—Reynolds, hearing that said 'Peter Bell' was coming out, took it into his head to write a skit upon it called 'Peter Bell.' He did it as soon as thought on ; it is to be published this morning and comes out before the real 'Peter Bell,' with this admirable motto from the 'Bold Stroke for a Wife' —"I am the real Simon Pure." It would be just as well to trounce Lord Byron in the same manner.'[1]

[1] See Buxton Forman's edition of "Shelley's Letters."

JOHN HAMILTON REYNOLDS

At a later date Keats wrote a review for the *Examiner*, in which he remarks :—

"It is plainly seen by one or two passages in this little skit, that the writer of it has felt the finer parts of Mr. Wordsworth's poetry, and perhaps expatiated with his more remote and sublimer muse. . . . We repeat, it is very unlucky: this Simon Pure is in points the very man : there is such a pernicious likeness in the scenery, such a pestilent humour in the rhymes and such an inveterate cadence in some of the stanzas."

JOHN HAMILTON REYNOLDS

Peter Bell: a Lyrical Ballad

[*Imitation—Wordsworth*]

VI

'TIS Peter Bell—'tis Peter Bell,
　　Who never stirreth in the day ;
His hand is wither'd—he is old !
On Sundays he is us'd to pray,
In winter he is very cold.[1]

.　　.　　.　　.　　.

XIV

Peter Bell doth lift his hand,
That thin hand, which in the light
Looketh like to oiled paper ;
Paper oiled,—oily bright,—
And held up to a waxen taper.

---

[1] Peter Bell resembleth Harry Gill in this particular : "His teeth they chatter, chatter, chatter." I should have introduced this fact in the text but that Harry Gill would not rhyme. I reserve this for my blank verse.

XV

The hand of Peter Bell is busy,
Under the pent-house of his hairs;
His eye is like a solemn sermon;
The little flea severely fares,
'Tis a sad day for the vermin.

XVI

He is thinking of the Bible—
Peter Bell is old and blest;
He doth pray and scratch away,
He doth scratch, and bitten, pray
To *flee* away, and be at rest.

XVII

At home his foster child is cradled—
Four brown bugs are feeding there; [1]
Catch as many, sister Ann,
Catch as many as you can [2]
And yet the little insects spare.

XVIII

Why should blessed insects die?
The flea doth skip o'er Betty Foy,
Like a little living thing;
Though it hath not fin or wing,
Hath it not a mortal joy?

[1] I have a similar idea in my poem "On Finding a Bird's Nest":
   "Look ! *five* blue eggs are gleaming there."

But the numbers are different, so I trust no one will differ with the numbers.

[2] I have also given these ideas before; but in thus printing them again, I neither tarnish their value, nor injure their novelty.

XIX

I the poet of the mountain,
Of the waterfall and fell,
I the mighty mental medlar,
I the lonely lyric pedlar,
I the Jove of Alice Fell.

XX

I the Recluse—a gentle man,[1]
A gentle man—a simple creature,
Who would not hurt, God shield the thing,
The merest, meanest May-bug's wing,
Am tender in my tender nature.

XXI

I do doat on my dear wife,
On the linnet, on the worm,
I can see sweet written salads
Growing in the Lyric Ballads,
And always find them green and firm.

[1] See my sonnet "To Sleep":

  "I surely not a man ungently made."

ROBERT SOUTHEY

1774–1843

PARODY was a subject alien to Southey's nature, yet the following elegies and sonnets have all the characteristics of the genuine stuff. They were written in mimicry of the "Della Cruscan versifiers," a band of writers which flourished about 1790. The chief figures of the movement were Robert Merry, a dilettante, who, by putting the signature "Della Crusca" to some verses entitled "Adieu and Recall to Love," gave his name to the movement, and Anna Matilda, parodied in "Rejected Addresses" under the name of Laura Matilda. That such writers should have attained to any degree of popularity, or that their literature should have been taken seriously, appears incredible ; yet such was the case. Their example was followed by scores of minor versifiers, and their poems, which were collected from *The World* and *The Oracle*, ran into four editions.

Southey's parodies of their style appeared rather too late to have great effect, for already the death-blow had been given to the school by William Gifford in his scathing satires, "The Baviad" and "The Mæviad," while the strained sentiment that inspired their style carried within itself the seed of its own destruction.

William Maginn aptly wrote that "the Della Cruscans talked nonsense without measure, were simple down to the lowest degree of silliness, and 'babbled of green fields' enough to make men sicken of summer."

The name *Shufflebottom* was suggested by the signature of Higginbottom which appeared under Coleridge's sonnet-parodies, included elsewhere in this volume.

ROBERT SOUTHEY

Love Elegies

By Abel Shufflebottom

[*Imitation—Della Crusca*]

The poet relates how he obtained Delia's pocket-handkerchief

'TIS mine! what accents can my joy declare?
  Blest be the pressure of the thronging rout!
Blest be the hand so hasty of my fair,
  That left the *tempting corner* hanging out!

I envy not the joy the pilgrim feels,
  After long travel to some distant shrine,
When to the relic of his saint he kneels,
  For DELIA'S POCKET-HANDKERCHIEF IS MINE.

When first with *filching fingers* I drew near
  Keen hope shot tremulous thro' every vein,
And when the finish'd deed removed my fear
  Scarce could my bounding heart its joy contain.

What tho' the eighth commandment rose to mind,
  It only served a moment's qualm to move,
For thefts like this it could not be design'd,
  The eighth commandment WAS NOT MADE FOR LOVE!

Here when she took the macaroons from me,
  She wiped her mouth to clean the crumbs so sweet;
Dear napkin! Yes, she wiped her lips in thee!
  Lips *sweeter* than the *macaroons* she eat.

And when she took that pinch of Mochabaugh
  That made my love so *delicately* sneeze,
Thee to her Roman nose applied I saw,
  And thou art doubly dear for things like these.

No washerwoman's filthy hand shall e'er
  Sweet pocket-handkerchief! thy worth profane;
For thou hast touched the *rubies* of my fair,
  And I will kiss thee o'er and o'er again.

Sonnet IV of the Amatory Poems of Abel Shufflebottom

[*Imitation—Della Crusca*]

I WOULD I were that portly gentleman
  With gold-laced hat and golden-headed cane,
Who hangs in Delia's parlour!   For whene'er
From books or needlework her looks arise,
On him CONVERGE THE SUNBEAMS OF HER EYES,
And he UNBLAMED may gaze upon MY FAIR,
And oft MY FAIR his FAVOUR'D form surveys.
O HAPPY PICTURE! still on HER to gaze;
I envy him! and jealous fear alarms,
Lest the STRONG *glance* of those *divinest* charms
WARM HIM TO LIFE, as in the ancient days,
When MARBLE MELTED in Pygmalion's arms.
I would I were that portly gentleman
With gold-laced hat and golden-headed cane.

HORACE SMITH

1779–1849

FOUR years younger than his brother, Horace Smith nevertheless made more stir in the world than the equally clever but less enterprising James Smith. He became a member of the Stock Exchange and afterwards a banker, amassing a considerable fortune which enabled him to indulge, after the fashion of a rich connoisseur, his taste for literature.

It is to Horace Smith that the "Rejected Addresses," which are without doubt the most notable parodies in the English language, owe their existence (see note to James Smith); but besides verse, Horace wrote many novels, one of which, "Brambletye House," obtained considerable fame, and is worthy of a better fate than the oblivion which surrounds it to-day. Of his parodies, those of Lord Byron, Sir Walter Scott, and Tom Moore are included in this volume, together with a slight travesty of Gray's "Elegy in a Country Churchyard," which appears in his collected works.

Cui Bono

[Imitation—Lord Byron]

I

SATED with home, of wife, of children tired,
   The restless soul is driven abroad to roam;
Sated abroad, all seen, yet nought admired,
The restless soul is driven to ramble home;
Sated with both, beneath new Drury's dome
The fiend Ennui awhile consents to pine,
   There growls, and curses, like a deadly Gnome,
Scorning to view fantastic Columbine,
Viewing with scorn and hate the nonsense of the Nine.

II

Ye reckless dupes, who hither wend your way
To gaze on puppets in a painted dome,
Pursuing pastimes glittering to betray,
Like falling stars in life's eternal gloom,
What seek ye here? Joy's evanescent bloom?
Woe's me! the brightest wreaths she ever gave
Are but as flowers that decorate a tomb.
Man's heart, the mournful urn o'er which they wave,
Is sacred to despair, its pedestal the grave.

III

Has life so little store of real woes,
That here ye wend to taste fictitious grief?
Or is it that from truth such anguish flows,
Ye court the lying drama for relief?
Long shall ye find the pang, the respite brief:
Or if one tolerable page appears
In folly's volume, 'tis the actor's leaf,
Who dries his own by drawing others' tears,
And, raising present mirth, makes glad his future years.

IV

Albeit, how like young Betty doth he flee!
Light as the mote that danceth in the beam,
He liveth only in man's present e'e;
His life a flash, his memory a dream,
Oblivious down he drops in Lethe's stream.
Yet what are they, the learned and the great?
Awhile of longer wonderment the theme!
Who shall presume to prophesy *their* date,
Where nought is certain, save the uncertainty of fate?

HORACE SMITH

V

This goodly pile, upheaved by Wyatt's toil,
Perchance than Holland's edifice more fleet,[1]
Again red Lemnos' artisan may spoil;
The fire-alarm and midnight drum may beat,
And all bestrewed ysmoking at your feet!
Start ye? perchance Death's angel may be sent,
Ere from the flaming temple ye retreat;
And ye who met, on revel idlesse bent,
May find, in pleasure's fane, your grave and monument.

VI

Your debts mount high—ye plunge in deeper waste;
The tradesman duns—no warning voice ye hear!
The plaintiff sues—to public shows ye haste;
The bailiff threats—ye feel no idle fear.
Who can arrest your prodigal career?
Who can keep down the levity of youth?
What sound can startle age's stubborn ear?
Who can redeem from wretchedness and ruth
Men true to falsehood's voice, false to the voice of truth?

VII

To thee, blest saint! who doffed thy skin to make
The Smithfield rabble leap from theirs with joy,[2]
We dedicate the pile—arise! awake!—
Knock down the Muses, wit and sense destroy,

[1] The old theatre was built by Holland the architect, and the new by Wyatt is still standing.   [2] Saint Bartholomew.

Clear our new stage from reason's dull alloy,
Charm hobbling age, and tickle capering youth
With cleaver, marrow-bone, and Tunbridge toy
While, vibrating in unbelieving tooth,[1]
Harps twang in Drury's walls, and make her boards a booth.

VIII

For what is Hamlet, but a hare in March?
And what is Brutus, but a croaking owl?
And what is Rolla?   Cupid steeped in starch,
Orlando's helmet in Augustine's cowl.
Shakespeare, how true thine adage, "fair is foul!"
To him whose soul is with fruition fraught,
The song of Braham[2] is an Irish howl,
Thinking is but an idle waste of thought,
And nought is everything, and everything is nought.

IX

Sons of Parnassus! whom I view above,
Not laurel-crown'd, but clad in rustic black;
Not spurring Pegasus through Tempe's grove,
But pacing Grub Street on a jaded hack;
What reams of foolscap, while your brains ye rack,
Ye mar to make again! for sure, ere long,
Condemned to tread the bard's time-sanction'd track,
Ye all shall join the bailiff-haunted throng,
And reproduce, in rags, the rags ye blot in song.

[1] A Jew's harp.
[2] Great singer of the day.

HORACE SMITH

x

So fares the follower in the Muses' train;
He toils to starve, and only lives in death;
We slight him, till our patronage is vain,
Then round his skeleton a garland wreathe,
And o'er his bones an empty requiem breathe—
Oh! with what tragic horror would he start,
(Could he be conjured from the grave beneath)
To find the stage again a Thespian cart,
And elephants and colts down-trampling Shakespeare's art.

xi

Hence, pedant Nature! with thy Grecian rules!
Centaurs (not fabulous) those rules efface;
Back, sister Muses, to your native schools;
Here booted grooms usurp Apollo's place,
Hoofs shame the boards that Garrick used to grace,
The play of limbs succeeds the play of wit,
Man yields the drama to the Hou'yn'm race,
His prompter spurs, his licenser the bit,
The stage a stable-yard, a jockey-club the pit.

xii

Is it for these ye rear this proud abode?
Is it for these your superstition seeks
To build a temple worthy of a god?
To laud a monkey, or to worship leeks!
Then be the stage, to recompense your freaks,
A motley chaos, jumbling age and ranks,
Where Punch, the lignum-vitæ Roscius, squeaks,
And Wisdom weeps and Folly plays his pranks,
And moody Madness laughs and hugs the chain he clanks.

HORACE SMITH

A Tale of Drury Lane

[*Imitation—Walter Scott*]

SURVEY this shield, all bossy bright—
  These cuisses twain behold !
Look on my form in armour dight
Of steel inlaid with gold ;
My knees are stiff in iron buckles,
Stiff spikes of steel protect my knuckles.
These once belong'd to sable prince,
Who never did in battle wince ;
With valour tart as pungent quince,
He slew the vaunting Gaul.
Rest there awhile, my bearded lance,
While from green curtain I advance
To yon footlights, no trivial dance,
And tell the town what sad mischance
Did Drury Lane befall.

THE NIGHT

On fair Augusta's[1] towers and trees
Flitted the silent midnight breeze,
Curling the foliage as it past,
Which from the moon-tipp'd plumage cast
A spangled light, like dancing spray,
Then reassumed its still array ;

[1] An old name for London.

HORACE SMITH

When, as night's lamp unclouded hung,
And down its full effulgence flung,
It shed such soft and balmy power
That cot and castle, hall and bower,
And spire and dome, and turret height,
Appear'd to slumber in the light.
From Henry's chapel,[1] Rufus' hall,[2]
To Savoy, Temple, and St. Paul,
From Knightsbridge, Pancras, Camden Town,
To Redriff, Shadwell, Horsleydown,
No voice was heard, no eye unclosed,
But all in deepest sleep reposed.
They might have thought, who gazed around
Amid a silence so profound,
  It made the senses thrill,
That 'twas no place inhabited,
But some vast city of the dead—
  All was so hush'd and still.

THE BURNING

As Chaos, which, by heavenly doom,
Had slept in everlasting gloom,
Started with terror and surprise
When light first flashed upon her eyes—
So London's sons in nightcap woke,
  In bedgown woke her dames;
For shouts were heard 'mid fire and smoke,
And twice ten hundred voices spoke—
  "The playhouse is in flames!"

[1] Henry VII's Chapel, Westminster.
[2] Better known as Westminster Hall.

And lo! where Catherine Street extends,
A fiery tail its lustre lends
    To every window-pane;
Blushes each spout in Martlet Court,
And Barbican, moth-eaten fort,[1]
And Covent Garden kennels sport,
    A bright ensanguined drain;
Meux's new brewhouse shows the light,
Rowland Hill's chapel, and the height
    Where patent shot they sell;[2]
The Tennis Court, so fair and tall,
Partakes the ray, with Surgeons' Hall,[3]
The ticket-porters' house of call,
Old Bedlam, close by London Wall,
    And Richardson's Hotel.

Nor these alone, but far and wide,
Across red Thames's gleaming tide,
To distant fields, the blaze was borne,
And daisy white and hoary thorn
In borrow'd lustre seem'd to sham
The rose or red Sweet Wil-li-am.

To those who on the hills around
Beheld the flames from Drury's mound,
    As from a lofty altar rise,
It seem'd that nations did conspire
To offer to the god of fire
    Some vast stupendous sacrifice!

[1] Remains of the tower existed till as late as the early eighteenth century. It was situated between Aldersgate Street and Golden Lane or Red Cross Street.

[2] A reference to Watts' Shot Factory, erected in 1789 off the river near Waterloo Bridge.   [3] This stood in the Old Bailey.

The summon'd firemen woke at call,
And hied them to their stations all :
Starting from short and broken snooze,
Each sought his pond'rous hobnailed shoes,
But first his worsted hosen plied,
Plush breeches next, in crimson dyed,
        His nether bulk embraced ;
Then jacket thick, of red or blue,
Whose massy shoulder gave to view
The badge of each respective crew,
        In tin or copper traced.
The engines thunder'd through the street,
Fire-hook, pipe, bucket, all complete,
And torches glared, and clattering feet
        Along the pavement paced.
And one, the leader of the band,
From Charing Cross along the Strand,
Like stag by beagles hunted hard,
Ran till he stopp'd at Vin'gar Yard.[1]
The burning badge his shoulder bore,
The belt and oilskin hat he wore,
The cane he had, his men to bang,
Show'd foreman of the British gang—
His name was Higginbottom.   Now
'Tis meet that I should tell you how
        The others came in view :
The Hand-in-Hand the race began,[2]

[1] A narrow passage adjoining Drury Lane, named from the vineyard which was once attached to Covent Garden.

[2] Historically correct, for the Hand-in-Hand Insurance Office was
one of the first such institutions to be founded.

Then came the Phoenix and the Sun,
Th' Exchange, where old insurers run,
    The Eagle, where the new ;
With these came Runford, Bumford, Cole,
Robins from Hockly in the Hole,
Lawson and Dawson, cheek by jowl,
    Crump from St. Giles's Pound :
Whitford and Mitford join'd the train,
Huggins and Muggins from Chick Lane,[1]
And Clutterbuck, who got a sprain
    Before the plug was found.

Hobson and Jobson did not sleep,
But ah ! no trophy could they reap,
For both were in the Donjon Keep
    Of Bridewell's gloomy mound !
E'en Higginbottom now was posed,
For sadder scene was ne'er disclosed ;
Without, within, in hideous show,
Devouring flames resistless glow,
And blazing rafters downward go,
And never halloo " Heads below ! "
    Nor notice give at all.
The firemen terrified are slow
To bid the pumping torrent flow,
    For fear the roof should fall.
Back, Robins, back ! Crump, stand aloof ;

---

[1] Hockley in the Hole was a neighbouring district to Clerkenwell;
St. Giles's Pound existed in the latter part of the eighteenth century
at the corner of Tottenham Court Road and Oxford Street ; Chick
Lane was subsequently West Street, Clerkenwell, and was pulled
down in 1857. All these were places of disrepute—"infamous
lurking-places of thieves."

116

Whitford, keep near the walls !
Huggins, regard your own behoof,
For, lo ! the blazing rocking roof
          Down, down, in thunder falls !
An awful pause succeeds the stroke,
And o'er the ruin's volumed smoke,
Rolling around its pitchy shroud,
Conceal'd them from th' astonished crowd.
At length the mist awhile was clear'd,
When, lo ! amid the wreck uprear'd,
Gradual a moving head appear'd,
          And Eagle firemen knew
'Twas Joseph Muggins, name revered,
          The foreman of their crew.
Loud shouted all in signs of woe,
"A Muggins ! to the rescue, ho !"
          And pour'd the hissing tide ;
Meanwhile the Muggins fought amain,
And strove and struggled all in vain,
For, rallying but to fall again,
          He totter'd, sunk, and died !
Did none attempt, before he fell,
To succour one they loved so well ?
Yes, Higginbottom did aspire
(His fireman's soul was all on fire)
          His brother chief to save ;
But ah ! his reckless generous ire
          Served but to share his grave !
'Mid blazing beams and scalding streams,
Through fire and smoke he dauntless broke
          Where Muggins broke before.

But sulphury stench and boiling drench
Destroying sight o'erwhelmed him quite,
  He sunk to rise no more.
Still o'er his head, while Fate he braved,
His whizzing water-pipe he waved;
"Whitford and Mitford, ply your pumps,
You, Clutterbuck, come, stir your stumps,
Why are you in such doleful dumps?
A fireman, and afraid of bumps!—
What are they fear'd on? fools, 'od rot 'em!"[1]
Were the last words of Higginbottom.

THE REVIVAL

Peace to his soul! new prospects bloom,
And toil rebuilds what fires consume!
Eat we and drink we, be our ditty,
"Joy to the managing committee!"
Eat we and drink we, join to rum
Roast beef and pudding of the plum;
Forth from thy nook, John Horner, come,
With bread of ginger brown thy thumb,
  For this is Drury's gay day:
Roll, roll thy hoop, and twirl thy tops,
And buy, to glad thy smiling chops,
Crisp parliament with lolly-pops,
  And fingers of the Lady.

Didst mark, how toil'd the busy train,
From morn to eve, till Drury Lane

[1] "'Charge, Chester, charge! On, Stanley, on!' were the last words of Marmion."

Leap'd like a roebuck from the plain?
Ropes rose and stooped, and rose again,
      And nimble workmen trod;
To realize bold Wyatt's plan
Rush'd many a howling Irishman;
Loud clatter'd many a porter-can,
And many a raggamuffin clan,
      With trowel and with hod.

Drury revives! her rounded pate
Is blue, is heavenly blue with slate;
She "wings the midway air," elate,
      As magpie, crow, or chough;
White paint her modish visage smears,
Yellow and pointed are her ears.
No pendent portico appears
Dangling beneath, for Whitebread's shears [1]
      Have cut the bauble off.

Yes, she exalts her stately head;
And, but that solid bulk outspread
Opposed you on your onward tread,
And posts and pillars warranted
That all was true that Wyatt said,
You might have deemed her walls so thick
Were not composed of stone or brick,
But all a phantom, all a trick,
Of brain disturb'd and fancy sick,
      So high she soars, so vast, so quick!

[1] The portico in question was vetoed by Whitbread, the manager of Drury Lane Theatre, on the ground of economy, but it was later erected facing Brydges Street under the lesseeship of Elliston.

119

HORACE SMITH

The Living Lustres

[*Imitation—Thomas Moore*]

I

O WHY should our dull retrospective addresses
    Fall damp as wet blankets on Drury Lane fire?
Away with blue devils, away with distresses,
    And give the gay spirit to sparkling desire!

II

Let the artists decide on the beauties of Drury,
    The richest to me is when woman is there;
The question of houses I leave to the jury,
    The fairest to me is the house of the fair.

III

When woman's soft smile all our senses bewilders,
    And gilds, while it carves, her dear form on the heart,
What need has New Drury of carvers and gilders?
    With Nature so bounteous, why call upon Art?

IV

How well would our actors attend to their duties,
    Our house save in oil, and our authors in wit,
In lieu of yon lamps, if a row of young beauties
    Glanced light from their eyes between us and the pit!

120

V

The apples that grew on the fruit-tree of knowledge
  By woman were pluck'd, and she still wears the prize,
To tempt us in theatre, senate, or college—
  I mean the love-apples that bloom in the eyes.

VI

There too is the lash which, all statutes controlling,
  Still governs the slaves that are made by the fair;
For man is the pupil, who, while her eye's rolling,
  Is lifted to rapture, or sunk in despair.

VII

Bloom, theatre, bloom, in the roseate blushes
  Of beauty illumed by a love-breathing smile!
And flourish, ye pillars,[1] as green as the rushes
  That pillow the nymphs of the Emerald Isle!

VIII

For dear is the Emerald Isle of the ocean,
  Whose daughters are fair as the foam of the wave,
Whose sons, unaccustom'd to rebel commotion,
  Tho' joyous, are sober—tho' peaceful, are brave.

IX

The shamrock their olive, sworn foe to a quarrel,
  Protects from the thunder and lightning of rows;
Their sprig of shillelagh is nothing but laurel,
  Which flourishes rapidly over their brows.

[1] This alludes to two massive pillars of verd antique which then
flanked the proscenium, but which have since been removed. Their
colour reminds the bard of the Emerald Isle, and this causes him
(*more suo*) to fly off at a tangent and Hibernicise the rest of the poem.

HORACE SMITH

X

Oh ! soon shall they burst the tyrannical shackles
   Which each panting bosom indignantly names,
Until not one goose at the capital cackles
   Against the grand question of Catholic claims.

XI

And then shall each Paddy, who once on the Liffey
   Perchance held the helm of some mackerel hoy,
Hold the helm of the state, and dispense in a jiffy
   More fishes than ever he caught when a boy.

XII

And those who now quit their hods, shovels, and barrows,
   In crowds to the bar of some ale-house to flock,
When bred to *our* bar shall be Gibbses and Garrows,[1]
   Assume the silk gown, and discard the smock-frock.

XIII

For Erin surpasses the daughters of Neptune,
   As Dian outshines each encircling star ;
And the spheres of the heavens could never have kept tune
   Till set to the music of Erin-go-bragh.

[1] Sir Vicary Gibbs was Attorney-General in 1807, while Sir William Garrow was preferred to the same office in 1813.

HORACE SMITH

HORACE SMITH

Evening, an Elegy

(By a poetical Carman)

[*Parody—T. Gray*]

APOLLO now, Sol's carman, drives his stud
    Home to the mews that's seated in the West,
And custom's clerks, like him, through Thames Street mud,
    Now westering wend, in Holland trousers dress'd.

So from the stands the empty carts are dragg'd,
    The horses homeward to their stable go,
And mine, with hauling heavy hogsheads fagg'd,
    Prepare to take the luxury of—" Wo ! "

Now from the slaughter-houses cattle roar,
    Knowing that with the morn their lives they yields,
And Mr. Sweetman's gig is at the door
    To take him to his house in Haekney Fields.

Closed are the gates of the West India Docks,
    Rums, Sugars, Coffees, find at length repose,
And I, with other careless carmen, flocks
    To the King's Head, the Chequers, or the Rose.

They smoke a pipe—the shepherd's pipe I wakes,
    Them skittles pleases—me the Muse invites,
They in their ignorance to drinking takes,
    I bless'd with learning, takes a pen and writes.

123

JAMES SMITH

1775–1839

What little fame
Is annexed to my name
Is derived from " Rejected Addresses "

wrote James Smith in his niece's album ; and certainly his name,
coupled with that of his brother Horace, will always be remembered
in connection with the volume of parodies which—planned, written,
and published within six weeks—is like to become immortal. The
event which suggested the work was the opening of the new Drury
Lane Theatre, an occasion necessitated by the total destruction of
the former building by fire. It was decided that the re-opening
should be celebrated by an inaugural ode, and a competition was
arranged by the Drury Lane Committee in order to obtain the
necessary material. A hundred and twelve addresses were sent
in, but none were chosen, and at length Lord Byron was prevailed
upon to write an especial inaugural address. Horace Smith then
conceived the idea of bringing out a book purporting to contain the
rejected odes by the best known authors. He communicated his
idea to his brother James, and, the one in Cheltenham and the other
in London, worked to such good purpose that they produced the
most remarkable series of parodies in the English language. Those
contributed by James are on Wordsworth, Crabbe, Southey, and
Coleridge, and of these the Wordsworth and Southey odes stand out
as pre-eminently successful. A number of verses by the author of
"The Baby's Debut" were published posthumously, and included
the delightful "Wee Joukydaidles," a masterpiece of charm and
happy expression.

James Smith was never married, and died at his house in Crane
Street, December 24th, 1839.

"The Rebuilding" is perhaps the masterpiece of the collection.

Apart from the imitation, there is sufficient incident in the poem itself to interest the reader; but added to this the curious measures of the original are admirably suggested, while throughout there is the mocking echo of Southey's magniloquent phrases, which, however, never break out into sonorous passages, but are cut short by the arbitrary arrangement of the lines, and so result in an anti-climax, not so much of sense as of sound. The following note by Mr. A. D. Godley to his edition of these parodies is interesting. He appends it to the passage commencing, "Descending, he twisted like Levy the Jew" :—

"If this parody has a fault, it is that the metre of 'Kehama' is not always suggested : the rhythm of that poem, with all its irregularities, is nearly always iambic—an anapæstic movement like that of these lines is of the rarest occurrence."

JAMES SMITH

The Rebuilding

[*Parody—Robert Southey*]

I AM a blessed Glendoveer :[1]
'Tis mine to speak, and yours to hear.
Midnight, yet not a nose
From Tower-hill to Piccadilly snored !
Midnight, yet not a nose
From Indra drew the essence of repose !
See with what crimson fury,
By Indra fann'd, the god of fire ascends the walls
of Drury !

Tops of houses blue with lead,
Bend beneath the landlord's tread.
Master and 'prentice, serving-man and lord,

[1] See Southey's "Curse of Kehama."

JAMES SMITH

Nailor and tailor,
Grazier and brazier,
Through streets and alleys poured—
All, all abroad to gaze,
And wonder at the blaze.
Thick calf, fat foot, and slim knee,[1]
Mounted on roof and chimney,
The mighty roast, the mighty stew
To see;
As if the dismal view
Were but to them a Brentford Jubilee.

Vainly, all-radiant Surya, sire of Phaeton
(By Greeks call'd Apollo[2])
Hollow

---

[1] This rhyme was inserted here to demonstrate the fact that, contrary to the received opinion, there was a possible rhyme to the word "chimney."

[2] Apollo. A gigantic wooden figure of this deity was erected on the roof. The writer (*horrescit referens !*) is old enough to recollect the time when it was first placed there. Old Bishop, then one of the masters of Merchant Taylors' School, wrote an epigram upon the occasion, which, referring to the aforesaid figure, concluded thus :—

"Above he fills up Shakespeare's place,
And Shakespeare fills up his below."

Very antithetical ; but quære as to the meaning ? The writer, like Pluto, "long puzzled his brain" to find it out, till he was immersed "in a lower deep" by hearing Madame de Staël say, at the table of the late Lord Dillon, "Buonaparte is not a man, but a system." Inquiry was made in the course of the evening of Sir James Mackintosh as to what the lady meant. He answered, "Mass ! I cannot tell." Madame de Staël repeats this apophthegm in her work on Germany. It is probably understood *there*.

126

JAMES SMITH

Sounds from thy harp proceed ;
    Combustible as reed,
The tongue of Vulcan licks thy wooden legs :
From Drury's top, dissever'd from thy pegs,
      Thou tumblest,
      Humblest,
Where late thy bright effulgence shone on high ;
While, by thy somerset excited, fly
      Ten million
      Billion
Sparks from the pit, to gem the sable sky.

Now come the men of fire to quench the fires ;
To Russell Street see Globe and Atlas run,
    Hope gallops first, and second Sun ;
      On flying heel,
    See Hand-in-Hand
     O'ertake the band !
    View with what glowing wheel
      He nicks
      Phœnix !

While Albion scampers from Bridge Street,
     Blackfriars—
    Drury Lane !   Drury Lane !
    Drury Lane !   Drury Lane !
They shout and they bellow again and again.
     All, all in vain !
     Water turns steam ;
     Each blazing beam
Hisses defiance to the eddying spout ;
It seems but too plain that nothing can put it out !

JAMES SMITH

Drury Lane! Drury Lane!
See Drury Lane expires!

Pent in by smoke-dried beams, twelve moons or more,
Shorn of his ray,
Surya in durance lay:
The workmen heard him shout,
But thought it would not pay,
To dig him out.
When lo! terrific Yamen, lord of hell,
Solemn as lead,
Judge of the dead,
Sworn foe to witticism,
By men call'd criticism,
Came passing by that way:
"Rise!" cried the fiend, "behold a sight of gladness!
Behold the rival theatre!
I've set O. P.[1] at her,
Who, like a bull-dog bold,
Growls and fastens on his hold.

---

[1] O. P.—This personage, who is alleged to have growled like a
bull-dog, requires rather a lengthened note, for the edification of the
rising generation. The "horns, rattles, drums," with which he is
accompanied, are no inventions of the poet. The new Covent
Garden Theatre opened on the 18th September, 1809, when a cry
of "Old Prices" (afterwards diminished to O. P.) burst out from
every part of the house. This continued and increased in violence
till the 23rd, when rattles, drums, whistles, and cat-calls having
completely drowned the voices of the actors, Mr. Kemble, the stage-
manager, came forward and said that a committee of gentlemen had
undertaken to examine the finances of the concern, and that until
they were prepared with their report the theatre would continue
closed. "Name them!" was shouted from all sides. The names

JAMES SMITH

"The many-headed rabble roar in madness;
  Thy rival staggers : come and spy her
Deep in the mud as thou art in the mire."
So saying, in his arms he caught the beaming one
              And crossing Russell Street,
              He placed him on his feet
'Neath Covent Garden dome.   Sudden a sound,
    As of the bricklayers of Babel, rose :
Horns, rattles, drums, tin trumpets, sheets of copper,
Punches and slaps, thwacks of all sorts and sizes,
From the knobb'd bludgeon to the taper switch,
Ran echoing round the walls ; paper placards
Blotted the lamps, boots brown with mud the benches ;
    A sea of heads roll'd roaring in the pit ;

were declared, viz. Sir Charles Price, the Solicitor-General, the
Recorder of London, the Governor of the Bank, and Mr. Angerstein.
"All shareholders!" bawled a wag from the gallery. In a few days
the theatre re-opened : the public paid no attention to the report of
the referees, and the tumult was renewed for several weeks with
even increased violence. The proprietors now sent in hired bruisers
to *mill* the refractory into subjection. This irritated most of their
former friends, and, amongst the rest, the annotator, who accord-
ingly wrote the song of "Heigh-ho, says Kemble," which was caught
up by the ballad-singers and sung under Mr. Kemble's house-windows
in Great Russell Street. A dinner was given at the Crown and
Anchor Tavern in the Strand to celebrate the victory obtained by
W. Clifford in his action against Brandon, the box-keeper, for as-
saulting him for wearing the letters O. P. in his hat. At this
dinner Mr. Kemble attended, and matters were compromised by
allowing the advanced price (seven shillings) to the boxes. The
writer remembers a former riot of a similar sort at the same theatre
(in the year 1792), when the price to the boxes was raised from five
shillings to six. That tumult, however, only lasted three nights.

JAMES SMITH

On paper wings O. P.'s
Reclin'd in lettered ease;
While shout and scoff,
"Ya! ya! off! off!"
Like thunderbolt on Surya's ear-drum fell,
And seemed to paint
The savage oddities of Saint
Bartholomew in hell.

Tears dimm'd the god of light—
"Bear me back, Yamen, from this hideous sight;
Bear me back, Yamen, I grow sick,
Oh! bury me again in brick;
Shall I on New Drury tremble,
To be O. P.'d like Kemble?
No,
Better remain by rubbish guarded,
Than in hubbubish groan placarded;
Bear me back, Yamen, bear me quick,
And bury me again in brick."
Obedient Yamen
Answered, "Amen,"
And did
As he was bid.

There lay the buried god, and Time
Seemed to decree eternity of lime;
But pity, like a dew-drop, gently prest
Almighty Veeshnoo's[1] adamantine breast:
He, the preserver, ardent still
To do whate'er he says he will,

[1] The late Mr. Whitbread.

From South Hill wing'd his way,
To raise the drooping lord of day.
All earthly spells the busy one o'erpower'd ;
He treats with men of all conditions,
Poets and players, tradesmen and musicians ;
Nay, even ventures
To attack the renters,
Old and new :
A list he gets
Of claims and debts,
And deems nought done while aught remains to do.[1]

Yamen beheld, and wither'd at the sight ;
Long had he aim'd the sunbeam to control,
For light was hateful to his soul :
"Go on !" cried the hellish one, yellow with spite,
"Go on !" cried the hellish one, yellow with spleen,
"Thy toils of the morning, like Ithaca's queen,
I'll toil to undo every night."
Ye sons of song, rejoice !
Veeshnoo has still'd the jarring elements,
The spheres hymn music ;
Again the god of day
Peeps forth with trembling ray,
Wakes, from their humid caves, the sleeping Nine
And pours at intervals a strain divine.
"I have an iron yet in the fire," cried Yamen,
"The vollied flame rides in my breath,
My blast is elemental death ;

[1] Nil actum reputans dum superesset agendum.

This hand shall tear your paper bonds to pieces ;
Ingross your deeds, assignments, leases,
 My breath shall every line erase
  Soon as I blow the blaze."

The lawyers are met at the Crown and Anchor,[1]
And Yamen's visage grows blanker and blanker ;
The lawyers are met at the Anchor and Crown,
 And Yamen's cheek is a russety brown ;
  Veeshnoo, now thy work proceeds ;
   The solicitor reads,
   And, merit of merit !
  Red wax and green ferret
Are fixed at the foot of the deeds !

  Yamen beheld and shiver'd ;
  His finger and thumb were cramp'd ;
  His ear by the flea in't was bitten,
When he saw by the lawyer's clerk written,
  Sealed and delivered, ⎫
  Being first duly stamped. ⎭

" Now for my turn !" the demon cries, and blows
A blast of sulphur from his mouth and nose.
  Ah ! bootless aim ! the critic fiend,
  Sagacious Yamen, judge of hell,
   Is judged in his turn ;
   Parchment won't burn !
His schemes of vengeance are dissolved in air,
  Parchment won't tear ! !

---

[1] At the top of Arundel Street, Strand, well known meeting-place
for political and other gatherings.

JAMES SMITH

Is it not written in the Himakoot[1] book
(That mighty Baly[2] from Kehama took)
  " Who blows on pounce
  Must the Swerga[3] renounce " ?
It is ! it is ! Yamen, thine hour is nigh :
  Like as an eagle claws an asp,
Veeshnoo has caught him in his mighty grasp,
And hurl'd him in spite of his shrieks and his squalls,
  Whizzing aloft, like the Temple fountain,
  Three times as high as Meru[4] mountain,
    Which is
  Ninety times as high as St. Paul's.
Descending, he twisted like Levy the Jew,[5]
  Who a durable grave meant
  To dig in the pavement
  Of Monument Yard :
To earth by the laws of attraction he flew,
  And he fell, and he fell
  To the regions of hell ;
Nine centuries bounced he from cavern to rock,

---

[1] Himakoot, " the holy mount, on high
    From mid-earth rising to mid-Heaven."
[2] The " righteous Judge " of the dead in Kehama.
[3] The Swerga is the Paradise of Indra, God of the Elements.
[4] The Central Mountain of the Earth, of prodigious size and precious material.
[5] Levy. An insolvent Israelite who [18th January, 1810] threw himself from the top of the Monument a short time before. An inhabitant of Monument Yard informed the writer that he happened to be standing at his door talking to a neighbour, and looking up at the top of the pillar, exclaimed, " Why, here's the flag coming down." " Flag ! " answered the other, " it's a man." The words were hardly uttered when the suicide fell within ten feet of the speaker.

And his head, as he tumbled, went nickety-nock,
  Like a pebble in Carisbrooke Well.
Now Veeshnoo turn'd round to a capering varlet,
  Array'd in blue and white and scarlet,
And cried, "Oh! brown of slipper as of hat!
  Lend me, Harlequin, thy bat!"
He seized the wooden sword, and smote the earth.

The Baby's Début

[Imitation—William Wordsworth]

MY brother Jack was nine in May,
  And I was eight on New Year's day;
    So in Kate Wilson's shop
Papa (he's my papa and Jack's)
Bought me, last week, a doll of wax,
  And brother Jack a top.

Jack's in the pouts, and thus it is,—
He thinks mine came to more than his;
  So to my drawer he goes,
Takes out the doll, and, O, my stars!
He pokes her head between the bars,
  And melts off half her nose!

Quite cross, a bit of string I beg,
And tie it to his peg-top's peg,
  And bang, with might and main,
Its head against the parlour-door:
Off flies the head, and hits the floor,
  And breaks a window-pane.

JAMES SMITH

This made him cry with rage and spite.
Well, let him cry, it serves him right.
    A pretty thing, forsooth!
If he's to melt, all scalding hot,
Half my doll's nose, and I am not
    To draw his peg-top's tooth!

Aunt Hannah heard the window break,
And cried, "O naughty Nancy Lake,
    Thus to distress your aunt:
No Drury Lane for you to-day!"
And while papa said, "Pooh, she may!"
    Mamma said, "No, she sha'n't!"

Well, after many a sad reproach,
They got into a hackney coach.
    And trotted down the street.
I saw them go: one horse was blind,
The tails of both hung down behind,
    Their shoes were on their feet.

The chaise in which poor brother Bill
Used to be drawn to Pentonville,
    Stood in the lumber-room:
I wiped the dust from off the top,
While Molly mopp'd it with a mop,
    And brushed it with a broom.

My uncle's porter, Samuel Hughes,
Came in at six to black the shoes,
    (I always talk to Sam:)

JAMES SMITH

So what does he, but takes, and drags
Me in the chaise along the flags,
    And leaves me where I am.

My father's walls are made of brick,
But not so tall, and not so thick
    As these ; and, goodness me !
My father's beams are made of wood,
But never, never half so good
    As those that now I see.

What a large floor ! 'tis like a town !
The carpet, when they lay it down,
    Won't hide it, I'll be bound ;
And there's a row of lamps !—my eye
How they do blaze !   I wonder why
    They keep them on the ground.

At first I caught hold of the wing,
And kept away ; but Mr. Thing-
    umbob, the prompter man,
Gave with his hand my chaise a shove,
And said, " Go on, my pretty love ;
    Speak to 'em, little Nan.

" You've only got to curtsey, whisp-
er, hold your chin up, laugh, and lisp,
    And then you're sure to take :
I've known the day when brats, not quite
Thirteen, got fifty pounds a night ;
    Then why not Nancy Lake ? "

But while I'm speaking, where's papa?
And where's my aunt? and where's mamma?
  Where's Jack? O, there they sit!
They smile, they nod; I'll go my ways,
And order round poor Billy's chaise,
  To join them in the pit.

And now, good gentlefolks, I go
To join mamma, and see the show;
  So, bidding you adieu,
I curtsey, like a pretty miss,
And if you'll blow to me a kiss,
  I'll blow a kiss to you.
    [*Blows a kiss and exit*

The Theatre

[*Imitation—Crabbe*]

'TIS sweet to view, from half-past five to six,
  Our long wax-candles, with short cotton wicks,
Touch'd by the lamplighter's Promethean art,
Start into light, and make the lighter start;

To see red Phoebus through the gallery-pane
Tinge with his beams the beams of Drury Lane;
While gradual parties fill our widen'd pit,
And gape, and gaze, and wonder, ere they sit.

At first, while vacant seats give choice and ease,
Distant or near, they settle where they please;
But when the multitude contracts the span,
And seats are rare, they settle where they can.

137

JAMES SMITH

Now the full benches to late-comers doom
No room for standing, miscall'd *standing room.*
Hark! the check-taker moody silence breaks,
And bawling "Pit full!" gives the check he takes;
Yet onward still the gathering numbers cram,
Contending crowders shout the frequent damn,
And all is bustle, squeeze, row, jabbering, and jam.

See to their desks Apollo's sons repair—
Swift rides the rosin o'er the horse's hair!
In unison their various tones to tune,
Murmurs the hautboy, growls the hoarse bassoon;
In soft vibrating sighs the whispering lute,
Tang goes the harpsichord, too-too the flute,
Brays the loud trumpet, squeaks the fiddle sharp,
Winds the French-horn, and twangs the tingling harp;
Till like great Jove, the leader, fingering in,
Attunes to order the chaotic din.
Now all seems hush'd—but, no, one fiddle will
Give half-ashamed, a tiny flourish still.
Foil'd in his crash, the leader of the clan
Reproves with frown the dilatory man:
Then on his candlestick thrice taps his bow,
Nods a new signal, and away they go.

Perchance, while pit and gallery cry, "Hats off!"
And awed Consumption checks his chided cough,
Some giggling daughter of the Queen of Love
Drops, 'reft of pin, her playbill from above:
Like Icarus, while laughing galleries clap,
Soars, ducks, and dives in air the printed scrap;

JAMES SMITH

But, wiser far than he, combustion fears,
And, as it flies, eludes the chandeliers;
Till, sinking gradual, with repeated twirl,
It settles, curling, on a fiddler's curl;
Who from his powder'd pate the intruder strikes,
And, for mere malice, sticks it on the spikes.

Say, why these Babel strains from Babel tongues?
Who's that calls "Silence!" with such leathern lungs?
He who, in quest of quiet, "Silence!" hoots,
Is apt to make the hubbub he imputes.
What various swains our motley walls contain!—
Fashion from Moorfields, honour from Chick Lane;
Bankers from Paper Buildings here resort,
Bankrupts from Golden Square and Riches Court;
From the Haymarket canting rogues in grain,
Gulls from the Poultry, sots from Water Lane;
The lottery-cormorant, the auction shark,
The full-price master and the half-price clerk;
Boys who long linger at the gallery door,
With pence twice five—they want but twopence more;
Till some Samaritan the twopence spares,
And sends them jumping up the gallery stairs.

Critics we boast who ne'er their malice balk,
But talk their minds—we wish they'd mind their talk;
Big-worded bullies, who by quarrels live—
Who give the lie, and tell the lie they give;
Jews from St. Mary Axe, for jobs so wary,
That of old clothes they'd even axe St. Mary;
And bucks with pockets empty as their pate,

JAMES SMITH

Lax in their gaiters, laxer in their gait ;
Who oft, when we our house lock up, carouse
With tippling tipstaves in a lock-up house.

Yet here, as elsewhere, Chance can joy bestow,
Where scowling Fortune seem'd to threaten woe.

John Richard William Alexander Dwyer
Was footman to Justinian Stubbs, Esquire ;
But when John Dwyer listed in the Blues,
Emanuel Jennings polish'd Stubbs's shoes.
Emanuel Jennings brought his youngest boy
Up as a corn-cutter—a safe employ ;
In Holywell Street, St. Pancras, he was bred
(At number twenty-seven, it is said),
Facing the pump, and near the Granby's Head ;
He would have bound him to some shop in town,
But with a premium he could not come down.
Pat was the urchin's name, a red-hair'd youth,
Fonder of purl and skittle-grounds than truth.
Silence, ye gods ! to keep your tongues in awe,
The Muse shall tell an accident she saw.

Pat Jennings in the upper gallery sat,
But, leaning forward, Jennings lost his hat :
Down from the gallery the beaver flew,
And spurn'd the one to settle in the two.

How shall he act ? Pay at the gallery-door
Two shillings for what cost, when new, but four ?
Or till half-price, to save his shilling, wait,
And gain his hat again at half-past eight ;

Now, while his fears anticipate a thief,
John Mullins whispers, "Take my handkerchief."
"Thank you," cried Pat; "but one won't make a line."
"Take mine," cried Wilson; and cried Stokes, "Take
    mine."
A motley cable soon Pat Jennings ties,
Where Spitalfields with real India vies.
Like Iris' bow, down darts the painted clue,
Starr'd, striped and spotted, yellow, red and blue,
Old calico, torn silk, and muslin new.
George Green below, with palpitating hand,
Loops the last 'kerchief to the beaver's band—
Up soars the prize! The youth, with joy unfeign'd,
Regain'd the felt, and felt what he regain'd;
While to the applauding galleries grateful Pat
Made a low bow, and touch'd the ransom'd hat.

PERCY BYSSHE SHELLEY

1792–1822

THAT the creator of "Prometheus Unbound" and "Adonais" could descend to the lowlier compositions of satirist and parodist, the poem of "Peter Bell the Third" sufficiently proves; but that the experience is rare is evinced by a letter to Mr. Ollier, the publisher in which he writes: "I think Peter is not bad in his way; but perhaps no one will believe in anything in the shape of a joke from me." If "Peter Bell" is a joke, it is certainly in rather a caustic vein. Here is an example :

> "For Peter did not know the town,
>   But thought as country readers do,
> For half a guinea or a crown,
> He bought oblivion or renown
>   From God's own voice in a review."

"Peter Bell" was suggested to the poet by the reviews in the *Examiner* of Reynolds' and Wordsworth's poems of the same name. There is no deep and awful purpose underlying the poem: it is simply a by-product of the poet's genius; written in a few days when the spirit was upon him as a set-off to the two other poems of that name. This idea is expressed in the introduction to the poem :

> "Peter Bell the First was Peter,
> Smugger, milder, softer, neater,
> Like the soul before it is
> Born from *that* world into *this*.
> The next Peter Bell was he,
> Pre-devote, like you and me,
> To good or evil as may come ;
> His was the severer doom,—
> For he was an evil cotter,
> And a polygamic potter.

> And the last is Peter Bell,
> Damned since our first parents fell,
> Damned eternally to Hell—
> Surely he deserves it well!"

Only an excerpt from the poem is given here.

PERCY BYSSHE SHELLEY

Peter Bell the Third

[Parody—W. Wordsworth]

I

AND Peter Bell, when he had been
   With fresh-imported hell-fire warmed.
Grew serious—from his dress and mien
'Twas very plainly to be seen
   Peter was quite reformed.

II

His eyes turned up, his mouth turned down;
   His accent caught a nasal twang;
He oiled his hair; there might be heard
The grace of God in every word
   Which Peter said or sang.

III

But Peter now grew old, and had
   An ill no doctor could unravel;
His torments almost drove him mad;
Some said it was a fever bad,
   Some swore it was the gravel.

143

IV

His holy friends then came about,
　　And with long preaching and persuasion
Convinced the patient that, without
The smallest shadow of a doubt,
　　　He was predestined to damnation.

V

They said : "Thy name is Peter *Bell*,
　　Thy skin is of a brimstone *hue ;*
Alive or dead—ay, sick or well—
The one God made to rhyme with *hell ;*
　　　The other, I think, rhymes with *you.*"

VI

Then Peter set up such a yell
　　The nurse who with some water gruel
Was climbing up the stairs as well
As her old legs could climb them, fell,
　　　And broke them both—the fall was cruel

VII

The parson from the casement leapt
　　Into the lake of Windermere :
And many an eel—though no adept
In God's right reason for it—kept
　　　Gnawing his kidneys half a year.

HORACE TWISS

1787–1849

BESIDES writing a small volume of parodies, from which the following examples have been taken, Twiss attained to some distinction as a politician. His first important literary work was a farewell address written for his aunt, Mrs. Siddons, which she recited on the stage 29th June, 1812. In June, 1811, Horace Twiss was called to the Bar, and he rose in his profession until in 1827 he became King's Counsel, in 1837 reader of his Inn, and in 1838 treasurer. In 1820 he was returned to Parliament as member for Wootton Bassett, and except for loss of his seat between 1831 and 1835 he made steady advancement, and in 1844 was rewarded for his labours with the Chancellorship of the Duchy of Lancaster. The period of inaction was occasioned by the passing of the Reform Bill. Twiss knew that this Bill would deprive him of his borough, and on the occasion of its second reading Macaulay relates that "the face of Twiss was as the face of a damned soul." In 1812 he brought out anonymously his "Posthumous Parodies of the Poets." In this volume Twiss has taken political life as his theme, just as Sir Isaac Hawkins Browne in the "Pipe of Tobacco" made his authors extol the fragrant weed.

All the parodies are distinguished by much wit and careful imitation, but particularly happy in his imitation of Jaques' famous speech in "As You Like It." There is, besides, a good parody on Milton, perhaps one of the best of the series, and the author aptly paraphrases Shakespeare in his peroration :—

> "Our parodies are ended. These our authors,
> As we foretold you, were all Spirits, and
> Are melted into air, into thin air.
> And, like the baseless fabric of these verses,
> The Critic's puff, the Trade's advertisements,

The Patron's promise, and the World's applause—
Yea, all the hopes of Poets—shall dissolve,
And, like this unsubstantial fable, fated,
Leave not a groat behind!"

HORACE TWISS

The Patriot's Progress

[*Parody—W. Shakespeare*]

         ST. STEPHEN's is a stage
And half the opposition are but players :
For clap-traps, and deceptions, and effects,
Fill up their thoughts throughout their many parts,
Their acts being sev'n.   At first the Demagogue,
Railing and mouthing at the hustings' front :
And then the cogging[1] Candidate, with beer,
Fibs, cringes, and cockades, giving to voters
Unwillingly a pledge.   And then the Member,
Crackling like furnace, with a flaming story
Made on the country's fall.   Then he turns Courtier,
Full of smooth words, and secret as a midwife,
Pleased with all rulers, zealous for the church,
Seeking the useful fame of orthodoxy,
Ev'n from the *Canon's* mouth.   And then a Secretary,
In fair white waistcoat, with boil'd chicken lin'd,
With placid smile, and speech of ready answer,
Lib'ral of promises and army contracts,
And so he rules the State.   The sixth act brings him
To be a snug retired old baronet,

---

[1] A term taken from the practice of cheating with loaded dice.

With riband red on breast, with star on side :
His early zeal for change a world too hot
For his cold age ; and his big eloquence,
Turning to gentler sonnets, obedient pipes—
And we must pay the piper.   Scene the last
That ends this comfortable history,
Is a fat pension and a pompous peerage,
With cash, with coronet—with all but conscience.

Fashion

[Parody—J. Milton]

HENCE, loath'd vulgarity,
  Of ignorance and native dullness bred,
    In low unwholesome shed,
'Mongst thieves and drabs, and street-sweeps asking charity:
  Find some suburban haunt,
Where the spruce 'prentice treats his flashy mate,
    And smoking cits debate :
Or at a dowdy rout, or ticket-ball,
    Giv'n at Freemasons' hall,
With tawdry clothes and liveries ever flaunt.
  But come thou nymph of slender waist,
Known early by the name of Taste,

.   .   .   .

      Haste thee, nymph, and bring with thee
      Steed and light-hung Tilbury,
      Undiscoverable rouge,
      Polished boots, and neckcloth huge,

147

(Such as might deck a Dandy's cheek,
And draw the gazers for a week).
Mackintosh's [1] racy phrase,
And wit, that peerless Ward [2] might praise.
Come, and let your steps be bent
With a lively measurement,
And bring the proper airs and graces,
That make their way in certain places:
And, if I give thee honour due,
Fashion, enroll me with the few,
With Spencer, [3] Sydney Smith and thee
In a select society:
To ride when many a lady fair, in
Her morning veil begins her airing,
And with the Nurse and Children stow'd
Drives down the Park, or Chelsea road:
Then to stop in spite of sorrow,
And through the window bid good-morrow
Of vis-à-vis, or barouchette,
Or half-open landaulette:
While little Burke, with lively din,
Scatters his stock of trifles thin;
And at the Bridge or Grosvenor Gate,
Briskly bids his horses wait;
Oft listening how the Catalani [4]

---

[1] Sir James Mackintosh (1765–1832) was a Scotch philosopher and writer.

[2] Nathaniel Ward (1578(?)–1653) was the author of a satirical work, "The Simple Cobbler of Agawam."

[3] Probably William Robert Spencer (1769–1834), a poet and leader of fashion. His chief poems were *vers de société* and ballads.

[4] Angelica Catalani (1779–1849), a very popular Italian singer.

Rouses at night th' applauding many.
In some opera of Mozart,
Winning the eye, the ear, the heart.
Then in the round room not unseen,
Attending dames of noble mien,
Right to the door in Market-lane,
Where chairmen range their jostling train,
And footmen stand with torch alight,
In their thousand liveries dight,
While the doorkeeper on the stairs
Bawls for the Marchionesses' chairs,
And young dragoons enjoy the crowd,
And dowagers inveigh aloud,
And lovers write a hasty scrawl
Upon the ticket of a shawl.
Straight mine eye hath caught new pleasures,
As the circling crowd it measures;
Virgins old with tresses grey,
That in corkscrew curls do stray;
Ladies, on whose softer breast,
Gallants receive a hope of rest;
Little feet with sandals tied,
Shallow heads and shoulders wide;
Necks and throats of lovely form,
Bosom'd high in tippet warm,
Where some beauty spreads her snare,
The envy of surrounding fair.
Hard by, the Op'ra being past,
To some small supper let me haste,
Where ladies, wits, and poets met,
Are at their various banquet set,

Of fifty little tempting messes,
Which the neat-handed Gunter dresses :
And there with satisfaction see
The pullet and the early pea,
Or, if the sultry dog-star reign,
The melon ice and cool champagne.
Sometimes to a late delight
Argyll [1] advertisements invite,
Where the wreathéd waltz goes round,
Or English tunes more briskly sound,
To twice a hundred feet or more,
Dancing on the chalky floor :
And wise mamma well pleased to see
Her daughter paired with high degree,
Stays till the daylight glares amain,
Then in the carriage home again,
With stories told of many bow,
And civil speech from so and so.
She was asked to dance, she said,
But scarcely down the middle led,
Because his Lordship only thought
How soonest to find out a spot,
Where seated by her side, unheard,
He whispered many a pretty word,
Such as no poet could excel !
Then, having paid his court so well,
Most manifestly meaning marriage,
He fetched the shawls and called the carriage,
Handed her from the crowded door
And watched her till she was seen no more.

[1] The Argyll Rooms.

Thus done the tales, the fluttering fair
Go up to bed and curl their hair.
Country houses please me too,
And the jocund Christmas crew,
Where chiefs of adverse politics
Awhile in social circle mix ;
And tenants come, whose county franchise
Connects them with the higher branches,
Since all the great alike contend
For votes, on which they all depend.
Let affability be there,
With cordial hand and friendly air,
And private play and glittering fête,
To make the rustic gentry prate,—
Such joys as fill young ladies' heads,
Who judge from books of masquerades.
Then will I to St. Stephen's stray,
If aught be moved by Castlereagh,
Or matchless Canning mean to roll
His thunders o'er the subject soul.
And sometimes, to divert my cares,
Give me some flirt, with joyous airs,
Married a girl, a widow now,
Such as will hear each playful vow,
Too young to lay upon the shelf :
Meaning—as little as myself :—
Still speaking, singing, walking, running,
With wanton heed and giddy cunning,
With a good mien to testify
Her converse with good company,
That Chesterfield might lift his eyes

HORACE TWISS

From the dark Tartarus where he lies,
Beholding, in her air and gait,
Graces that almost compensate
The blunders of his awkward son,
And half the harm his book has done.
These delights if thou canst give
Taste with thee I mean to live.

Modern Parodists

WILLIAM EDMONSTOUNE AYTOUN

1813–1865

WILLIAM AYTOUN was the descendant of that Sir Roger Aeton (him-self a poet and a patron of poets) whose dust lies near the steps ascending King Henry VII's Chapel, Westminster Abbey. His father was Writer to the Signet, and the young Aytoun was educated at Edinburgh Academy and University with a view to entering the profession of the law. But the poetic blood of his forefathers was in the veins of the young man, and he was anxious to devote his energies to literature ; in fact, at the early age of seventeen he published a book of poems entitled : "Poland, Homer and other Poems." He wisely decided, however, that the profession of the law afforded more chance of success to one who had to depend on his energies for his livelihood, and after some months spent at Aschaffenburg he entered his father's office, was admitted a Writer to the Signet in 1835, and was called to the Bar in 1840.

He did not forsake literature altogether, for a little later he was collaborating with (Sir) Theodore Martin in "The Bon Gaultier Ballads," a volume of humorous verse, marked by splendid diction and sparkling wit, which was readily welcomed by the public. It is from these ballads that the parodies chosen for this volume have been selected. Many of the poems are the joint work of Aytoun and Martin, and amongst these is "The Lay of the Lovelorn," to which Aytoun contributed some of the best lines. It is certainly the best parody in the whole collection. Sir Theodore Martin, in his preface to the sixteenth edition, gives Aytoun as the sole author of "La Mort d'Arthur" and "A Midnight Meditation." Both poems are good, though they do not reach to that high level of parody which distinguishes many of the other contributions. Since, how-ever, they alone are the undisputed work of William Aytoun they must be admitted here ; but their author was a prince of parodists, as his burlesque poem "Firmilian" sufficiently testifies. He wrote, besides, "The Lays of the Scottish Cavaliers," in which he makes good his position as an original poet of great distinction. As a man he was noted for his genial and kindly disposition. He died at Blackhills, near Elgin, in 1865.

The Puff Poetical

["WE have often thought of entering the lists against Robins (famous for his imaginative advertisements of properties for sale). It may be vanity, but we think we could trump him. Robins amplifies well, but we think we could trump him." Thereupon "Bon Gaultier" proceeds to illustrate his views by the following rhyming advertisements.—"*Bon Gaultier Ballads*."]

WILLIAM EDMONSTOUNE AYTOUN

La Mort d'Arthur

[*Parody—Tennyson*]

SLOWLY, as one who bears a mortal hurt,
  Through which the fountain of his life runs dry,
Crept good King Arthur down unto the lake.
A roughening wind was bringing in the waves
With cold dull plash and plunging to the shore,
And a great bank of clouds came sailing up
Athwart the aspect of the gibbous moon,
Leaving no glimpse save starlight, as he sank,
With a short stagger, senseless on the stones.

No man yet knows how long he lay in swound ;
But long enough it was to let the rust
Lick half the surface of his polished shield,
For it was made by far inferior hands
Than forged his helm, his breastplate and his greaves,
Whereon no canker lighted, for they bore
The magic stamp of Mechi's Silver Steel.

A Midnight Meditation

[*Parody—Bulwer Lytton*]

FILL me once more the foaming pewter up !
    Another board of oysters, ladye mine !
To-night Lucullus with himself shall sup.
    These mute inglorious Miltons[1] are divine !
    And as I here in slippered ease recline,
Quaffing of Perkin's Entire my fill,
I sigh not for the lymph of Aganippe's rill.[2]

A noble inspiration fires my brain,
    Caught from Old England's fine time-hallowed drink ;
I snatch the pot again and yet again,
    And as the foaming fluids shrink and shrink,
    Fill me once more, I say, up to the brink !
This makes strong hearts—strong heads attest its charm—
This nerves the might that sleeps in Britain's brawny arm

[1] The most highly reputed oysters of the day.
[2] A well, whose waters possessed the power of inspiration, situated at the foot of Mount Helicon.

But these remarks are neither here nor there.
  Where was I ? Oh, I see—old Southey's dead !
They'll want some bard to fill the vacant chair,
    And drain the annual butt—and oh, what head
    More fit with laurel to be garlanded
Than this, which, curled in many a fragrant coil,
Breathes of Castalia's [1] streams, and best Macassar oil !

I know a grace is seated on my brow,
  Like young Apollo's with his golden beams—
There should Apollo's bays be budding now :—
    And in my flashing eyes the radiance beams,
    That marks the poet in his waking dreams,
When, as his fancies cluster thick and thicker,
He feels the trance divine of poesy and liquor.

They throng around me now, those things of air
  That from my fancy took their being's stamp :
There Pelham [2] sits and twirls his glossy hair,
    There Clifford [2] leads his pals upon the tramp ;
    There pale Zanoni, [2] bending o'er his lamp,
Roams through the starry wilderness of thought,
Where all is everything, and everything is nought.

Yes, I am he who sang how Aram [2] won
  The gentle ear of pensive Madeline !
How love and murder hand in hand may run,
    Cemented by philosophy serene,
    And kisses bless the spot where gore has been !

[1] A well on Mount Parnassus dedicated to Apollo and the Muses.
[2] Characters which not only occur in, but have occasioned the titles of several of Lord Lytton's novels.

WILLIAM EDMONSTOUNE AYTOUN

Who breathed the melting sentiment of crime,
And for the assassin waked a sympathy sublime!

Yes, I am he, who on the novel shed
   Obscure philosophy's enchanting light!
Until the public, 'wildered as they read,
   Believed they saw that which was not in sight—
   Of course 'twas not for me to set them right;
For in my nether heart convinced I am,
Philosophy's as good as any other flam.

Novels three-volumed I shall write no more—
   Somehow or other now they will not sell;
And to invent new passions is a bore—
   I find the Magazines pay quite as well.
   Translating's simple, too, as I can tell,
Who've hawked at Schiller [1] on his lyric throne,
And given the astonished bard a meaning all my own.

Moore, Campbell, Wordsworth, their best days are grassed:
   Battered and broken are their early lyres,—
Rogers, a pleasant memory of the past,
   Warmed his young hands at Smithfield's martyr fires,
   And, worth a plum, nor bays nor butt desires.
But these are things which suit me to the letter,
For though this Stout is good, old Sherry's greatly better.

---

[1] A reference to Lytton's translation of Schiller's "Poems and Ballads."

WILLIAM EDMONSTOUNE AYTOUN

A fico for your small poetic ravers,
 Your Hunts, your Tennysons, your Milnes,[1] and these!
Shall they compete with him who wrote "Maltravers,"
 Prologue to "Alice or the Mysteries"?
 No! Even now my glance prophetic sees
My own high brow girt with the bays about.
What ho! within there, ho! another pint of STOUT!

---

[1] Probably a reference to Richard Monckton Milnes, afterwards Lord Houghton, a distinguished poet and politician. The names of other poets are too well known to require annotation.

ROBERT BARNABAS BROUGH

1828–1860

ROBERT BROUGH started his career as a clerk in Manchester. He subsequently removed to Liverpool, where he started a satiric journal entitled *The Liverpool Lion*, and for the rest of his life he was associated with the Press. Some of his work has been illustrated by George Cruikshank, for whose *Comic Annual* he wrote the following parody of Edgar Allan Poe's "Raven." His verses are justly described by the late Joseph Knight as "of their epoch." In his work Brough is neat, and can be very humorous, but he lacks the sparkle which is apparent among latter-day humorists; nevertheless, he is the best writer of a style of verse which was very popular fifty years ago, and as representative of this class he should not be forgotten.

The Vulture

[*Parody—E. A. Poe*]

AN ORNITHOLOGICAL STUDY

THE Vulture is the most cruel, deadly, and voracious of birds of prey. He is remarkable for his keen scent, and for the tenacity with which he invariably clings to the victim on whom he has fixed his grip. He is not to be shaken off whilst the humblest pickings remain. He is usually to be found in an indifferent state of feather.—*New Translation of Cuvier.*

Once upon a midnight chilling, as I held my feet unwilling
O'er a tub of scalding water, at a heat of ninety-four ;
Nervously a toe in dipping, dripping, slipping, then out-
    skipping,
Suddenly there came a ripping, whipping, at my cham-
    bers door.
"'Tis the second floor," I mutter'd, "flipping at my
    chambers door—
            Wants a light—and nothing more ! "

Ah ! distinctly I remember, it was in the chill November,
And each cuticle and member was with influenza sore ;
Falt'ringly I stirr'd the gruel, steaming, creaming o'er the
    fuel,
And anon removed the jewel that each frosted nostril
    bore,
Wiped away the trembling jewel that each redden'd
    nostril bore—
            Nameless here for evermore !

And I recollect a certain draught that fann'd the window
    curtain
Chill'd me, fill'd me, with the horror of two steps across
    the floor,
And, besides, I'd got my feet in, and a most refreshing
    heat in,
To myself I kept repeating—" If I answer to the door—
Rise to let the ruffian in who seems to want to burst the
    door,
            I'll be——" that and something more.

Presently the row grew stronger; hesitating then no longer,
"Really, Mister Johnson, blow it!—your forgiveness I
  implore,
Such an observation letting slip, but when a man's just
  getting
Into bed, you come upsetting nerves and posts of cham-
  bers door,
Making such a row, forgetting"—Spoke a voice beyond
  the door:
   "'Tisn't Johnson"—nothing more!

Quick a perspiration clammy bathed me, and I uttered
  "Dammy!"
(Observation wrested from me, like the one I made before)
Back upon the cushions sinking, hopelessly my eyes, like
  winking,
On some stout for private drinking, ranged in rows upon
  the floor,
Fix'd—and on an oyster barrel (full) beside them on the
  floor,
   Look'd and groan'd, and nothing more.

Open then was flung the portal, and in stepp'd a hated
  mortal,
By the moderns call'd a VULTURE (known as *Sponge* in
  days of yore),
Well I knew his reputation! cause of all my agitation—
Scarce a nod of salutation changed, he pounced upon the
  floor;
Coolly lifted up the oysters and some stout from off the
  floor,
   Help'd himself, and took some more!

Then this hungry beast untiring fix'd his gaze with fond
   admiring
On a piece of cold boil'd beef, I meant to last a week or
   more,
Quick he set to work devouring—plates, in quick succession, scouring—
Stout with every mouthful show'ring—made me ask, to
   see it pour,
If he quite enjoy'd his supper, as I watch'd the liquid pour;
               Said the Vulture " Never more."

Much disgusted at the spacious *vacuum* by this brute
   voracious
Excavated in the beef—(he'd eaten quite enough for four)—
Still, I felt relief surprising when at length I saw him
   rising,
That he meant to go surmising, said I, glancing at the
   door—
" Going ? Well, I won't detain you—mind the stairs and
   shut the door——"
               " Leave you, Tomkins !—never more."

Startled by an answer dropping hints that he intended
   stopping
All his life—I knew him equal to it if he liked, or more—
Half in dismal earnest, half in joke, with an attempt at
   laughing,
I remarked that he was chaffing, and demanded of the
   bore,
Ask'd what this disgusting, nasty, greedy, vile, intrusive
   bore
               Meant in croaking " Never more ? "

But the Vulture not replying, took my bunch of keys, and trying
Sev'ral, found at length the one to fit my private cupboard door ;
Took the gin out, fill'd the kettle ; and with a *sang froid* to nettle
Any saint, began to settle calmly down the grate before,
Really as he meant departing at the date I named before,
      Of never, never more !

Then I sat engaged in guessing what this circumstance distressing
Would be likely to result in, for I knew that long before
Once (it served me right for drinking) I had told him that if sinking
In the world, my fortunes linking to his own, he'd find my door
Always open to receive him, and it struck me now that door
      He would pass, p'raps never more !

Suddenly the air was clouded, all the furniture enshrouded
With the smoke of vile tobacco—this was worse than all before ;
" Smith ! " I cried (in not offensive tones, it might have been expensive,
For he knew the art defensive, and could costermongers floor) ;
" Recollect it's after midnight, *are* you going ?—mind the floor."
      Quoth the Vulture, " Never more ! "

"Smith!" I cried (the gin was going, down his throat in
  rivers flowing),
"If you want a bed, you know there's quite a nice hotel
  next door,
Very cheap. I'm ill—and, joking set apart, your horrid
  smoking
Irritates my cough to choking. Having mentioned it before,
Really, you should not compel one—*Will* you mizzle—
  as before?"
  Quoth the Vulture, "Never more!"

"Smith!" I cried, "that joke repeating merits little
  better treating
For you than a condemnation as a nuisance and a bore.
Drop it, pray, it isn't funny; I've to mix some rum and
  honey—
If you want a little money, take some and be off next
  door;
Run a bill up for me if you like, but *do* be off next door."
  Quoth the Vulture, "Never more!"

"Smith!" I shriek'd—the accent humbler dropping, as
  another tumbler
I beheld him mix, " be off! you drive me mad—it's
  striking four.
Leave the house and something in it; if you go on at
  the gin, it
Won't hold out another minute. Leave the house and
  shut the door—
Take your beak from out my gin, and take your body
  through the door!"
  Quoth the Vulture, "Never more!"

And the Vulture never flitting—still is sitting, still is
sitting,
Gulping down my stout by gallons, and my oysters by the
score ;
And the beast, with no more breeding than a heathen
savage feeding,
The new carpet's tints unheeding, throws his shells upon
the floor.
And his smoke from out my curtains, and his stains from
out my floor,
Shall be shifted never more !

I'm a Shrimp !

[Parody—"I'm afloat, I'm afloat"]

I'M a shrimp !   I'm a shrimp, of diminutive size :
    Inspect my antennae, and look at my eyes ;
I'm a natural syphon, when dipped in a cup,
For I drain the contents to the latest drop up.
I care not for craw-fish, I heed not the prawn,
From a flavour especial my fame has been drawn ;
Nor e'en to the crab or the lobster do yield,
When I'm properly cook'd and efficiently peeled.
Quick ! quick ! pile the coals—let your saucepan be deep,
For the weather is warm, and I'm sure not to keep ;
Off, off with my head—split my shell into three—
I'm a shrimp ! I'm a shrimp—to be eaten with tea.

FRANCIS BRET HARTE

1839–1902

BRET HARTE was born in Albany, New York, but at the age of fifteen migrated to California. At different periods of his life he was teacher, miner, printer, express messenger, editor of *The Golden Era*, Secretary to the San Francisco Mint, and finally editor of *The Overland Monthly*, in which paper appeared some of his best-known tales, *e.g.* "The Luck of Roaring Camp." Gifted with perception, imagination, and poetic feeling, Bret Harte united the two attracting qualities of humour and pathos. In parody, pathos takes a very subordinate position; it is for the laughter-maker to prove his prowess, and Bret Harte is at his merriest in such poems as the "Ode to the Pliocene Skull," and "The Lost Tails of Miletus."

The Lost Tails of Miletus

[*Imitation—E. B. Lytton*]

HIGH on the Thracian hills, half hid in the billows
    of clover,
Thyme, and the asphodel blooms, and lulled by Pactolian [1]
    streamlet,
She of Miletus [2] lay ; and beside her an aged satyr
Scratched his ear with his hoof, and playfully mumbled
    his chestnuts.

[1] A river of Lydia with golden sands.
[2] One of the greatest cities of Asia Minor, built on the banks of the Mæander, and noted for its valuable flocks.

168

Vainly the Maenid and the Bassarid [1] gambolled about
her,
The free-eyed Bacchante sang, and Pan—the renowned,
the accomplished—
Executed his difficult solo. In vain were his gambols
and dances ;
High o'er the Thracian hills, rose the voice of the
shepherdess, wailing.

"Ai ! for the fleecy flocks, the meek-nosed, the passion-
less faces ;
Ai ! for the tallow-scented, the straight-tailed, the high-
stepping ;
Ai ! for the timid glance, which is that which the rustic
sagacious,
Applies to him who loves but may not declare his
passion ! "

Her then Zeus answered low : " O daughter of song
and sorrow,—
Hapless tender of sheep,—arise from thy long lamenta-
tion !
Since thou canst not trust fate, nor behave as becomes a
Greek maiden,
Look and behold thy sheep." And lo ! they returned
to her tailless.

[1] Another of the titles by which the frenzied worshippers of
Bacchus were known.

FRANCIS BRET HARTE

Mrs. Judge Jenkins

[Being the only genuine sequel to " Maud Müller "]

[*Parody—Whittier*]

MAUD MÜLLER, all that summer day,
    Raked the meadows sweet with hay ;

Yet, looking down the distant lane,
She hoped the judge would come again.

But when he came, with smile and bow,
Maud only blushed, and stammered, " Ha-ow ? "

And spoke of her " pa," and wondered whether
He'd give consent they should wed together.

Old Müller burst in tears, and then
Begged that the judge would lend him "ten " ;

For trade was dull and wages low,
And the " crops " this year were somewhat slow.

And ere the languid summer died,
Sweet Maud became the Judge's bride.

But on the day that they were mated,
Maud's brother Bob was intoxicated ;

And Maud's relations, twelve in all,
Were very drunk at the judge's ball.

And when the summer came again,
The young bride bore him babies twain.

And the judge was blest, but thought it strange
That bearing children made such a change :

For Maud grew broad and red and stout :
And the waist that his arm once clasped about

Was more than he now could span.   And he
Sighed as he pondered, ruefully,

How that which in Maud was native grace
In Mrs. Jenkins was out of place ;

And thought of the twins, and wished that they
Looked less like the man who raked the hay

On Müller's farm, and dreamed with pain
Of the day he wandered down the lane.

And, looking down that dreary track,
He half regretted that he came back.

For, had he waited, he might have wed
Some maiden fair and thoroughbred ;

For there be women fair as she,
Whose verbs and nouns do more agree.

Alas for maiden ! alas for judge !
And the sentimental,—that's one-half " fudge " ;

For Maud soon thought the judge a bore,
With all his learning and all his lore.

And the judge would have bartered Maud's fairface
For more refinement and social grace.

If, of all words of tongue and pen,
The saddest are, " It might have been,"

More sad are these we daily see :
" It is, but hadn't ought to be."

A Geological Madrigal

[*Parody—Shenstone*]

I HAVE found out a gift for my fair ;
  I know where the fossils abound,
Where the footprints of *Aves* declare
  The birds that once walked on the ground ;
Oh, come, and—in technical speech—
  We'll walk this Devonian shore,
Or on some Silurian beach
  We'll wander, my love, evermore.

I will show thee the sinuous track
  By the slow-moving annelid made,
Or the Trilobite that, further back,
  In the old Potsdam sandstone was laid ;
Thou shalt see, in his Jurassic tomb,
  The Plesiosaurus embalmed ;
In his Oolitic prime and his bloom,
  Iguanodon safe and unharmed !

You wished—I remember it well,
  And I loved you the more for the wish—
For a perfect cystedian shell,
  And a *whole* holocephalic fish.
And oh, if Faith's strata contains
  In its lowest Silurian drift,
Or palæozoic remains
  The same,—'tis your lover's free gift !

Then come, love, and never say nay,
  But calm all your maidenly fears ;
We'll note, love, in one summer's day
  The record of millions of years ;
And though the Darwinian plan
  Your sensitive feelings may shock ;
We'll find the beginning of man,—
  Our fossil ancestors, in rock !

The Willows

[*Parody—E. A. Poe*]

THE skies they were ashen and sober,
  The streets they were dirty and drear ;
It was night in the month of October,
  Of my most immemorial year ;
Like the skies I was perfectly sober,
  And I stopped at the mansion of Shear,—
At the Nightingale,—perfectly sober,
  And the willowy woodland, down here.

FRANCIS BRET HARTE

Here, once in an alley Titanic
  Of Ten-pins, I roamed with my soul,—
  Of Ten-pins,—with Mary, my soul ;
They were days when my heart was volcanic,
  And impelled me to frequently roll,
  And made me resistlessly roll,
Till my ten-strikes created a panic
  In the realms of the Boreal pole,
Till my ten-strikes created a panic
  With the monkey atop of his pole.

I repeat, I was perfectly sober,
  But my thoughts they were palsied and sere,—
  My thoughts were decidedly queer ;
For I knew not the month was October,
  And I marked not the night of the year ;
I forgot that sweet *morceau* of Auber
  That the band oft performed down here,
And I mixed the sweet music of Auber
  With the Nightingale's music of Shear.

And now as the night was senescent,
  And the star-dials pointed to morn,
  And car-drivers hinted of morn,
At the end of the path a liquescent
  And bibulous lustre was born ;
'Twas made by the bar-keeper present,
  Who mixéd a duplicate horn,—
His two hands describing a crescent
  Distinct with a duplicate horn.

And I said : " This looks perfectly regal,
  For it's warm, and I know I feel dry,—
  I am confident that I feel dry ;
We have come past the emu and eagle,
  And watched the gay monkey on high ;
Let us drink to the emu and eagle,—
  To the swan and the monkey on high,—
  To the eagle and monkey on high ;
For this bar-keeper will not inveigle,—
  Bully boy with the vitreous eye ;
He surely would never inveigle,—
  Sweet youth with the crystalline eye."

But Mary, uplifting her finger,
  Said, " Sadly this bar I mistrust,—
  I fear that this bar does not trust.
O hasten !   O let us not linger !
  O fly,—let us fly,—ere we must ! "
In terror she cried, letting sink her
  Parasol till it trailed in the dust,—
In agony sobbed, letting sink her
  Parasol till it trailed in the dust,—
  Till it sorrowfully trailed in the dust.

Then I pacified Mary and kissed her,
  And tempted her into the room,
  And conquered her scruples and gloom ;
And we passed to the end of the vista,
  And were stopped by the warning of doom,—
  By some words that were warning of doom ;

And I said, "What is written, sweet sister,
    At the opposite end of the room?"
She sobbed, as she answered, "All liquors
    Must be paid for ere leaving the room."

Then my heart it grew ashen and sober,
    As the streets were deserted and drear,—
For my pockets were empty and drear;
And I cried, "It was surely October,
    On this very night of last year,
    That I journeyed—I journeyed down here,—
    That I brought a fair maiden down here,
    On this night of all nights in the year,
    Ah! to me that inscription is clear;
Well I know now, I'm perfectly sober,
    Why no longer they credit me here,—
Well I know now that music of Auber,
    And this Nightingale, kept by one Shear.

North Beach

[*Imitation—Spenser*]

LO! where the castle of bold Pfeiffer throws
    Its sullen shadow on the rolling tide,—
No more the home where joy and wealth repose
But now where wassailers in cells abide;
See yon long quay that stretches far and wide,
Well known to citizens as wharf of Meiggs;
There each sweet Sabbath walks in maiden pride
Then pensive Margaret, and brave Pat, whose legs
Encased in broad cloth oft keep time with Peg's.

FRANCIS BRET HARTE

Here cometh oft the tender nursery maid
While in her ear her love his tale doth pour.
Meantime her infant doth her charge evade,
And rambleth sagely on the sandy shore
Till the sly sea crab, low in ambush laid,
Seizeth his leg and biteth him full sore.
Ah me! what sounds the shuddering echoes bore
When his small treble mixed with Ocean's roar.

Hard by there stands an ancient hostelrie
And at its side a garden, where the bear,
The stealthy catamount, and coon agree
To work deceits on all who gather there ;
And when Augusta—that unconscious fair—
With nuts and apples plieth Bruin free,
Lo! the green parrot claweth her back hair,
And the grey monkey grabbeth fruits that she
On her gay bonnet wears, and laugheth loud in glee !

SHIRLEY BROOKS

1816–1874

CHARLES WILLIAM SHIRLEY BROOKS was born in London, April 29th, 1816. He started life as a student of law, but at length determined to embark on a literary career. For some time he was on the staff of the *Morning Chronicle*, during which period he found time to write both novels and plays; later he became leader-writer to the *Illustrated London News*, and soon afterwards began writing for *Punch*, becoming its editor on the death of Mark Lemon in 1870. During his period of editorship he wrote a large number of verses, which were collected and published posthumously under the title, "Poems of Wit and Humour." Of his parodies the best is assuredly his "critique" of Longfellow's "Hiawatha," which appeared in 1856, but the sonnet in imitation of Martin Tupper is of almost equal excellence, though lacking the direct criticism which gives an added interest to the former parody.

The Song of Hiawatha

[*Parody—H. W. Longfellow*]

YOU, who hold in grace and honour
   Hold as one who did you kindness
When he published former poems,
Sang Evangeline the noble,
Sang the golden Golden Legend,
Sang the song the voices utter,
Crying in the night and darkness,
Sang how unto the Red Planet

SHIRLEY BROOKS

Mars he gave the Night's First Watches,
Henry Wadsworth, whose adnomen
(Coming awkward for the accents
Into this his latest rhythm)
Write we as Protracted Fellow,
Or in Latin, Longus Comes—
Buy the Song of Hiawatha.

Should you ask me, Is the poem
Worthy of its predecessors,
Worthy of the sweet conceptions
Of the manly, nervous diction
Of the phrase, concise or pliant,
Of the songs that sped the pulses
Of the songs that gemmed the eyelash,
Of the other works of Henry?
I should answer, I should tell you,
You may wish that you may get it—
Don't you wish that you may get it?

Should you ask me, Is it worthless,
Is it bosh, and is it bunkum;
Merely facile, flowing nonsense,
Easy to a practised rhythmist,
Fit to charm a private circle,
But not worth the print and paper
David Brogue hath here expended?
I should answer, I should tell you
You're a fool and most presumptuous;
Hath not Henry Wadsworth writ it,
Hath not Punch commanded "Buy it"?

SHIRLEY BROOKS

Should you ask me, What's its nature?
Ask me, What's the kind of Poem?
Ask me in respectful language,
Touching your respectful beaver,
Kicking back your manly hind leg,
Like to one who sees his betters;
I should answer, I should tell you,
'Tis a poem in this metre,
And embalming the traditions,
Tables, rites, and superstitions
Of the various tribes of Indians.
From the land of the Ogibways,
From the land of the Dacotahs,
From the mountains, moors, and fenlands
Where the heron, the Shuh-shuh-gar
Finds its sugar in the rushes.
From the fast decaying nations
Which our gentle Uncle Samuel
Is improving, very smartly
From the face of all creation,
Off the face of all creation.
Should you ask me by what story
By what action, plot or fiction,
All these matters are connected?
I should answer, I should tell you,
Go to Bogue's and buy the poem
Published neatly at one shilling,
Published sweetly at five shillings.

SHIRLEY BROOKS

Sonnet CCCI

[*Parody—Tupper*]

MR. PUNCH has the pleasure to announce that in consequence of the unexampled success of Mr. Martin F. Tupper's new volume, "Three Hundred Sonnets," the former has entered into an arrangement with the latter for a new series of those delightful compositions. The slight delay in completing the negotiation arose solely from the Poet's supposition that, having written upon every conceivable place, thing, boy, girl, baby, and other article in any way connected with himself, he might find a lack of subject. But . . . Mr. P. states with delight that the supply is again turned on.

To my Five New Kittens

SOFT little beasts, how pleasantly ye lie
    Snuggling and snoozling by your purring sire,
   Mother I mean (but sonnet-rhymes require
A shorter word, and boldly I defy
Those who would tie the bard by pedant rule).
   O kittens, you're not thinking, I'll be bound,
   How three of you had yesterday been drowned
But that my little boy came home from school,
And begged your lives though Cook remonstrance made
Declaring we were overrun with cats,
That licked her cream dish and her butter pats,
But Childhood's pleadings won me, and I said—
O Cook, we'll keep the innocents alive ;
They're five consider and you've fingers five.

181

SHIRLEY BROOKS

More Luck to Honest Poverty

[Parody—Robert Burns]

MORE luck to honest poverty,
    It claims respect, and a' that;
But honest wealth's a better thing,
    We dare be rich for a' that.
        For a' that, and a' that,
            And spooney cant and a' that,
        A man may have a ten-pun note,
            And be a brick for a' that.

What though on soup and fish we dine,
    Wear evening togs and a' that,
A man may like good meat and wine
    Nor be a knave for a' that.
        For a' that, and a' that,
            Their fustian talk and a' that,
        A gentleman, however clean,
            May have a heart for a' that.

A prince can make a belted knight,
    A marquis, duke and a' that,
And if the title's earned, all right,
    Old England's fond of a' that.
        For a' that, and a' that,
            Their balderdash and a' that,
        A name that tells of service done,
            Is worth the wear for a' that.

SHIRLEY BROOKS

Then let us pray that come it may,
 And come it will for a' that,
That common sense may take the place
 Of common cant and a' that.
  For a' that, and a' that,
   Who cackles trash and a' that,
  Or be he lord, or be he low,
   The man's an ass for a' that.

CUTHBERT BEDE

1827–1889

The Reverend Edward Bradley was one of a humorist circle of friends which included Cruikshank and Mark Lemon. He was twenty-three when he commenced writing for the Press, but he was not long before he was widely known as "Cuthbert Bede," the author of "Mr. Verdant Green," a book which has met with universal approval, so much so that M. Taine, the writer of "Notes sur l'Angleterre," has drawn upon it for his remarks on the lighter side of University life. From his "Shilling Book of Beauty," which was published in 1856, a parody of Lord Lytton's versification is inserted here. The humour may appear to modern ideas a little thin, but the poem is a good skit on the original, and the quips it contains are admirably turned.

On a Toasted Muffin

[Imitation—Bulwer Lytton]

OBJECT belov'd! when day to eve gives place,
    And Life's best nectar thy fond vot'ry sips,
How sweet to gaze upon thy shining face,
    And press thy tender form unto my lips!

Fair as the Naiad of the Grecian stream,
    And beautiful as Oread of the lawn;
Bright-beaming as the iv'ry-palac'd dream,
    And melting as the dewy Urns of Dawn.

CUTHBERT BEDE

For thee I strike the sounding Lyre of Song,
    And hymn the Beautiful, the Good, the True;
The dying notes of thankfulness prolong,
    And light the Beacon-fires of Praise for you.

Butter'd Ideal of Life's coarser food!
    Thou calm Egeria [1] in a world of strife!
Antigone [2] of crumpets! mild as good,
    Decent in death, and beautiful in life!

Fairest where all is *fare!* shine on me still,
    And gild the dark To-Morrow of my days;
In public Marts and crowded Senates thrill
    My soul with Tea-time thoughts and Muffin lays.

[1] Egeria was the wife and adorer of the great Kuma Pompilius, Rome's second king, and greatly assisted him by her sage counsel.

[2] The noble daughter of Œpidus. After witnessing the ruin of her house, which she was powerless to prevent, she killed herself.

ROBERT BUCHANAN

1841–1901

THE work of Robert Buchanan has never received that consideration to which it is justly entitled. His star was eclipsed by a constellation of lights of greater magnitude, which included Browning, Tennyson, Swinburne, and the many great men who flourished in the latter half of the nineteenth century. He further increased his unfortunate position by his hostile attitude towards the accepted poets, an attitude clearly indicated in the following parody which appeared in the *Spectator* for September 15th, 1865. But whatever may be the opinions of Robert Buchanan, he was undeniably a great humorist and a great humanist, and wrote vigorous and skilled verse, instinc with poetry. Such poems as "The Wake of O'Hara" and "The Wedding of Shon McLean" prove this, while his constructive and satirical skill is shown to great advantage in the following parody.

The Session of the Poets

[*Parody—Sir John Suckling*]

AT the Session of Poets held lately in London,
    The Bard of Freshwater was voted the chair;
With his tresses unbrush'd, and his shirt-collar undone,
    He loll'd at his ease like a good-humour'd Bear;
"Come, boys!" he exclaimed, "we'll be merry together!"
    And lit up his pipe with a smile on his cheek;
While with eye like a skipper's cock'd up at the weather,
    Sat the Vice-Chairman Browning, thinking in Greek.

ROBERT BUCHANAN

The company gather'd embraced great and small bards,
  Both strong bards and weak bards, funny and grave,
Fat bards and lean bards, little and tall bards,
  Bards who wear whiskers and others who shave.
Of books, men and things, was the bards' conversation—
  Some praised *Ecce Homo*,[1] some deemed it so-so—
And then there was talk of the state of the nation
  And when the unwash'd would devour Mister Lowe.[2]

Right stately sat Arnold—his black gown adjusted
  Genteelly, his Rhine wine deliciously iced,—
With puddingish English serenely disgusted,
  And looking in vain (in the mirror) for " Geist " ; [3]
He heark'd to the Chairman, with " Surely ! " and
  " Really ? "
Aghast at both collar and cutty of clay,—
Then felt in his pocket and breathed again freely
  On touching the leaves of his own classic play.

Close at hand lingered Lytton, whose Icarus-winglets [4]
  Had often betrayed him in regions of rhyme—
How glitter'd the eye underneath the grey ringlets,
  A hunger within it unlessened by time !

---

[1] An allusion to the late Dean Farrar's book of that name.

[2] Robert Lowe (1811–1892), afterwards Viscount Sherbrooke, was an eminent politician. He interested himself keenly in the advancement of education.

[3] A catch-word much used at one time by literary enthusiasts to express spirituality, or rather " the divine spark."

[4] Icarus, son of Daedalus, attempted to fly with wings attached to his shoulders, but the heat of the sun melted the wax by which they were fastened and he fell into the Ægean Sea.

ROBERT BUCHANAN

Remoter sat Bailey,—satirical, surly—
  Who studied the language of Goethe too soon,
Who sang himself hoarse to the stars very early,
  And crack'd a weak voice with too lofty a tune.

How name all that wonderful company over?—
  Prim Patmore, mild Alford—and Kingsley also?
Among the small sparks who was realler than Lover?
  Among misses, who sweeter than Miss Ingelow?
There sat, looking mooney, conceited and narrow,
  Buchanan,—who, finding when foolish and young
Apollo asleep on a coster-girl's barrow,
  Straight dragged him away to see somebody hung.

What was said? What was done? Was there prosing
    or rhyming?
  Was nothing noteworthy in deed or in word?
Why, just as the hour for the supper was chiming
  The only event of the evening occurred.
Up jumped, with his neck stretching out like a gander,
  Master Swinburne, and squeal'd glaring out through
    his hair,
"All virtue is bosh! Hallelujah for Landor!
  I disbelieve wholly in everything!—there!"

With language so awful he dared then to treat 'em,—
  Miss Ingelow fainted in Tennyson's arms,
Poor Arnold rushed out crying "Sæcl' inficetum!"
  And great bards and small bards were full of alarms;
Till Tennyson, flaming, and red as a gipsy,
  Struck his fist on the table and uttered a shout,
"To the door with the boy! Call a cab! He is tipsy!"
  And they carried the naughty young gentleman out.

CHARLES STUART CALVERLEY

1813–1884

FROM the age of fifteen, when he entered Harrow, Calverley's career was a series of successes. True, he was removed from Oxford for non-observance of authority, but he quickly atoned for this outburst of high spirits by a brilliant course at Cambridge, where he was finally installed as Fellow of his College (Christ's). While he was still young his good nature and ready wit had won him many friends, and when he published, in 1862, his "Verses and Translations," he was not long in attaining a much wider popularity. As a writer his keen humour and satiric wit are conspicuous, but with these qualities are combined thorough poetic technique and a delicate sense of rhythm. His verse has, therefore, great fluency and literary "flavour," which place the writer in the forefront of parodists. Most of his imitations were prompted by a spirit of humorous caricature, but in his masterpiece, "The Cock and the Bull," he was actuated by deeper motives. His sense of clearness and poetic simplicity was offended by Browning's elaborate methods of poetry, and his protest against these methods found expression in this masterpiece of parody, which was published in "Fly Leaves" in 1872.

The Cock and the Bull

[Imitation—Browning]

YOU see this pebble-stone ? It's a thing I bought
    Of a bit of a chit of a boy i' the mid o' the day—
I like to dock the smaller parts-o'-speech,
As we curtail the already cur-tail'd cur

(You catch the paronomasia, play 'po' words?)
Did, rather, i' the pre-Landserian days.
Well, to my muttons.   I purchased the concern,
And clapt it i' my poke, having given for same
By way o' chop, swop, barter or exchange—
"Chop" was my snickering dandiprat's own term—
One shilling and fourpence, current coin o' the realm.
O-n-e one and f-o-u-r four
Pence, one and fourpence—you are with me, sir?—
What hour it skills not : ten or eleven o' the clock,
One day (and what a roaring day it was
Go shop or sight-see—bar a spit o' rain!)
In February, eighteen sixty-nine,
Alexandrina Victoria, Fidei
Hm—hm—how runs the jargon? being on throne.

Such, sir, are all the facts, succinctly put,
The basis or substratum—what you will—
Of the impending eighty thousand lines.
"Not much in 'em either," quoth perhaps simple Hodge.
But there's a superstructure.   Wait a bit.

Mark first the rationale of the thing :
Hear logic rivel and levigate the deed.
That shilling—and for matter o' that, the pence—
I had o' course upo' me—wi' me say—
(*Mecum*'s the Latin, make a note o' that)
When I popp'd pen i' stand, scratch'd ear, wiped snout,
(Let everybody wipe his own himself)
Sniff'd—tch!—at snuffbox ; tumbled up, he-heed,
Haw-haw'd (not hee-haw'd, that's another guess thing :)

Then fumbled at, and stumbled out of, door,
I shoved the timber ope wi' my omoplat;
And *in vestibulo*, i' the lobby to wit,
(Iacobi Facciolati's rendering, sir,)
Donn'd galligaskins, antigropeloes,[1]
And so forth; and, complete with hat and gloves,
One on and one a-dangle i' my hand,
And ombrifuge (Lord love you!) case o' rain,
I flopp'd forth, 'sbuddikins! on my own ten toes,
(I do assure you there be ten of them),
And went clump-clumping up hill and down dale
To find myself o' the sudden i' front o' the boy.
Put case I hadn't 'em on me, could I ha' bought
This sort-o'-kind-o'-what-you-might-call toy,
This pebble-thing, o' the boy-thing? Q.E.D.
That's proven without aid from mumping Pope,
Sleek porporate or bloated Cardinal.
(Isn't it, old Fatchaps? You're in Euclid, now.)
So, having the shilling—having i' fact a lot—
And pence and halfpence, ever so many o' them,
I purchased, as I think I said before,
The pebble (*lapis, lapidis, -di, -dem, -de*—
What nouns 'crease short i' the genitive, Fatchaps, eh?)
O' the boy, a bare-legg'd beggarly son of a gun,
For one-and-fourpence. Here we are again.

Now Law steps in, bigwigg'd, voluminous-jaw'd;
Investigates and re-investigates.
Was the transaction illegal? Law shakes head.
Perpend, sir, all the bearings of the case.

[1] Long riding boots for wet weather.

At first the coin was mine, the chattel his.
But now (by virtue of the said exchange
And barter) *vice versa* all the coin,
Per juris operationem, vests
I' the boy and his assigns till ding o' doom ;
In sæcula sæculo-o-o-orum ;
I think I hear the Abate mouth out that.)
To have and hold the same to him and them . . .
Confer some idiot on Conveyancing.
Whereas the pebble and every part thereof,
And all that appertaineth thereunto,
Quodcunque pertinet ad eam rem,
(I fancy, sir, my Latin's rather pat)
Or shall, will, may, might, can, could, would or should,
(*Subandi cætera*—clap me to the close—
For what's the good of law in a case o' the kind ?)
Is mine to all intents and purposes.
This settled, I resume the thread o' the tale.

Now for a touch o' the vendor's quality.
He says a gen'lman bought a pebble of him,
(This pebble i' sooth, sir, which I hold i' my hand)—
And paid for't *like* a gen'lman, on the nail.
" Did I o'ercharge him a ha'penny ?   Devil a bit.
Fiddlepin's end !   Get out, you blazing ass !
Gabble o' the goose.   Don't bugaboo-baby *me* !
Go double or quits ?   Yah ! tittup ! what's the odds ? "
—There's the transaction view'd i' the vendor's light.

Next ask that dumpled hag, stood snuffling by,
With her three frowsy blowsy brats o' babes,
The scum o' the kennel, cream o' the filth-heap—Faugh !

Aie, aie, aie, aie! ὀτοτοτοτοτοῖ,
('Stead which we blurt out Hoighty toighty now)—
And the baker and the candlestickmaker, and Jack and
    Gill,
Blear'd Goody this and queasy Gaffer that.
Ask the schoolmaster. Take schoolmaster first.

He saw a gentleman purchase from a lad
A stone, and pay for it *rite*, on the square,
And carry it off *per saltum*, jauntily,
Propria quæ maribus, gentleman's property now
(Agreeably to the law explain'd above),
In proprium usum, for his private ends.
The boy he chuck'd a brown i' the air, and bit
I' the face the shilling: heaved a thumping stone
At a lean hen that ran cluck clucking by,
(And hit her, dead as nail i' post o' door,)
Then abiit—what's the Ciceronian phrase?—
Excessit, evasit, erupit—off slogs boy;
Off like bird, *avi similis*—(you observed
The dative? Pretty i' the Mantuan!) [1]—*Anglice*
Off in three flea skips. *Hactenus*, so far,
So good, *tam bene. Bene, satis, male*—,
Where was I with my trope 'bout one in a quag?
I did once hitch the syntax into verse:
Verbum personale, a verb personal,
Concordat—ay, "agrees," old Fatchaps—*cum*
Nominativo, with its nominative,
Genere, i' point o' gender, *numero*,
O' number, *et persona*, and person. *Ut*,

---

[1] A title for Virgil, who was born in Mantua.

Instance : *Sol ruit*, down flops sun, *et* and,
Montes umbrantur, out flounce mountains.   Pah !
Excuse me, sir, I think I'm going mad.
You see the trick on 't though, and can yourself
Continue the discourse *ad libitum*.
It takes up about eighty thousand lines,
A thing imagination boggles at :
And might, odds-bobs, sir ! in judicious hands,
Extend from here to Mesopotamy.

Ode to Tobacco

[*Parody—Longfellow*]

THOU who, when fears attack,
    Bidst them avaunt, and Black
Care, at the horseman's back
        Perching, unseatest ;
Sweet, when the morn is gray ;
Sweet, when they've cleared away
Lunch ; and at close of day
        Possibly sweetest :

I have a liking old
For thee, though manifold
Stories, I know, are told,
        Not to thy credit ;
How one (or two at most)
Drops make a cat a ghost—
Useless, except to roast—
        Doctors have said it :

CHARLES STUART CALVERLEY

How they who use fusees
All grow by slow degrees
Brainless as chimpanzees,
        Meagre as lizards :
Go mad, and beat their wives ;
Plunge (after shocking lives)
Razors and carving knives
        Into their gizzards.

Confound such knavish tricks !
Yet I know five or six
Smokers who freely mix
        Still with their neighbours ;
Jones—(who, I'm glad so say,
Asked leave of Mrs. J.)—
Daily absorbs a clay
        After his labours.

Cats may have had their goose
Cooked by tobacco-juice ;
Still why deny its use
        Thoughtfully taken ?
We're not as tabbies are :
Smith, take a fresh cigar !
Jones, the tobacco-jar !
        Here's to thee, Bacon !

LEWIS CARROLL

1833–1898

WHILE the mathematical works of the Reverend Charles Dodgson are known only to scientists, the name of Lewis Carroll still stands, still signifies the laureate of mirth. "Alice in Wonderland," which was published in 1865, is a treasure-house of "inspired nonsense," and it is a nimble mind that can keep pace with its exuberant gaiety. In this book appeared some famous parodies, such as "You are old, Father William"—of which it is not too much to say that it has helped to immortalise the original by Southey— "Beautiful Soup," "How doth the Little Crocodile?" and many others.

Lewis Carroll published several other works of a humorous nature, notably, "Rhyme and Reason," "Sylvie and Bruno," "The Hunting of the Snark" and the sequel to "Alice," "Through the Looking-Glass."

Father William

[*Parody—Southey*]

"YOU are old, Father William," the young man said,
   "And your hair has become very white;
And yet you incessantly stand on your head,
   Do you think at your age it is right?"

"In my youth," Father William replied to his son,
   "I feared it might injure the brain,
But now that I'm perfectly sure I have none,
   Why, I do it again and again."

"You are old," said the youth, "as I mentioned before,
    And have grown most uncommonly fat;
Yet you turned a back somersault in at the door,
    Pray, *what* is the reason of that?"

"In my youth," said the sage, as he shook his grey
      locks,
    "I kept all my limbs very supple,
By the use of this ointment—one shilling the box,
    Allow me to sell you a couple."

"You are old," said the youth, "and your jaws are too
      weak
    For anything tougher than suet,
Yet you finished the goose, with the bones and the beak,
    Pray, how did you manage to do it?"

"In my youth," said his father, "I took to the law,
    And argued each case with my wife,
And the muscular strength which it gave to my jaw
    Has lasted the rest of my life."

"You are old," said the youth, "one would hardly
      suppose
    That your eye was as steady as ever;
Yet you balanced an eel on the end of your nose,—
    What made you so *awfully* clever?"

"I have answered three questions and that is enough,"
    Said his father; "don't give yourself airs.
Do you think I can listen all day to such stuff?
    Be off, or I'll kick you downstairs!"

LEWIS CARROLL

[Parody—Watts]

HOW doth the little crocodile
    Improve his shining tail,
And pour the waters of the Nile
    On every shining scale !

How cheerfully he seems to grin,
    How neatly spreads his claws,
And welcomes little fishes in
    With gently smiling jaws.

[Parody—Miss Anne Taylor]

TWINKLE, twinkle, little bat !
    How I wonder what you're at !
Up above the world you fly,
Like a tea-tray in the sky.

The Voice of the Lobster

[Parody—Watts]

" 'TIS the voice of the Lobster : I heard him declare
    ' You have baked me too brown, I must sugar my
        hair.'
As a duck with its eyelids, so he with his nose
Trims his belt and his buttons, and turns out his toes.

198

When the sands are all dry, he is gay as a lark,
And will talk in contemptuous tones of the Shark :
But, when the tide rises and sharks are around,
His voice has a timid and tremulous sound.

" I passed by his garden, and marked, with one eye,
How the Owl and the Panther were sharing a pie ;
The Panther took pie-crust, and gravy, and meat,
While the Owl had the dish as its share of the treat.
When the pie was all finished, the Owl, as a boon,
Was kindly permitted to pocket the spoon ;
While the Panther received knife and fork with a growl,
And concluded the banquet by——"

Turtle Soup

[Parody—Ann Taylor]

BEAUTIFUL soup, so rich and green,
        Waiting in a hot tureen !
Who for such dainties would not stoop ?
Soup of the evening, beautiful Soup ?
Soup of the evening, beautiful Soup ?
        Beau-ootiful Soo-oop !
        Beau-ootiful Soo-oop !
Soo-oop of the e-e-evening,
        Beautiful, beautiful Soup !

Beautiful Soup ! Who cares for fish,
Game, or any other dish ?
Who would not give all else for two p-

-ennyworth only of beautiful Soup?
Pennyworth only of beautiful Soup?
    Beau-ootiful Soo-oop!
    Beau-ootiful Soo-oop!
Soo-oop of the e-e-evening,
    Beautiful, beauti-FUL SOUP!

The Lobster Quadrille

[Parody—Mary Howitt]

"WILL you walk a little faster?" said a whiting to
    a snail,
There's a porpoise close behind us, and he's treading on
    my tail.
See how eagerly the lobsters and the turtles all advance!
They are waiting on the shingle—will you come and join
    the dance?
    Will you, won't you, will you, won't you, will you join
        the dance?
    Will you, won't you, will you, won't you, won't you
        join the dance?

"You can really have no notion how delightful it will be
When they take us up and throw us, with the lobsters,
    out to sea!"
But the snail replied "Too far, too far!" and gave a look
    askance—
Said he thanked the whiting kindly, but he would not
    join the dance.

Would not, could not, would not, could not, would not
    join the dance,
Would not, could not, would not, could not, could not
    join the dance.

"What matters it how far we go?" his scaly friend
    replied;
"There is another shore, you know, upon the other side.
The further off from England the nearer is to France—
Then turn not pale, beloved snail, but come and join the
    dance.
    Will you, won't you, will you, won't you, will you join
        the dance?
    Will you, won't you, will you, won't you, won't you
        join the dance?"

Hiawatha's Photographing [1]

[Parody—Longfellow]

FROM his shoulder Hiawatha
    Took the camera of Rosewood
Made of sliding folding rosewood;
Neatly put it all together.
In its case it lay compactly,
Folded into nearly nothing;
But he opened out the hinges,
Pushed and pulled the joints and hinges,

---

[1] The author was one of the earliest amateur photographers, and it is to him that we owe a photograph of the Rossetti Family, whose intimate friend he was.

Till it looked all squares and oblongs
Like a complicated figure
In the Second Book of Euclid.
This he perched upon a Tripod—
Crouched beneath its dusky cover—
Stretched his hand, enforcing silence—
Saith, " Be motionless, I beg you ! "

Mystic, awful was the process.
    All the family in order
Sat before him for their pictures :
Each in turn as he was taken,
Volunteered his own suggestions,
His ingenious suggestions.
    First the Governor, the Father :
He suggested velvet curtains
Looped about a massy pillar ;
And the corner of a table,
Of a rosewood dining-table.
He would hold a scroll of something,
Hold it firmly in his left hand ;
He would keep his right hand buried
(Like Napoleon) in his waistcoat ;
He would contemplate the distance
With a look of pensive meaning
As of ducks that die in tempests.
    Grand, heroic was the motion :
Yet the picture failed entirely :
Failed because he moved a little,
Moved, because he couldn't help it.
    Next, his better half took courage ;

LEWIS CARROLL

She would have *her* picture taken.
She came dressed beyond description,
Dressed in jewels and in satin
Far too gorgeous for an empress.
Gracefully she sat down sideways,
With a simper scarcely human,
Holding in her hand a bouquet
Rather larger than a cabbage.
All the while that she was sitting,
Still the lady chattered, chattered,
Like a monkey in the forest.
"Am I sitting still?" she asked him.
"Is my face enough in profile?
Shall I hold the bouquet higher?
Will it come into the picture?"
And the picture failed completely.

 Next the son the stunning Cantab:
He suggested curves of beauty,
Curves pervading all his figure,
Which the eye might follow onward,
Till they centred in the breast-pin,
Centred in the golden breast-pin.
He had learnt it all from Ruskin
(Author of "The Stones of Venice,"
"Seven Lamps of Architecture,"
"Modern Painters," and some others);
And perhaps he had not fully
Understood his author's meaning,
But, whatever was the reason,
All was fruitless, as the picture
Ended in an utter failure.

Next to him the eldest daughter :
She suggested very little,
Only asked if he would take her
With her look of "passive beauty."

Her idea of passive beauty
Was a squinting of the left eye,
Was a drooping of the right eye,
Was a smile that went up sideways
To the corner of the nostrils.

Hiawatha, when she asked him,
Took no notice of the question,
Looked as if he hadn't heard it,
But, when pointedly appealed to,
Smiled in his peculiar manner,
Coughed and said it "didn't matter,"
Bit his lip and changed the subject.
Nor in this was he mistaken
As the picture failed completely.

So in turn the other sisters.
Last the youngest son was taken :
Very rough and thick his hair was,
Very round and red his face was,
Very dusty was his jacket,
Very fidgety his manner ;
And his overbearing sisters
Called him names he disapproved of,
Called him Johnny, "Daddy's Darling,"
Called him Jacky, "Scrubby School-boy,"
And, so awful was the picture
In comparison the others
Seemed to the bewildered fancy

To have partially succeeded.
   Finally my Hiawatha
Tumbled all the tribe together,
("Grouped" is not the right expression),
And, as happy chance would have it
Did at last obtain a picture
Where the faces all succeeded :
Each came out a perfect likeness.

   Then they joined and all abused it,
Unrestrainedly abused it,
As the worst and ugliest picture
They could possibly have dreamed of.
"Giving one such strange expressions—
Sullen stupid pert expressions.
Really anyone would take us
(Anyone that did not know us)
For the most unpleasant people ! "
(Hiawatha seemed to think so,
Seemed to think it not unlikely).
All together rang their voices,
Angry loud discordant voices,
As of dogs that howl in concert,
As of cats that wail in chorus.

   But my Hiawatha's patience,
His politeness and his patience,
Unaccountably had vanished,
And he left that happy party.
Neither did he leave them slowly,
With the calm deliberation
Of a photographic artist :
But he left them in a hurry,

Left them in a mighty hurry,
Stating that he would not stand it,
Stating in emphatic language
What he'd be before he'd stand it.
Hurriedly he packed his boxes,
Hurriedly the porter trundled
On a barrow all the boxes :
Hurriedly he took his ticket,
Hurriedly the train received him :
Thus departed Hiawatha.

PHOEBE CARY

1824–1871

PHOEBE and her elder sister Alice were the two daughters of a man of good position living near Cincinnati, Ohio. In early life they encountered much opposition to the indulgence of their taste for letters, and were further hampered by the dearth of literature in this then half-developed land. In 1852 the sisters removed to New York City, and from that time their reputation as writers gradually increased, until they eventually became prominent members of the literary world. Horace Greeley, Robert Owen, and Bayard Taylor were among their intimate friends. "Poems and Parodies," the work of Phoebe Cary, from which the following extracts are taken, was published in Boston, 1854.

Jacob

[*Parody —Wordsworth*]

HE dwelt among "Apartments let"
    About five stories high ;
A man, I thought, that none would get,
    And very few would try.

A boulder, by a larger stone
    Half hidden in the mud,
Fair as a man when only one
    Is in the neighbourhood.

He lived unknown, and few could tell
    When Jacob was not free ;
But he has got a wife, and, Oh !
    The difference to me.

The Wife

HER washing ended with the day,
    Yet lived she at its close,
And passed the long, long night away,
    In darning ragged hose.

But when the sun in all his state
    Illumed the eastern skies,
She passed about the kitchen grate
    And went to making pies.

[Parody—Shakespeare]

THAT very time I saw, (but thou coulds't not,)
    Walking between the garden and the barn,
Reuben, all armed ; a certain aim he took
At a young chicken, standing by a post,
And loosed his bullet smartly from his gun,
As he would kill a hundred thousand hens.
But I might see young Reuben's fiery shot
Lodged in the chaste board of the garden fence,
And the domesticated fowl passed on
In henly meditation, bullet free.

PHOEBE CARY

There's a Bower of Bean-Vines

[*Parody—Moore*]

THERE'S a bower of bean-vines in Benjamin's yard,
  And the cabbages grow round it, planted for greens;
In the time of my childhood 'twas terribly hard
  To bend down the bean-poles, and pick off the beans.

That bower and its products I never forget,
  But oft when my landlady presses me hard,
I think, are the cabbages growing there yet,
  Are the bean-vines still bearing in Benjamin's yard?

No, the bean-vines soon withered that once used to wave,
  But some beans had been gathered, the last that hung on,
And a soup was distilled in a kettle, that gave
  All the fragrance of summer when summer was gone.

Thus memory draws from delight, ere it dies,
  An essence that breathes of it, awfully hard;
And thus good to my taste as 'twas then to my eyes,
  Is that bower of bean-vines in Benjamin's yard.

MORTIMER COLLINS

1827–1876

MORTIMER COLLINS was a man of rare good humour, and his happy nature combined with his literary success made life for him a pleasure, in which his soul took delight, and his genial spirit is apparent in all his writings. He was a most facile and prolific writer, and was, moreover, never too busy to pen some dainty note (usually in verse) or some humorous doggerel to one or other of his numerous friends. These included Locker-Lampson, Edmund Yates, and more especially R. D. Blackmore, the author of "Lorna Doone." Amongst his better-known works are "Sweet Anne Page," which appeared in 1868, and is partially autobiographical; "The Ivory Gate," and the most successful of his works, "The Secret of Long Life," 1871. All the principal papers of the day received contributions from his pen.

Mortimer Collins was a fluent writer of light verse, perhaps too fluent to attain a literary reputation, for his facility encouraged him to write carelessly, and so to depreciate the value of his more finished work, which is often of great excellence. His parody of Swinburne is singularly happy.

Salad

[Imitation—Swinburne]

O COOL in the summer is salad
    And warm in the winter is love;
And a poet shall sing you a ballad
    Delicious thereon and thereof.

MORTIMER COLLINS

A singer am I, if no sinner,
    My muse has a marvellous wing,
And I willingly worship at Dinner
    The Sirens of Spring.

Take endive—like love it is bitter,
    Take beet—for like love it is red :
Crisp leaf of the lettuce shall glitter,
    And cress from the rivulet's bed :
Anchovies, foam-born, like the lady
    Whose beauty has maddened this bard ;
And olives, from groves that are shady,
    And eggs—boil 'em hard.

Salad

[*Imitation—Alfred Tennyson*]

KING ARTHUR, growing very tired indeed,
    Of wild Tintagel, now that Launcelot
Had gone to Jersey or to Jericho,
And there was nobody to make a rhyme,
And Cornish girls were christened Jennifer,
And the Round Table had grown rickety,
Said unto Merlin (who had been asleep
For a few centuries in Broceliande,
But woke, and had a bath, and felt refreshed) :
" What shall I do to pull myself together ? "
Quoth Merlin, " Salad is the very thing,
And you can get it at the *Cheshire Cheese*."
King Arthur went there ; *verily* I believe

211

That he has dined there every day since then.
Have you not marked the portly gentleman
In his cool corner, with his plate of greens?
The great knight Launcelot prefers the *Cock*,
Where port is excellent (in pints) and waiters
Are portlier than kings, and steaks are tender,
And poets have been known to meditate—
Ox-fed orating ominous ostasticks.

CHARLES DICKENS

1812–1870

THE great Boz was not given to speaking "in numbers," though certain of his songs appear scattered throughout his world-famous novels. Only one parody of his is known, however, and that was written to Mark Lemon (who had been ill), inviting him to pay the writer and his family a visit at Brighton. In the letter which accompanied the poem he bade him "get a clean pocket-handkerchief ready for the close of Copperfield No. 3—simple and quiet, but very natural and touching—Evening Bore." The song is signed T. Sparkler, while pressure is brought to bear on the recipient by the signatures of the rest of the party—Catherine Dickens, Annie Leech, Georgina Hogarth, Mary Dickens, Katie Dickens, and John Leech.

New Song

[*Parody of a Song*—"Lesbia hath a Beaming Eye"]

LEMON is a little hipped,
    And this is Lemon's true position—
He is not pale, he's not white-lipped,
Yet wants a little fresh condition.
Sweeter 'tis to gaze upon
Old Ocean's rising, falling billers,
Than on the Houses every one
That form the street called Saint Anne's Willers.
    Oh my Lemon, round and fat,
    Oh my bright, my right, my tight 'un,
    Think a little what you're at—
    Don't stay at home, but come to Brighton!

CHARLES DICKENS

Lemon has a coat of frieze,
But all so seldom Lemon wears it,
That it is a prey to fleas,
And ev'ry moth that's hungry, tears it.
Oh, that coat's the coat for me,
That braves the railway sparks and breezes,
Leaving ev'ry engine free
To smoke it, till its owner sneezes!
    Then my Lemon, round and fat,
    L., my bright, my right, my tight 'un,
    Think a little what you're at—
    On Tuesday first, come down to Brighton!

OLIVER WENDELL HOLMES

1809–1894

W<small>HILE</small> Oliver Wendell Holmes was by profession a physician, to all the world he is best known as the author of "The Autocrat at the Breakfast Table," and of the companion volumes, "The Poet at the Breakfast Table" and "The Professor at the Breakfast Table." A kindly spirit and a graceful humour characterise his writings, and it is these qualities which make for the success of his parodies.

Evening

BY A TAILOR

[Imitation—Bryant]

DAY hath put on his jacket, and around
   His burning bosom buttoned it with stars.
Here will I lay me on the velvet grass,
That is like padding to earth's meagre ribs,
And hold communion with the things about me.
Ah me ! how lovely is the golden braid
That binds the skirt of night's descending robe !
The thin leaves, quivering on their silken threads,
Do make a music like to rustling satin,
As the light breezes smooth her downy nap.

Ha ! what is this that rises to my touch,
So like a cushion ?   Can it be a cabbage ?
It is, it is that deeply injured flower,
Which boys do flout us with—but yet I love thee,

Thou giant rose, wrapped in a green surtout.
Doubtless in Eden thou didst blush as bright
As these thy puny brethren; and thy breath
Sweetened the fragrance of her spicy air;
But now thou seemest like a bankrupt beau,
Stripped of his gaudy hues and essences,
And growing portly in his sober garments.

Is it a swan that rides upon the water?
Oh, no, it is that other gentle bird,
Which is the patron of our noble calling.
I well remember in my early days,
When these young hands first closed upon a goose;[1]
I have a scar upon my thimble finger
Which chronicles the hour of young ambition.
My father was a tailor, and his father,
And my sire's grandsire, all of them were tailors.
They had an ancient goose—it was an heirloom
From some remoter tailor of our race.
It happened I did see it on a time
When none was near and I did deal with it,
And it did burn me, oh, most fearfully.

It is a joy to straighten out one's limbs,
And leap elastic from the level counter,
Leaving the petty grievances of earth,
The breaking thread, the din of clashing shears,
And all the needles that do wound the spirit,
For such a pensive hour of soothing silence.

[1] A tailor's smoothing iron, so called from the shape of the handle, which is like a goose's neck.

Kind nature, shuffling in her loose undress,
Lays bare her shady bosom. I can feel
With all around me; I can hail the flowers
That sprig earth's mantle,—and yon quiet bird
That rides the stream is to me as a brother.
The vulgar know not all the hidden pockets
Where nature stows away her loveliness.
But this unnatural posture of the legs
Cramps my extended calves, and I must go
Where I can coil them in their wonted fashion.

The September Gale

[*Parody—Campbell*]

I'M not a chicken; I have seen
    Full many a chill September,
And though I was a youngster then,
    That gale I well remember;

The day before, my kite-string snapped
    And I, my kite pursuing,
The wind whisked off my palm-leaf hat;—
    For me two storms were brewing!

It came as quarrels sometimes do,
    When married folks get clashing;
There was a heavy sigh or two,
    Before the fire was flashing,—

OLIVER WENDELL HOLMES

A little stir among the clouds,
    Before they rent asunder,—
A little rocking of the trees,
    And then came on the thunder.

Lord! how the ponds and rivers boiled,
    And how the shingles rattled!
And oaks were scattered on the ground,
    As if the Titans battled;

And all above was in a howl,
    And all below a clatter,—
The earth was like a frying-pan
    Or some such hissing matter.

It chanced to be our washing day,
    And all our things were drying;
The storm came roaring through the lines,
    And set them all a-flying;

I saw the shirts and petticoats
    Go riding off like witches;
I lost, ah! bitterly I wept,—
    I lost my Sunday breeches!

I saw them straddling through the air,
    Alas! too late to win them;
I saw them chase the clouds, as if
    The devil had been in them;

They were my darlings and my pride,
    My boyhood's only riches,—
" Farewell, farewell," I faintly cried,—
    " My breeches! O my breeches!"

OLIVER WENDELL HOLMES

That night I saw them in my dreams,
   How changed from what I knew them!
The dews had steeped their faded threads,
   The wind had whistled through them!

I saw the wide and ghastly rents
   Where demon claws had torn them;
A hole was in their amplest part,
   As if an imp had worn them.

I have had many happy years
   And tailors kind and clever,
But those young pantaloons have gone
   Forever and forever!

And not till fate has cut the last
   Of all my earthly stitches,
This aching heart shall cease to mourn
   My loved, my long-lost breeches.

THOMAS HOOD (THE YOUNGER)

1835–1874

PERHAPS the writer of "A Catch" is better known to the public as "Tom" Hood, the name by which he chose to distinguish himself from his father, the famous humorist of the early part of the nineteenth century. From an early age Tom Hood earned his living by his pen, and was only twenty-three when he was made editor of the *Liskeard Gazette*. From here he was admitted as a clerk into the War Office, but relinquished his appointment for the editorship of *Fun*. Without the exuberant fancy or the poetic force of his father, the younger Hood was an elegant writer of light verse, which by reason of its fluency and irresponsible gaiety does not make great demand on the deeper qualities of the writer, and for this very reason is refreshing to the reader. In "The Catch" Hood has admirably parodied his original "A Match" by Swinburne, reproducing faithfully the peculiarities of this style of versification; equally admirable, and for the same reason, is the travesty of Browning, entitled "Poets and Linnets," which also appeared in *Fun*.

Poets and Linnets

[*Imitation—Robert Browning*]

WHERE'ER there's a thistle to feed a linnet
    And linnets are plenty, thistles rife—
Or an acorn cup to catch dew-drops in it,
There's ample promise of further life.
Now, mark how we begin it.

220

For linnets will follow, if linnets are minded,
As blows the white feather parachute;
And ships will reel by the tempest blinded—
By, ships, and shiploads of men to boot!
How deep whole fleets you'll find hid.

And we'll blow the thistle-down hither and thither,
Forgetful of linnets and men, and God.
The dew! for its want an oak will wither—
By the dull hoof into the dust is trod,
And then who strikes the cithar?

But thistles were only for donkeys intended,
And that donkeys are common enough is clear.
And that drop! what a vessel it might have befriended,
Does it add any flavour to Glugabib's beer?
Well, there's my musing ended.

A Catch

[Parody—Swinburne]

IF you were queen of bloaters,
    And I were king of soles,
The sea we'd wag our fins in
Nor heed the crooked pins in
The water dropt by boaters,
    To catch our heedless joles;
If you were queen of bloaters—
    And I were king of soles.

THOMAS HOOD (THE YOUNGER)

If you were LADY MILE-END,
    And I were DUKE of Bow,
We'd marry and we'd quarrel,
And then, to point the moral
Should LORD PENZANCE his file lend,
    Our chains to overthrow;
If you were LADY MILE-END,
    And I were DUKE of Bow.

If you were chill November,
    And I were sunny June,
I'd not with love pursue you;
For I should be to woo you
(You're foggy, pray remember)
    A most egregious spoon;
If you were chill November,
    And I were sunny June.

If you were cook to Venus,
    And I were J 19,
When missus was out dining,
    Our suppetites combining,
We'd oft contrive between us
    To keep the platter clean;
If you were cook to Venus,
    And I were J 19.

If you were but a jingle,
    And I were but a rhyme,
We'd keep this up for ever,
Nor think it very clever,

THOMAS HOOD (THE YOUNGER)

A grain of sense to mingle
    At times with simple chime ;
If you were but a jingle,
    And I were but a rhyme.

ANDREW LANG

1844–1912

THE recent death of this brilliant writer is a serious loss to modern literature, for few there are who can reach that mastery of expression and that varied knowledge which marked out Andrew Lang from among his contemporaries. Perhaps his most noteworthy achievement was his little book of "Ballads and Verses of Old France," which he brought out when he was twenty-eight. It was his first book, and it immediately made a name for its author; not without reason either, for it is a very "box where sweets compacted lie." From that time to the week after his death a continual stream of histories, belles-lettres, poems, articles, and reviews flowed from his pen. The following poems are taken from a little book of "Jubilee Odes by Bards that were Silent," which appeared in 1887.

Ode of Jubilee

[Imitation—Swinburne]

ME, that have sung and shrieked, and foamed in praise
    of Freedom,
      Me do you ask to sing [1]
Parochial pomps, and waste, the wail of Jubileedom
      For Queen, or Prince, or King!

.   .   .   .   .

[1] Swinburne's political creed was Republicanism in its most uncompromising form.

ANDREW LANG

Nay, by the foam that fleeting oars have feathered,
   In Grecian seas;
Nay, by the winds that barques Athenian weathered—
   By all of these
I beg you each be mute, Bards tamed and tethered,
   And fee'd with fees.

For you the laurel smirched, for you the gold, too,
   Of Magazines;
For me the Spirit of Song, unbought, unsold to
   Pale Priests or Queens!
For you the gleam of gain, the fluttering cheque
   Of Mr. Knowles,[1]
For me, to soar above the ruins and wreck
   Of Snobs and "Souls"!

When aflush with the dew of the dawn, and the
   Rose of the Mystical Vision,
The spirit and soul of the Men of the
   Future shall rise and be free,
They shall hail me with hymning and harping,
   With eloquent Art and Elysian,—
The Singer who sung not but spurned them,
   The slaves that could sing "Jubilee";
   With pinchbeck lyre and tongue,
   Praising their tyrant sung,
They shall fail and shall fade in derision,
   And wind on the ways of the sea!

[1] At that time the editor of the *Nineteenth Century* magazine.

ANDREW LANG

Jubilee before Revolution

[Imitation—Wm. Morris[1]]

" TELL me, O Muse of the Shifty, the Man who
    wandered afar,"
So have I chanted of late, and of Troy burg wasted of
    war—[2]
Now of the sorrows of Menfolk that fifty years have been,
Now of the Grace of the Commune I sing, and the days
    of a Queen !
Surely I curse rich Menfolk, "the Wights of the Whirl-
    wind " may they—
This is my style of translating, Ἁρπυίαι,—snatch them
    away !
The Rich Thieves rolling in wealth that make profit of
    labouring men,
Surely the Wights of the Whirlwind shall swallow them
    quick in their den !
O baneful, O wit-straying, in THE Burg of London ye
    dwell,
And ever of Profits and three per cent. are the tales ye tell,
But the stark, strong Polyphemus shall answer you back
    again,
Him whom " No man slayeth by guile and not by main."

---

[1] William Morris was an ideal socialist, and brought all his
powerful intellect and noble character to the furtherance of a cause
that he held very much to heart.

"Scenes from the Fall of Troy," written about 1865.

226

ANDREW LANG

(By "main" I mean "main force," if aught at all do I mean.

In the Greek of the blindfold Bard it is simpler the sense
   to glean.)

You Polyphemus shall swallow and fill his mighty maw,

What time he maketh an end of the Priests, the Police,
   and the Law,

And then, ah, who shall purchase the poems of old that
   I sang,

Who shall pay twelve-and-six for an epic in Saga slang?

But perchance even "Hermes the Flitter" could scarcely
   expound what I mean,

And I trow that another were fitter to sing you a song for
   a Queen.

HENRY S. LEIGH

1837–1883

HENRY LEIGH, son of the artist and author of the same name, became a writer at an early age, and later turned his attention to the drama. He was a clever linguist, and translated many French comic operas for the stage. His most noteworthy achievement was, however, "The Carols of Cockayne," a volume of humorous verse which was published in 1869, and from which the following parodies have been selected.

Only Seven

(Parody—Wordsworth)

I MARVELLED why a simple child,
　That lightly draws its breath,
Should utter groans so very wild,
　And look as pale as Death.

Adopting a parental tone,
　I ask'd her why she cried;
The damsel answered with a groan,
　"I've got a pain inside!

"I thought it would have sent me mad
　Last night about eleven."
Said I, "What is it makes you bad?
How many apples have you had?"
　She answered, "Only seven!"

"And are you sure you took no more,
  My little maid?" quoth I;
"Oh, please, sir, mother gave me four,
  But they were in a pie!"

"If that's the case," I stammer'd out,
  "Of course you've had eleven."
The maiden answered with a pout,
  "I ain't 'ad more nor seven!"

I wonder'd hugely what she meant,
  And said, "I'm bad at riddles;
But I know where little girls are sent
  For telling tarodiddles.

"Now, if you won't reform," said I,
  "You'll never go to Heaven."
But all in vain; each time I try,
That little idiot makes reply,
  "I ain't 'ad more nor seven!"

POSTSCRIPT

To borrow Wordsworth's name was wrong,
  Or slightly misapplied;
And so I'd better call my song,
  "Lines after Ache-Inside."

HENRY S. LEIGH

'Twas Ever Thus

[Parody—Moore]

I NEVER rear'd a young gazelle,
  (Because, you see, I never tried) ;
But had it known and loved me well,
  No doubt the creature would have died.
My rich and aged Uncle John
  Had known me long and loves me well,
But still persists in living on—
  I would he were a young gazelle.

I never loved a tree or flower ;
  But, if I had, I beg to say
The blight, the wind, the sun, or shower
  Would soon have withered it away.
I've dearly loved my Uncle John,
  From childhood to the present hour,
And yet he will go living on—
  I would he were a tree or flower !

HENRY S. LEIGH

Saragossa

[*Imitation—Moore*]

PEPITA, my paragon, bright star of Arragon;
   Listen, dear, listen ; your Cristobal sings.
From my cot that lies buried a short way from Lerida
   Love and a diligence lent me their wings.
Swift as a falcon I flew to thy balcony.
   (Is it bronchitis ?   I can't sing a bar.)
Greet not with merriment Love's first experiment ;
   Listen, Pepita !   I've brought my *catarrh*.

Manuel the matador may, like a flat, adore
   Donna Dolores : I pity his choice,
For they say that her governor lets neither lover nor
   Anyone else hear the sound of her voice.
Brother Bartolomé (stoutish Apollo) may
   Sigh for Sabina—you'll pardon this cough ?—
And Isabel's votary, Nunez the notary,
   Vainly—(that sneeze again ?   Loved one, I'm Off !)

HENRY S. LEIGH

Châteaux d' Espagne

[*Parody—E. A. Poe*]

ONCE upon an evening weary, shortly after Lord
　Dundreary
With his quaint and curious humour set the town in such
　a roar,
With my shilling I stood rapping—only very gently
　tapping—
For the man in charge was napping—at the money-taker's
　door.
It was Mr. Buckstone's playhouse, where I linger'd at the
　door ;
　　Paid half price and nothing more.

Most distinctly I remember, it was just about September—
Though it might have been in August, or it might have
　been before—
Dreadfully I fear'd the morrow.　Vainly had I sought to
　borrow ;
For (I own it to my sorrow) I was miserably poor,
And the heart is heavy laden when one's miserably poor.
　(I have been so once before.)

I was doubtful and uncertain, at the rising of the curtain,
If the piece would prove a novelty, or one I'd seen before ;
For a band of robbers drinking in a gloomy cave, and
　clinking

232

With their glasses on the table, I had witness'd o'er and
    o'er ;
Since the half-forgotten period of my innocence was o'er ;
    Twenty year ago or more.

Presently my doubt grew stronger. I could stand the
    thing no longer,
" Miss," said I, " or Madam, truly your forgiveness I
    implore,
Pardon my apparent rudeness. Would you kindly have
    the goodness
To inform me if this drama is from Gaul's enlighten'd
    shore ? "
For I know that plays are often brought us from the
    Gallic shore ;
    Adaptations—nothing more !

So I put the question lowly ; and my neighbour answer'd
    slowly,
" It's a British drama wholly, written quite in days of
    yore.
'Tis an Andalusian story of a castle old and hoary,
And the music is delicious, though the dialogue be
    poor ! "
And I could not help agreeing that the dialogue *was*
    poor
    (Very flat, and nothing more).

But at last a lady entered, and my interest grew
    center'd
In her figure, and her features and the costume that she
    wore.

And the slightest sound she utter'd was like music ; so I
    mutter'd
To my neighbour, " Glance a minute at your playbill I
    implore.
Who's that rare and radiant maiden ?   Tell, oh, tell me,
    I implore."
    Quoth my neighbour, " Nelly Moore."

Then I ask'd in quite a tremble—it was useless to
    dissemble—
" Miss, or Madam, do not trifle with my feelings any
    more ;
Tell me who, then, was the maiden, that appear'd so
    sorrow laden
In the room of David Garrick, with a bust above the
    door ? "
(With a bust of Julius Cæsar up above the study door.)
    Quoth my neighbour, " Nelly Moore."

.   .   .   .   .

I've her photograph from Lacy's ; that delicious little
    face is
Smiling on me as I'm sitting (in a draught from yonder
    door),
And often in the nightfalls, when a precious little light
    falls
From the wretched tallow candles on my gloomy second
    floor
(For I have not got the gaslight on my gloomy second
    floor),
    Comes an echo, " Nelly Moore ! "

CHARLES GODFREY LELAND

1824–1903

THIS versatile American writer is perhaps better known as "Hans Breitmann," the author of a series of comical ballads purporting to be written by a German-American. Leland was well equipped for such a task, as his college days were spent at Heidelberg, Munich, and Paris, and when he started work as a journalist he contributed largely to the *Knickerbocker Magazine*. He wrote much and on varied topics, from "The Poetry and Mystery of Dreams" (1855) to a Manual, "Mending and Repairing" (1885), or the work from which the following parody is taken, "Pidgin-English Sing-song" (1876). In inserting the parody in this curious collection of songs, Leland pointed out that it had appeared anonymously in one of the periodicals of his day; but since it was he who introduced it into the world of letters, it has been thought best to insert it in this collection under his name.

Top-side Galow

[*Parody—Longfellow*]

THAT nightey-tim begin chop-chop[1]
　　One young man walkey, no can stop,
Maskee[2] snew, maskee ice,
He cal*l*y flag with chop[3] so nice
　　Top-side galow![4]

[1] *Chop-chop* = quickly.
[2] *Maskee* = a word of lax significance; used here to mean "in spite of."
[3] *Chop* = inscription.　　[4] *Top-side galow* = Excelsior.

He muchee so*ll*y—one piecee[1] eye
Look-see sharp—so—all-same my,
He talkey largey—talkee st*l*ong,
Too muchee curio[2]—all-same gong,
      Top-side galow !

Inside house he can see *l*ight,
And eve*l*y *l*oom got fire all *l*ight,
He lookee plenty ice more high
Insidee mouth he plenty c*l*y,
      Top-side galow !

Olo man talkee, " No can walk,
By'mby *l*ain come—ve*ll*y dark
Hab got water, ve*ll*y wide,"
Maskee, my must go top-side,
      Top-side galow !

" Man-man,"[3] one girley talkee he,
" What for you go top-side look-see ? "
And one tim more he plenty c*l*y,
But 'àllo-tim walkee plenty high,
      Top-side galow !

" Take care t'hat spoilum[4] t*l*ee, young man,
Take care t'hat ice.   He want man-man."
T'hat[5] coolie chin-chin[6] he, " Good-night ! "
He talkee my can go all *l*ight
      Top-side galow !

[1] *One-Piecee* = a or an.   [2] *Curio* = odd.
[3] *Man-man* = slowly.   [4] *Spoilum* = rotten, decayed.
[5] *T'hat* = the usual way of pronouncing ' *that.* '
[6] *Chin-chin* = to salute, bow, or worship.

236

CHARLES GODFREY LELAND

Joss-pidgin-man[1] he soon begin
Morning-tim t'hat Joss[2] chin-chin.
He no man see, him plenty fear,
Cos some man talkee he can hear
      Top-side galow!

T'hat young man die, one large dog see
Too muchee bobbe/y[3] findee he.
He hand blong colo—all-same ice,[4]
Hab got he flag with chop so nice,
      Top-side galow!

MORAL

You too muchee laugh! What for sing.
I tlnk so you no savvy t'hat ling!
Supposey you no blong clever inside
More betta *you* go walk top-side,
      Top-side galow!

This anonymous parody was published first in *Macmillan's Magazine*.

[1] *Joss-pidgin-man* = clergyman.
[2] *Joss*-idol (from Portuguese *Dios*).
[3] *Bobbery* = fuss, trouble, uproar.
[4] *He hand blong colo—all-same ice* = his hand is deadly, cold and quite frozen.

ARTHUR CLEMENT HILTON

1851–1877

The Light Green

THE little green pamphlet, which purports, according to the super-scription on cover and title page, to be "A superior and High-Class Periodical supported only by well known and Popular Writers," appeared at Cambridge in 1872. It was an organ for the publication of some very clever parodies in prose and verse chiefly from the pen of Arthur Clement Hilton. The promise shown by this young writer was destined never to reach fulfillment, for he died while still a very young man. Many of the verses, such as the "Vulture and the Husbandman" and "The Heathen Pass-ee," deal with phases or episodes of University life. Of more general interest are the "Octopus" by "Sin-burn" and "Ding-Dong" by "Rosina Christetti." Both of these parodies are masterpieces.

Octopus

[Parody—Swinburne]

STRANGE beauty, eight limbed and eight handed,
   Whence camest to dazzle our eyes?
With thy bosom bespangled and banded
   With the hues of the seas and the skies;
Is thy home European or Asian,
   O mystical monster marine?
Part molluscous and partly crustacean,
      Betwixt and between.

238

ARTHUR CLEMENT HILTON

Wast thou born to the sound of sea trumpets ?
  Hast thou eaten and drunk to excess
Of the sponges—thy muffins and crumpets,
  Of the seaweed—thy mustard and cress ?
Hast thou nurtured in caverns of coral,
  Remote from reproof or restraint ?
Art thou innocent, art thou immoral,
        Sinburnian or Saint ?

Lithe limbs curling free as a creeper
  That creeps in a desolate place,
To enrol and envelop the sleeper
  In a silent and stealthy embrace ;
Cruel beak craning forward to bite us,
  Our juices to drain and to drink,
Or to whelm us in waves of Cocytus,
        Indelible ink !

Oh breast that 'twere rapture to writhe on !
  Oh arms 'twere delicious to feel
Clinging close with the crush of the Python
  When she maketh her murderous meal !

In thy eight-fold embraces enfolden
  Let our empty existence escape,
Give us death that is glorious and golden,
  Crushed all out of shape !

Ah thy red lips, lascivious and luscious,
  With death in their amorous kiss !
Cling round us and clasp us, and crush us,
  With bitings of agonised bliss ;

We are sick with the poison of pleasure,
    Dispose us the potion of pain ;
Ope thy mouth to its uttermost measure,
    And bite us again !

The Vulture and the Husbandman [1]

[Parody—Lewis Carroll]

THE rain was raining cheerfully,
    As if it had been May,
The Senate-House appeared inside
    Unusually gay ;
And this was strange, because it was
    A Viva-Voce day.

The men were sitting sulkily,
    Their paper work was done,
They wanted much to go away
    To ride or row or run ;
" It's very rude," they said, " to keep
    Us here and spoil our fun."

The papers they had finished lay
    In piles of blue and white,
They answered everything they could,
    And wrote with all their might,
But though they wrote it all by rote,
    They did not write it right.

[1] The vulture because it is known as a voracious bird of prey, and the husbandman because he alone is an expert in the art of ploughing.

The Vulture and the Husbandman
  Beside these piles did stand ;
They wept like anything to see
  The work they had in hand :
" If this were only finished up,"
  Said they, " it would be grand ! "

" If seven D's or seven C's
  We give to all the crowd,
Do you suppose," the Vulture said,
  " That we could get them ploughed ? "
" I think so," said the Husbandman,
  " But pray don't talk so loud."

" Oh, Undergraduates, come up,"
  The Vulture did beseech,
" And let us see if you can learn
  As well as we can teach ;
We cannot do with more than two,
  To have a word with each."

Two Undergraduates came up,
  And slowly took a seat ;
They knit their brows, and bit their thumbs,
  As if they found them sweet ;
And this was odd, because you know
  Thumbs are not good to eat.

" The time has come," the Vulture said,
  " To talk of many things—
Of Accidence and Adjectives,
  And names of Jewish kings ;
How many notes a sackbut has,
  And whether shawms have strings."

" Please, Sir," the Undergraduates said,
   Turning a little blue,
" We did not know that was the sort
   Of thing we had to do."
" We thank you much," the Vulture said ;
   " Send up another two."

Two more came up, and then two more,
   And more, and more, and more,
And some looked upwards at the roof,
   Some down upon the floor,
But none were any wiser than
   The pair that went before.

" I weep for you," the Vulture said ;
   " I deeply sympathize !"
With sobs and tears he gave them all
   D's of the largest size,
While at the Husbandman he winked
   Out of his streaming eyes.

" I think," observed the Husbandman,
   " We're getting on too quick ;
Are we not putting down the D's
   A little bit too thick ? "
The Vulture said with much disgust,
   " Their answers make me sick."

" Now, Undergraduates," he cried,
   " Our fun is nearly done ;
Will anybody else come up ? "
   But answer came there none ;
And this was scarcely odd, because
   They'd ploughed them every one !

ARTHUR CLEMENT HILTON

The Heathen Pass-ee

[*Parody—Bret Harte*]

WHICH I wish to remark,
   And my language is plain,
That for plots that are dark
   And not always in vain,
The Heathen Pass-ee is peculiar,
   And the same I would rise to explain.

I would also premise
   That the term of Pass-ee
Most fitly applies,
   As you probably see,
To one whose vocation is passing
   The "ordinary B.A. degree."

Tom Crib was his name,
   And I shall not deny
In regard to the same
   What that name might imply,
That his face it was trustful and childlike,
   And he had the most innocent eye.

Upon April the First
   The Little-Go fell,
And that was the worst

Of the gentleman's sell,
For he fooled the Examining Body
   In a way I'm reluctant to tell.

The candidates came
   And Tom Crib soon appeared ;
It was Euclid, the same
   Was " the subject he feared " ;
But he smiled as he sat by the table
   With a smile that was wary and weird.

Yet he did what he could,
   And the papers he showed
Were remarkably good,
   And his countenance glowed
With pride when I met him soon after
   As he walked down the Trumpington Road.

We did not find him out,
   Which I bitterly grieve,
For I've not the least doubt
   That he'd placed up his sleeve
Mr. Todbunker's excellent Euclid,
   The same with intent to deceive.

But I shall not forget
   How the next day or two
A stiff paper was set
   By Examiner U——
On Euripides' tragedy, Bacchæ,
   A subject Tom " partially knew."

ARTHUR CLEMENT HILTON

But the knowledge displayed
   By that Heathen Pass-ee,
And the answers he made
   Were quite frightful to see,
For he rapidly floored the whole paper
   By about twenty minutes to three.

Then I looked up at U——
   And he gazed upon me,
I observed, "This won't do";
   He replied, "Goodness me!
We are fooled by this artful young person."
   And he sent for that Heathen Pass-ee.

The scene that ensued
   Was disgraceful to view,
For the floor it was strewed
   With a tolerable few
Of the "tips" that Tom Crib had been hiding
   For the "subject he partially knew."

On the cuff of his shirt
   He had managed to get
What we hoped had been dirt,
   But which proved, I regret,
To be notes on the rise of the Drama,
   A question invariably set.

In his various coats
   We proceeded to seek,
Where we found sundry notes

And—with sorrow I speak—
One of Bohn's publications, so useful
    To the student of Latin or Greek.

In the crown of his cap
    Were the Furies and Fates,
And a delicate map
    Of the Dorian States,
And we found in his palms, which were hollow,
    What are frequent in palms—that is, dates;

Which is why I remark,
    And my language is plain,
That for plots that are dark
    And not always in vain,
The Heathen Pass-ee is familiar,
    Which the same I am free to maintain.

Ding Dong

[*Parody—Christina Rossetti*]

DING dong, Ding dong,
    There goes the Gong,
Dick, come along,
    'Tis time for dinner.
Wash your face,
Take your place,
Where's your grace,
    You little sinner?

" Like an apple ? "
    " Yes I should,
Nice, nice, nicey !
    Good, good, good ! "

" Manners miss,
    Please behave,
Those who ask,
    Shan't have."

" Those who don't
    Don't want.
I'll eat it,
    You shan't."

Baby cry,
Wipe his eye.
Baby good,
Give him food.
Baby sleepy,
Go to bed.
Baby naughty,
Smack his head !

Poor little thrush,
Found dead in a bush !
When did he die ?
He is rather high.
Bury him deep,
He won't keep.
Bury him well,
Or he'll smell.

What have horns?
Cows and moons.
What have crests?
Cocks and spoons.
What are nice?
Ducks and peas.
What are nasty?
Bites of fleas.
What are fast?
Tides and times.
What are slow?
Nursery Rhymes.

FREDERICK LOCKER-LAMPSON

1821–1895

"London Lyrics," first published in 1857, and "Lyra Elegantiarum" (1867), are the two most notable works of Frederick Locker-Lampson, perhaps better known as Frederick Locker. The first book, which in its many editions contains the greater part of his original verse, is composed chiefly of "*Vers de Société*," after the dainty lyrics of the days of Prior and Swift. Occupied as Frederick Locker-Lampson was with the cultivation of this style, it was only very rarely that he attempted parody. Perhaps his most successful imitation was "On a Human Skull," although more generally known is his travesty of Tennyson's "Lord of Burleigh"—"The Unfortunate Miss Bailey." There is a marked difference in his treatment of these two subjects, and certainly the parody of Waller is a masterpiece, for the imitator has entered without effort into the whole spirit of his original.

A Human Skull[1]

[*Parody—Edmund Waller*]

A HUMAN Skull! I bought it passing cheap,
    No doubt 'twas dearer to its first employer!
I thought mortality did well to keep
    Some mute memento of the Old Destroyer.

[1] In our last month's magazine you may remember that there were some verses about a portion of a skeleton. Did you remark how the poet and human proprietor of the human skull at once settled the sex of it, and determined off-hand that it must have belonged to a woman? Such skulls are locked up in many gentle-

249

Time was, some may have prized its blooming skin ;
    Here lips were woo'd perhaps in transport tender ;
Some may have chuck'd what was a dimpled chin
    And never had my doubt about its gender.

Did she live yesterday or ages back ?
    What colour were the eyes when bright and waking ?
And were your ringlets fair or brown or black,
    Poor little head ! that long has done with aching ?

It may have held (to shoot some random shots)
    Thy brains, Eliza Fry ! or Baron Byron's ;
The wits of Nelly Gwynne, or Doctor Watts,—
    Two quoted bards.   Two philanthropic sirens.

But this I trust is clearly understood ;
    If man or woman,—if adored or hated—
Whoever own'd this skull was not so good
    Nor quite so bad as many may have stated.

    .   .   .   .

Who love can need no special type of Death ;
    He bares his awful face too soon, too often ;
Immortelles bloom in Beauty's bridal wreath,
    And does not yon green elm contain a coffin ?

men's hearts and memories. Bluebeard, you know, had a whole
museum of them—as that imprudent little wife found out to her
cost. And, on the other hand, a lady, we suppose, would select here
of the sort which had carried beards in the flesh.—"Adventures of
Philip on his Way through the World," *Cornhill Magazine*, January,
1861, p. 18. Note by F. L.-L.

O True-Love mine, what lines of care are these?
  The heart still lingers with its golden hours;
But fading tints are on the chestnut trees,
  And where is all that lavish wealth of flowers?

The end is near. Life lacks what once it gave,
  Yet Death hath promises that call for praises;
A very worthless rogue may dig the grave,
  But hands unseen will dress the turf with daisies.

The Unfortunate Miss Bailey

[Parody—Tennyson]

WHEN he whispers, "O Miss Bailey,
    Thou art brightest of the throng!"
She makes murmur, softly, gaily—
    "Alfred, I have loved thee long."

Then he drops upon his knees, a
    Proof his heart is soft as wax;
She's—I don't know who; but he's a
    Captain bold from Halifax.

Though so loving, such another
    Artless bride was never seen;
Coachee thinks that she's his mother—
    Till they get to Gretna Green.

There they stand by him attended,
    Hear the sable smith rehearse
That which links them, when 'tis ended,
    Tight for better or for worse.

FREDERICK LOCKER-LAMPSON

Now her heart rejoices—ugly
    Troubles need disturb her less—
Now the Happy Pair are snugly
    Seated in the night express.

So they go with fond emotion,
    So they journey through the night;
London is their land of Goschen—
    See its suburbs are in sight!

Hark, the sound of life is swelling,
    Pacing up, and racing down;
Soon they reach her simple dwelling—
    Burley street, by Somers Town.

What is there to so astound them?
    She cries "Oh!" for he cries "Hah!"
When five brats emerge—confound them!
    Shouting out, "Mamma!"—"Papa!"

While at this he wonders blindly,
    Nor their meaning can divine,
Proud she turns them round, and kindly,
    "All of these are mine and thine!"

.   .   .   .

Here he pines and grows dyspeptic,
    Losing heart he loses pith—
Hints that Bishop Tait's a sceptic,
    Swears that Moses was a myth.

FREDERICK LOCKER-LAMPSON

Sees no evidence in Paley,
  Takes to drinking ratafia :
Shies the muffins at Miss Bailey,
  While she's pouring out the tea.

One day, knocking up his quarters,
  Poor Miss Bailey found him dead,
Hanging in his knotted garters,
  Which she knitted ere they wed.

ROBERT MURRAY

1863–1894

HAD Robert Murray lived a little longer there is no doubt that he would have been accorded a high place amongst the writers of his day. But the young poet was dead before his song reached the public ear, and before confidence in his own powers had cause to develop the tentative efforts of the beginner into the skilled and certain ease of the matured writer. As it was, after he left St. Andrews in 1889, he found the road to a literary livelihood, let alone success, very difficult and steep. In the end the struggle was too great, and a constitution never very robust gave way to consumption, of which he died "in the early hours of 1894," and it was his own harsh experiences which prompted him to write—

> "Every critic in the town
> Runs the minor poet down ;
> Every critic—don't you know it ?
> Is himself a minor poet."

As to whether Robert Murray knew the art of parody the reader will be able to judge for himself ; but that two opinions could exist about such splendid nonsense as the "Tennysonian Fragment" or "Andrew M'Crie" is surely impossible.

College life, more especially life at St. Andrews, is largely the subject of Murray's poems, for it was at this University that the poet spent his most happy years and gathered in his most lively experiences.

ROBERT MURRAY

ROBERT MURRAY

A Tennysonian Fragment

[*Parody—Tennyson*]

SO in the village inn the poet dwelt;
  His honey-dew was gone; only the pouch,
His cousin's work, her empty labour, left.
But still he sniffed it, still a fragrance clung
And lingered all about the broidered flowers.
Then came his landlord, saying in broad Scotch,
"Smoke plug, mon," whom he looked at doubtfully.
Then came the grocer saying, "Hae some Twist
At tippence," whom he answered with a qualm.
But when they left him to himself again,
Twist, like a fiend's breath from a distant room
Diffusing through the passage, crept; the smell
Deepening had power upon him, and he mixt
His fancies with the billow-lifted bay
Of Biscay and the rolling of a ship.
And on that night he made a little song,
And called his song "The Song of Twist and Plug,"
And sang it, scarcely could he make or sing.

" Rank is black plug, though smoked in wind and rain;
And rank is twist, which gives no end of pain;
I know not which is ranker; no, not I.

" Plug, art thou rank? then milder twist must be;
Plug, thou art milder: rank is twist to me.
O Twist, if plug be milder, let me buy.

"Rank twist that seems to make me fade away,
Rank plug that navvies smoke in loveless clay,
I know not which is ranker; no, not I.

"I fain would purchase flake, if that could be;
I needs must purchase plug, ah, woe is me!
Plug and a cutty, a cutty, let me buy."

The Poet's Hat

[Parody—Tennyson]

THE rain had fallen, the Poet arose,
    He passed through the doorway into the street;
A strong wind lifted his hat from his head,
    And he uttered some words that were far from sweet.
And then he started to follow the chase,
    And put on a spurt that was wild and fleet,
It made the people pause in a crowd
    And lay odds as to which would beat.

The street-cad scoffed as he hunted the hat,
    The errand-boy shouted hooray!
The scavenger stood with his broom in his hand,
    And smiled in a very rude way;
And the clergyman thought, "I have heard many words,
    But never until to-day,
Did I hear any words that were quite so bad
    As I heard that young man say.

ROBERT MURRAY

Andrew M'Crie

[*Parody—Edgar Allan Poe*]

IT was many and many a year ago,
    In a city by the sea,
That a man there lived whom I happened to know
    By the name of Andrew M'Crie;
And this man he slept in another room
    But ground and had meals with me.

I was an ass and he was an ass,
    In this city by the sea;
But we ground in a way that was more than a grind,
    I and Andrew M'Crie;
In a way that the idle semi-s [1] next door
    Declared was shameful to see.

And this was the reason that, one dark night,
    In this city by the sea,
A stone flew in at the window, hitting
    The milk-jug and Andrew M'Crie.
And once some low-bred tertians [2] came,
    And bore him away from me,
And shoved him into a private house
    Where the people were having tea.

[1] Second year undergraduates.
[2] Third year undergraduates.

ROBERT MURRAY

Professors, not half so well up in their work,
   Went envying him and me—
Yes!—that was the reason, I always thought
   (And Andrew agreed with me),
Why they ploughed us both at the end of the year,
   Chilling and killing poor Andrew M'Crie.

But his ghost is more terrible far than the ghosts
   Of many more famous than he—
   Of many more gory than he—
And neither visits to foreign coasts,
   Nor tonics, can ever set free
Two well-known Profs. from the haunting wraith
   Of the injured Andrew M'Crie.

For at night, as they dream, they frequently scream,
   "Have mercy, Mr. M'Crie!"
And at morn they will rise with bloodshot eyes,
   And the very first thing they will see,
When they dare to descend to their coffee and rolls,
Sitting down on the scuttle, the scuttle of coals,
   With a volume of notes on its knee,
   Is the spectre of Andrew M'Crie.

DANTE GABRIEL ROSSETTI

1828–1882

It would be vain to search through the poetical works of the great poet-painter for the following sonnet, which is included in one of the volumes of his letters edited by his brother, William Michael Rossetti. It is the only parody extant of the author, and is of additional interest from the uncommon method employed in the writing. Rossetti has faithfully kept to the word-sounds of his original, and although he has altered the sense, he has gained his end by a series of clever puns ; for example :—Kraken—MacCracken ; his shadowy side—the shady side ; Huge sponges—Through spungings ; secret cell—secret sell. The subject of Rossetti's good-natured witticism is an art dealer who was a patron of the Pre-Raphaelite Brotherhood and a friend as well as a patron of Rossetti himself. No doubt Rossetti was struck with the similarity between the surname of his patron and the title of Tennyson's sonnet, and in one of his moods of happy inspiration evolved this remarkable parody.

Mac Cracken

[Parody—Tennyson]

GETTING his pictures, like his supper, cheap,
    Far Far away in Belfast by the Sea,
His watchful, one-eyed, uninvaded sleep
Mac Cracken sleepeth. While the P.R.B.[1]
Must keep the shady side, he walks a swell
Through spungings of perennial growth and height
And far away, in Belfast out of sight,

[1] Pre-Raphaelite Brotherhood.

DANTE GABRIEL ROSSETTI

By many an open "do" and secret sell
Fresh daubers he makes swift to scarify,
And fleece with pliant shears the slumbering "green."
There he has lied, though aged, and will lie
Fattening on ill got pictures in his sleep,
Till some Pre-Raphaelite prove for him too deep.
Then once by Hunt[1] and Ruskin[2] to be seen,
Insolvent he will turn, and in the Queen's Bench[3] die.

[1] Holman Hunt, one of the most earnest exponents of the Pre-Raphaelite school of painting.

[2] Ruskin, the art-critic and writer, who was himself an ardent supporter of Pre-Raphaelitism, and at one time the close friend of Rossetti.

[3] The debtors' prison.

THE SHOTOVER PAPERS

OR ECHOES FROM OXFORD

1874–1875

SUCH is the title of the little quarto magazine, issued at Oxford and devoted to the publication of current parodies. These are chiefly of topical interest, but perhaps the prose imitations are better than those in verse. Nevertheless no apology is needed for including the following specimens in this anthology. They are dexterous, witty, and, without attempting the more critical functions of the art, are sufficiently close to their originals to be considered good parody.

Truthful James Again

[*Parody—Bret Harte*]

DO I sleep?   Do I dream?
　　'Tis the Cherwell, no doubt.
Can this be a stream?
　　Or is sewers about?
Is deodorization a failure?
　　Or is sanitation played out?

Which expressions are strong,
　　But stronger, I think,
If you e'er stray along
　　The Cherwell's foul brink
You'll say is the smell of Cherwell—
　　You might call it "stink."

And I looked and behold
    There came an old don,
And he said, " It is cold,"
    But as he passed on
He grunted out, " Typhoid by Jingo ! "
    And then he was gone.

.   .   .   .   .

So I ask, Do I dream ?
    It's the Cherwell, no doubt,
Can *this* be a stream ?
    Or is sewers about ?
Is deodorization a failure ?
    Or is sanitation played out ?

In the Schools at Oxford

[*Parody—Tennyson*]

BUTCHER boys shouted without,
    —Within was writing for thee,
Shadows of three live men
    Talked as they walked into me,
Shadows of three live men and you were one of
    the three.

Butcher boys sang in the streets,
    The Bobby was far away,
Butcher boys shouted and sang
    In their usual maddening way.
Still in the Schools quite courteous you were
    torturing men all the day.

262

Two dead men I have known
    Examiners settled by me.
Two dead men have I scored,
    Now I will settle with thee.
Three dead men must I score, and thou art the
        last of the three.

Blue Moonshine

[Parody—O'Shaughnessy]

MINGLED aye with fragrant yearnings,
    Throbbing in the mellow glow,
Glint the silvery spitits burnings,
    Pearly blandishments of woe.

Ay! for ever and for ever,
    While the love-lorn censers sweep,
While the jasper winds disever,
    Amber like, the crystal deep;

Shall the soul's delirious slumber
    Sea green vengeance of a kiss,
Touch despairing crags to number
    Blue infinities of bliss.

THE SHOTOVER PAPERS

Horae Tennysonianae

I

[Parody—Tennyson]

THE Cup with trembling hand he grasps,
    Close to his thirsty lips he clasps,
Ringed with its pewter rim—he gasps.

The eddying floor beneath him crawls,
He clutches at the flying walls,
Then like a lump of lead he falls.

JAMES KENNETH STEPHEN

1859–1892

WITH the death of James Kenneth Stephen, at the early age of thirty-three, a career of exceptional brilliance and great promise was brought to a close. From the time he went to Eton in 1871 as second of the King's Scholars to his election at Cambridge, as Fellow of his college (King's), his progress is marked by the attainment of many a prize and scholarship, the finale of which was the Whewell Scholarship in International Law, gained in 1882. In the next year, besides obtaining his Fellowship, he was appointed Tutor in History to the future Duke of Clarence. In 1885 he was called to the Bar, and soon after began to contribute to the *St. James's Gazette*. In 1888 he founded and edited a weekly paper entitled *The Reflector*, and in the autumn of the same year was appointed Clerk of Assize for South Wales, but this post he resigned two years later to take up the duties of a coach at Cambridge, and it was here that he brought out his two volumes of humorous verse, "Lapsus Calami" and "Quo Musa tendis?" In these two slender books are contained some of the finest modern parodies, notably "of R. B." and the splendid sonnet in imitation of William Wordsworth.

No parodist has more nearly approached his original or has combined so much keen criticism with so much genuine mirth; but most remarkable of all the qualities of these parodies is the easy flow of verse. Every poem is a masterpiece of construction : no halting lines, no strained endeavours or obvious "corners," but natural, keen, melodious sense,—or nonsense !

JAMES KENNETH STEPHEN

A Sonnet

[*Parody—Wordsworth*]

TWO voices are there : one is of the deep ;
    It learns the storm-cloud's thunderous melody,
Now roars, now murmurs with the changing sea,
Now bird-like pipes, now closes soft in sleep :
And one is of an old half-witted sheep
Which bleats articulate monotony,
And indicates that two and one are three,
That grass is green, lakes damp, and mountains steep :
And, Wordsworth, both are thine : at certain times
Forth from the heart of thy melodious rhymes,
The form and pressure of high thoughts will burst :
At other times—good Lord ! I'd rather be
Quite unacquainted with the A B C
Than write such hopeless rubbish as thy worst.

JAMES KENNETH STEPHEN

Of R. B.

[Imitation—Browning]

BIRTHDAYS? yes, in a general way;
  For the most if not for the best of men :
You were born (I suppose) on a certain day :
So was I : or perhaps in the night : what then ?

Only this : or at least, if more,
  You must know, not think it, and learn, not speak :
There is truth to be found on the unknown shore,
And many will find where few will seek.

For many are called and few are chosen,
  And the few grow many as ages lapse :
But when will the many grow fat : what dozen
Is fused into one of Time's hammer-taps ?

A bare brown stone in a babbling brook :—
  It was wanton to hurt it there, you say :
And the moss, which clung in the sheltered nook
(Yet the stream runs cooler), is washed away.

That begs the question : many a prater
  Thinks such a suggestion a sound " stop thief ! "
Which, may I ask, do you think the greater,
Sergeant-at-arms or a Robber Chief ?

And if it were not so ? still you doubt ?
Ah ! yours is a birthday indeed if so.
There were something to write a poem about,
If one thought a little.   I only know.

P.S.

There's a Me Society down at Cambridge,
Where my works, *cum notis variorum*,
Are talked about ; well, I require the same bridge
That Euclid took toll at as *Asinorum*.

And, as they have got through several ditties
I thought were as stiff as a brick-built wall,
I've composed the above, and a stiff one *it* is,
A bridge to stop asses at, once for all.

Ode on a Retrospect of Eton College

[Parody—Gray]

YE bigot spires, ye Tory towers,
　　That crown the watery lea,
Where grateful science still adores
　　The Aristocracy :
A happy usher once I strayed
Beneath your lofty elm-trees' shade,
　　With mind untouched by guilt or woe :
But mad ambition made me stray
Beyond the round of work and play
　　Wherein we ought to go.

JAMES KENNETH STEPHEN

My office was to teach the young
    Idea how to shoot :
But, ah ! I joined with eager tongue
    The political dispute :
I ventured humbly to suggest
That all things were not for the best
    Among the Irish peasantry :
And finding all the world abuse
My simple unpretending views,
    I thought I'd go and see.

I boldly left the College bounds,
    Across the sea I went,
To prove the economic grounds
    Of Irish discontent.
My constant goings to and fro
Excited some alarm and so
    Policemen girded up their loins,
And, from his innocent pursuits,—
Morose, unsympathetic brutes—
    They snatched a fearful Joynes.

Escaped, I speedily returned
    To teach the boys again :
But ah, my spirit inly burned
    To think on Ireland's pain.
Such wrongs must out : and then, you see,
My own adventures might not be
    Uninteresting to my friends :
I therefore ventured to prepare
A little book, designed with care,
    To serve these humble ends.

JAMES KENNETH STEPHEN

Our stern head-master spoke to me
     Severely :— " You appear
(Horresco referens) to be
     A party pamphleteer.
If you *must* write, let Cæsar's page
Or Virgil's poetry engage
     Your all too numerous leisure hours :
But now annihilate and quash
This impious philanthropic bosh :
     Or quit these antique towers."

It seems that he who dares to write
     Is all unfit to teach :
And literary fame is quite
     Beyond an usher's reach.
I dared imprisonment in vain :
The little bantling of my brain
     I am compelled to sacrifice.
The moral, after all, is this :—
That here, where ignorance is bliss,
     'Tis folly to be wise.

ALGERNON CHARLES SWINBURNE

1837–1909

THE career of this brilliant poet and man of letters is too well known to need repetition here; nor has time sufficiently mellowed his work for the critic to be able to obtain its full flavour, but there is no doubt that he will always rank amongst the greatest of the later nineteenth-century writers. "Nephelidia" is taken from a small collection of parodies which he published anonymously under the title of "The Heptalogia, or the Seven against Sense, a Cap with Seven Bells," and is remarkable as being a very true imitation of his own style and manner of versification.

Nephelidia

[Imitation—A. C. Swinburne]

FROM the depth of the dreamy decline of the dawn
    through a notable nimbus of nebulous moonshine,
  Pallid and pink as the palm of the flag-flower that
    flickers with fear of the flies as they float,
Are they looks of our lovers that lustrously lean from a
    marvel of mystic miraculous moonshine,
  These that we feel in the blood of our blushes that
    thicken and threaten with throbs through the throat?
Thicken and thrill as a theatre thronged at appeal of an
    actor's appalled agitation,
  Fainter with fear of the fires of the future than pale
    with the promise of pride in the past;

Flushed with the famishing fullness of fever that reddens
    with radiance of rathe recreation,
    Gaunt as the ghastliest of glimpses that gleam through
        the gloom of the gloaming when ghosts go aghast?
Nay, for the nick of the tick of the time is a tremulous
    touch on the temples of terror,
    Strained as the sinews yet strenuous with strife of the
        dead who is dumb as the dust-heaps of death:
Surely no soul is it, sweet as the spasm of erotic emotional
    exquisite error,
    Bathed in the balms of beatified bliss, beatific itself by
        beatitude's breath.
Surely no spirit or sense of a soul that was soft to the spirit
    and soul of our senses
    Sweetens the stress of suspiring suspicion that sobs in
        the semblance and sound of a sigh;
Only this oracle opens Olympian, in mystical moods and
    triangular tenses—
    " Life is the lust of a lamp for the light that is dark till
        the dawn of the day when we die."
Mild is the mirk and monotonous music of memory,
    melodiously mute as it may be,
    While the hope in the heart of a hero is bruised by the
        breach of men's rapiers, resigned to the rod;
Made meek as a mother whose bosom-beats bound with
    the bliss-bringing bulk of a balm-breathing baby,
As they grope through the graveyard of creeds, under
    skies growing green at a groan for the grimness
    of God.
Blank is the book of his bounty beholden of old, and its
    binding is blacker than bluer:

ALGERNON CHARLES SWINBURNE

Out of blue into black is the scheme of the skies, and
    their dews are the wine of the bloodshed of things ;
Till the darkling desire of delight shall be free as a fawn
    that is freed from the fangs that pursue her,
  Till the heart-beats of hell shall be hushed by a hymn
    from the hunt that has harried the kennel of kings.

BAYARD TAYLOR

1825–1878

BAYARD TAYLOR was the son of a well-to-do farmer, and was born in Chester, Pennsylvania. At the age of seventeen he was apprenticed to a printer, and had already contributed several poems to different papers. In 1844 he published, through Griswold, his first book, entitled "Ximena and Other Poems," and this venture brought him to the notice of the *New York Tribune*, which commissioned certain articles that were to be sent to the paper from Europe. This, with several other commissions, enabled him to undertake a voyage to France, Germany, and England, which lasted two years, and only cost him £100. He returned to America in 1846 and published his letters in volume form under the title "Views a-foot, or Europe seen with Knapsack and Staff"; six editions were sold within the year, and Taylor's reputation was made.

The "Diversions of the Echo Club" appeared as a series of articles in the *Atlantic Monthly*. The main idea of the book is that of parody, for the Club, as the title shows, is founded for the sake of "echoing" the works of the best-known authors. The members meet together certain nights of the week, when certain poets are chosen and their names distributed by lot to the various members, each of whom has to produce an imitation of the style of poet named as his model.

There is a second principle underlying the first idea of parody, for the author states in his preface that each of the chief characters represents a type of critic.

The Ancient—the calmer judicial temper which comes of age and liberal study.

Zoilus—derived from the *Homeromastix* or *Scourge of Homer*, the carping cynical critic.

Galahad—the young sensation impressive element.

The Gannet—brilliancy, love of technical effect without principle.

BAYARD TAYLOR

The Shrimp-Gatherers

[Imitation—Jean Ingelow]

SCARLET spaces of sand and ocean,
  Gulls that circle and winds that blow;
Baskets and boats and men in motion,
  Sailing and scattering to and fro.

Girls are waiting, their wimples adorning
  With crimson sprinkles the broad gray flood;
And down the beach the blush of the morning
  Shines reflected from moisture and mud.

Broad from the yard the sails hang limpy;
  Lightly the steersman whistles a lay;
Pull with a will, for the nets are shrimpy,
  Pull with a whistle, our hearts are gay!

Tuppence a quart; there are more than fifty!
  Coffee is certain, and beer galore:
Coats are corduroy, minds are thrifty,
  Won't we go it on sea and shore!

See, behind, how the hills are freckled
  With low white huts, where the lasses bide!
See, before, how the sea is speckled
  With sloops and schooners that wait the tide!

Yarmouth fishers may rail and roister,
  Tyne-side boys may shout, " Give way ! "
Let them dredge for the lobster and oyster,
  Pink and sweet are our shrimps to-day !

Shrimps and the delicate periwinkle,
  Such are the sea-fruits lasses love :
Ho ! to your nets till the blue stars twinkle,
  And the shutterless cottages gleam above !

The Lay of Macaroni

[Imitation—Swinburne]

AS a wave that steals when the winds are stormy,
  From creek to cave of the curving shore,
Buffeted, blown, and broken before me,
  Scattered and spread to its sunlit core :
As a dove that dips in the dark of maples
  To sip the sweetness of shelter and shade,
I kneel in thy nimbus, O noon of Naples,
  I bathe in thy beauty, by thee embayed.

What is it ails me that I should sing of her ?
  The queen of the flashes and flames that were !
Yea, I have felt the shuddering sting of her,
  The flower-sweet throat and the hands of her !
I have swayed and sung to the sound of her psalters,
  I have danced her dances of dizzy delight,
I have hallowed mine hair to the horns of her altars,
  Between the nightingale's song and the night !

BAYARD TAYLOR

What is it, Queen, that now I should do for thee?
   What is it now I should ask at thine hands?
Blow of the trumpets thine children once blew for thee?
   Break from thine feet and thine bosom the bands?
Nay, as sweet as the songs of Leone Leoni,
   And gay as her garments of gem-sprinkled gold,
She gives me mellifluous, mild macaroni,
   The choice of her children when cheeses are old!

And over we hover, as if by the wings of it,
   Frayed in the furnace by flame that is fleet,
The curious coils and the strenuous strings of it,
   Dropping, diminishing down as I sat;
Lo! and the beautiful Queen, as she brings of it,
   Lifts me the links of the limitless chain,
Bidding mine mouth chant the splendidest things of it,
   Out of the wealth of my wonderful brain!

Behold! I have done it: my stomach is smitten
   With sweets of the surfeit her hands have unrolled.
Italia, mine cheeks with thine kisses are bitten:
   I am broken with beauty, stabbed, slaughtered, and sold!
No man of thy millions is more macaronied,
   Save mighty Mazzini, than musical Me:
The souls of the Ages shall stand as astonied,
   And faint in the flame I am fanning for thee!

BAYARD TAYLOR

Ode to a Jar of Pickles

[*Imitation—Keats*]

A SWEET, acidulous, dawn-reaching thrill
    Pervades my sense : I seem to see or hear
The lushy garden-grounds of Greenwich Hill
    In autumn, when the crispy leaves are sere :
And odours haunt me of remotest spice
    From the Levant or musky-aired Cathay,
Or from the saffron-fields of Jericho,
      Where everything is nice :
    The more I sniff, the more I swoon away,
And what else mortal palate craves, forego.

Odours unsmelled are keen, but those I smell
    Are keener ; wherefore let me sniff again !
Enticing walnuts, I have known ye well
    In youth, when pickles were a passing pain ;
Unwitting youth, that craves the candy stem,
    And sugar-plums to olives doth prefer,
And even licks the pots of marmalade
      When sweetness clings to them :
    But now I dream of ambergris and myrrh,
Tasting these walnuts in the poplar shade.

Lo ! hoarded coolness in the heart of noon,
    Plucked with its dew, the cucumber is here,
As to the Dryad's parching lips a boon,
    And crescent bean-pods, unto Bacchus dear ;

And, last of all, the pepper's pungent globe,
   The scarlet dwelling of the sylph of fire,
Provoking purple draughts ; and, surfeited,
      I cast my trailing robe
   O'er my pale feet, touch up my tuneless lyre,
And twist the Delphic wreath to suit my head.

Here shall my tongue in other wise be soured
   Than fretful men's in parched and palsied days ;
And, by the mid-May's dusky leaves embowered,
   Forget the fruitful blame, the scanty praise.
No sweets to them who sweet themselves were born,
   Whose natures ooze with lucent saccharine ;
Who, with sad repetition soothly cloyed,
      The lemon-tinted morn
   Enjoy, and find acetic twilight fine :
Wake I, or sleep ? The pickle-jar is void.

Sir Eggnogg

[*Imitation—Tennyson*]

FORTH from the purple battlements he fared.
   Sir Eggnogg of the Rampant Lily, named
From that embrasure of his argent shield
Given by a thousand leagues of heraldry
On snuffy parchments drawn,—so forth he fared,
By bosky boles and autumn leaves, he fared,
Where grew the juniper with berries black,
The sphery mansions of the future gin.

But naught of this decoyed his mind, so bent
On fair Miasma, Saxon-blooded girl,
Who laughed his loving lullabies to scorn,
And would have snatched his hero-sword to deck
Her haughty brow, or warm her hands withal,
So scornful she : and thence Sir Eggnogg cursed
Between his teeth, and chewed his iron boots
In spleen of love.   But ere the morn was high
In the robustious heaven, the postern-tower
Clang to the harsh, discordant, slivering scream
Of the tire-woman, at the window bent
To dress her crispèd hair.   She saw, ah woe !
The fair Miasma, overbalanced, hurled
O'er the flamboyant parapet which ridged
The muffled coping of the castle's peak,
Prone on the ivory pavement of the court,
Which caught and cleft her fairest skull, and sent
Her rosy brains to fleck the Orient floor.
This saw Sir Eggnogg, in his stirrups poised,
Saw he and cursed, with many a deep-mouthed oath,
And, finding nothing more could reunite
The splintered form of the fair Miasma, rode
On his careering palfrey to the wars,
And there found death, another death than hers.

BAYARD TAYLOR

Cimabuella

[*Imitation—D. G. Rossetti*]

FAIR-TINTED cheeks, clear eyelids drawn
 In crescent curves above the light
Of eyes, whose dim, uncertain dawn
 Becomes not day : a forehead white
Beneath long yellow heaps of hair :
She is so strange she must be fair.

Had she sharp, slant-wise wings outspread,
 She were an angel ; but she stands
With flat dead gold behind her head,
 And lilies in her long thin hands :
Her folded mantle, gathered in,
Falls to her feet as it were tin.

Her nose is keen as pointed flame ;
 Her crimson lips no thing express ;
And never dread of saintly blame
 Held down her heavy eyelashes :
To guess what she were thinking of,
Precludeth any meaner love.

An azure carpet, fringed with gold,
 Sprinkled with scarlet spots, I laid
Before her straight, cool feet unrolled :
 But she nor sound nor movement made
(Albeit I heard a soft, shy smile,
 Printing her neck a moment's while) ;

And I was shamed through all my mind
    For that she spake not, neither kissed,
But stared right past me.   Lo! behind
    Me stood, in pink and amethyst,
Sword-girt and velvet-doubleted,
A tall, gaunt youth, with frowzy head,

Wide nostrils in the air, dull eyes,
    Thick lips that simpered, but, ah me!
I saw, with most forlorn surprise,
    He was the Thirteenth Century!
I but the Nineteenth : then despair
Curdled beneath my curling hair.

O, Love and Fate!   How could she choose
    My rounded outlines, broader brain,
And my resuscitated Muse?
    Some tears she shed, but whether pain
Or joy in him unlocked their source,
I could not fathom which, of course.

But I from missals, quaintly bound,
    With cither and with clavichord
Will sing her songs of sovran sound :
    Belike her pity will afford
Such faint return as suits a saint
So sweetly done in verse and paint.

BAYARD TAYLOR

Angelo Orders his Dinner

[*Imitation—Browning*]

I, ANGELO, obese, black-garmented,
  Respectable, much in demand ; well fed
With mine own larder's dainties,—where, indeed,
Such cakes of myrrh or fine alyssum seed,
Thin as a mallow-leaf embrowned o' the top,
Which, cracking, lets the ropy, trickling drop
Of sweetness touch your tongue, or potted vests
Which my recondite recipe invests
With cold conglomerate tidbits—ah, the bill !
(You say,) but given it were mine to fill
My chests, the case so put were yours, we'll say,
(This counter, here, your post, as mine to-day,)
And you've an eye to luxuries, what harm
In smoothing down your palate with the charm
Yourself concocted ?   There we issue take ;
And see ! as thus across the rim I break
This puffy paunch of glazed embroidered cake,
So breaks, through use, the lust of watering chaps
And craveth plainness : do I so ?   Perhaps ;
But that's my secret.   Find me such a man
As Lippo yonder, built upon the plan
Of heavy storage, double-navelled, for
From his own giblets' oils, an Ararat
Uplift o'er water, sucking rosy draughts
From Noah's vineyard,— . . . crisp, enticing wafts

Yon kitchen now emits, which to your sense
Somewhat abate the fear of old events,
Qualms to the stomach,—I, you see, am slow
Unnecessary duties to forego,—
You understand?   A venison haunch, *haut gout*,
Ducks that in Cimbrian olives mildly stew,
And sprigs of anise, might one's teeth provoke
To taste, and so we wear the complex yoke
Just as it suits,—my liking, I confess,
More to receive, and to partake no less,
Still more obese, while through thick adipose
Sensation shoots, from testing tongue to toes
Far-off, dim-conscious, at the body's verge,
Where the froth-whispers of its waves emerge
On the untasting sand.   Stay, now ! a seat
Is bare : I, Angelo, will sit and eat.

By the Sea

[*Imitation (lyrical)*—*R. Browning*]

IS it life or is it death ?
    A whiff of the cool soft scum,
As the whole sea puffed its breath
    Against you,—blind and dumb,
This way it answereth.

Nearer the sands it shows
    Spotted and leprous tints ;
But stay ! yon fisher knows
    Rock-tokens, which evince
How high the tide arose.

BAYARD TAYLOR

How high? In you and me
  'Twas falling then, I think;
Open your heart's eyes, see
  From just so slight a chink
The chasm that now must be.

You sighed and shivered then,
  Blue ecstasies of June
Around you, shouts of fishermen,
  Sharp wings of sea-gulls, soon
To dip—the clock struck ten!

Was it the cup too full,
  To carry it you grew
Too nervous, the wine's hue too dull,
  (Dulness, misjudged, untrue!)
Love's flower unfit to cull?

You should have held me fast
  One moment, stopped my pace,
Crushed down the feeble, vast
  Suggestions of embrace,
And so be crowned at last.

But now! . . . Bare-legged and brown
  Bait-diggers delve the sand,
Tramp i' the sunshine down
  Burnt-ochre vestured land.
And yonder stares the town.

A heron screams! I shut
　　This book of scurf and scum,
Its final page uncut;
　　The sea-beast blind and dumb,
Done with his bellowing! All but!

The Promissory Note[1]

[Parody—E. A. Poe]

IN the lonesome latter years,
　　(Fatal years!)
To the dropping of my tears
Danced the mad and mystic spheres
In a rounded, reeling rune,
　　'Neath the moon,
To the dripping and the dropping of my tears.

Ah my soul is swathed in gloom,
　　(Ulalume!)
In a dim Titanic tomb,
For my gaunt and gloomy soul
Ponders o'er the penal scroll
O'er the parchment (not a rhyme),
Out of place—out of time,—
I am shredded, shorn, unshifty,
　　(O, the fifty!)
And the days have passed, the three,
　　Over me!
And the debit and the credit are as one to him and me!

[1] Greeley's only autograph of Poe was a signature to a promissory note for fifty dollars.

'Twas the random runes I wrote
At the bottom of the note
  (Wrote and freely,
  Gave to Greeley),
In the middle of the night
On the yellow, moonless night,
When the stars were out of sight,
When my pulses, like a knell,
  (Israfel!)
Danced with dim and dying fays
O'er the ruins of my days,
O'er the dimeless, timeless days,
When the fifty, drawn at thirty,
Seeming thrifty, yet the dirty
Lucre of the market, was the most that I could raise!

  Fiends controlled it,
  (Let him hold it!)
Devils held for me the inkstand and the pen;
Now the days of grace are o'er,
  (Ah, Lenore!)
I am but as other men;
What is time, time, time,
To my rare and runic rhyme,
To my random, reeling rhyme,
By the sands along the shore,
Where the tempest whispers, "Pay him!" and I
 answer "Never more!"

WILLIAM MAKEPEACE THACKERAY

1811–1863

SEVERAL instances are to be found in Thackeray's verse of burlesque songs which bear the rough impress of parody, but in the two following poems the great author reaches nearest the finished production. The first example, as in the case of Dickens's only parody, is the travesty of a popular song. The second has a peculiar interest, as it is based on the author's own song of "The Willows" (see the Appendix). Thackeray, it must be noted, has focussed his attention on reducing the theme of his original poem to an absurdity, and has paid little regard to the form and the metre of his copy, although he has contrived in his parody to suggest the lyrical measure of his more serious poem.

The Willow-Tree

[Parody—Thackeray]

L ONG by the willow-tree
   Vainly they sought her,
Wild rang the mother's screams
   O'er the gray water.
" Where is my lovely one ?
   Where is my daughter ?

" Rouse, thee, sir constable—
   Rouse thee, and look.
Fisherman, bring your net,
   Boatman, your hook ;
Beat in the lily beds,
   Dive in the brook."

Vainly the constable
  Shouted and called her ;
Vainly the fisherman
  Beat the green alder ;
Vainly he threw the net,
  Never it hauled her !

Mother beside the fire
  Sat, her night-cap in ;
Father, in easy-chair,
  Gloomily napping ;
When at the window-sill
  Came a light tapping.

And a pale countenance
  Looked through the casement :
Loud beat the mother's heart,
  Sick with amazement,
And at the vision which
  Came to surprise her !
Shrieking in an agony—
  " Lor ! it's Elizar ! "

Yes, 'twas Elizabeth ;
  Yes, 'twas their girl ;
Pale was her cheek, and her
  Hair out of curl.
" Mother ! " the loved one,
  Blushing, exclaimed,
" Let not your innocent
  Lizzy be blamed.

U

WILLIAM MAKEPEACE THACKERAY

" Yesterday, going to Aunt
  Jones's to tea,
Mother, dear mother, I
  Forgot the door-key !
And as the night was cold,
  And the way steep,
Mrs. Jones kept me to
  Breakfast and sleep."

Whether her pa and ma
  Fully believed her,
That we shall never know ;
  Stern they received her ;
And for the work of that
  Cruel, though short night,—
Sent her to bed without
  Tea for a fortnight.

MORAL

Hey diddle diddlety,
  Cat and the fiddlety,
Maidens of England take
  Caution by she !
Let love and suicide
  Never tempt you aside,
And always remember to take the door-key.

WILLIAM MAKEPEACE THACKERAY

Old-Fashioned Fun

[Parody—"*When this Old Hat was New*"]

WHEN that old joke was new,
   It was not hard to joke,
And puns we now pooh-pooh,
   Great laughter would provoke.
True wit was seldom heard,
   And humour shown by few,
When reign'd King George the Third,
   And that old joke was new.

It passed indeed for wit
   Did this achievement rare,
When down your friend would sit,
   To steal away his chair ;
You brought him to the floor,
   You bruised him black and blue,
And this would cause a roar,
   When your old joke was new.

HENRY DUFF TRAILL

1842–1900

MUCH of this author's really brilliant work is buried in the accumulated wilderness of those files of newspapers which "have their day and cease to be." *The Pall Mall Gazette, The St. James's,* and *The Saturday Review* were the chief *media* for the publication of many of Traill's leaders, literary reviews, and essays. Some of these have been rescued from an unmerited oblivion by republication in collected form, under the titles of "Recaptured Rhymes" (1882), "Saturday Songs" (1890), "Number Twenty" (1892), and "The New Fiction" (1897); but the most important of his works were his biographies of Sterne and Coleridge, which were contributed to the "English Men of Letters" series, and "The Life of Sir John Franklin." In 1876 Traill published an anonymous pamphlet which proved him no mere 'prentice hand in the art of burlesque. It purported to be "The Comment of the Canaan Journals on the Israelitish Question," and contained some remarkably clever parodies of the styles of the leading London newspapers. Unfortunately, much of Traill's work is topical, a fact which precludes its appearance in a general anthology, but the following parodies have been taken from "Recaptured Rhymes," and are, we trust, fairly representative of the writer's style.

Before concluding this note, mention should be made of "The Ants' Nest," a poem of a serious nature which Sidney Low considers to be "one of the finest philosophical and reflective poems of the last twenty years of the nineteenth century."

H. D. Traill died suddenly, in the full vigour of his intellect, of heart disease, February 21st, 1900.

HENRY DUFF TRAILL

After Dilettante Concetti

[*Parody—D. G. Rossetti*]

" WHY do you wear your hair like a man,
                    Sister Helen ?
This week is the third since you began."
" I'm writing a ballad ; be still if you can,
                    Little brother.
          (*O Mother Carey, mother !*
What chickens are these between sea and heaven !) "

" But why does your figure appear so lean,
                    Sister Helen ?
And why do you dress in sage, sage green ? "
" Children should never be heard, if seen,
                    Little brother !
          (*O Mother Carey, mother !*
What fowls are a-wing in the stormy heaven !) "

" But why is your face so yellowy white,
                    Sister Helen ?
And why are your skirts so funnily tight ? "
" Be quiet, you torment, or how can I write,
                    Little brother ?
          (*O Mother Carey, mother !*
How gathers thy train to the sea from the heaven !) "

293

HENRY DUFF TRAILL

" And who's Mother Carey, and what is her train,
                          Sister Helen ?
And why do you call her again and again ? "
" You troublesome boy, why that's the refrain,
                          Little brother.
          (*O Mother Carey, mother !*
What work is toward in the startled heaven ?) "

" And what's a refrain ?   What a curious word,
                          Sister Helen !
Is the ballad you're writing about a sea-bird ? "
" Not at all ; why should it be ?   Don't be absurd,
                          Little brother.
          (*O Mother Carey, mother !*
Thy brood flies lower as lowers the heaven.) "

          (*A big brother speaketh :*)
" The refrain you've studied a meaning had,
                          Sister Helen !
It gave strange force to a weird ballad.
But refrains have become a ridiculous ' fad,'
                          Little brother.
          And *Mother Carey, mother,*
Has a bearing on nothing in earth or heaven.

" But the finical fashion has had its day,
                          Sister Helen.
And let's try in the style of a different lay
To bid it adieu in poetical way,
                          Little brother.
          So Mother Carey, mother !
Collect your chickens and go to—heaven."

(A pause. Then the big brother singeth, accompanying himself in a plaintive wise on the triangle :)

"Look in my face.   My name is Used-to-was ;
    I am also called Played-out and Done-to-death,
    And It-will-wash-no-more.   Awakeneth
Slowly, but sure awakening it has,
The common sense of man ; and I, also !
    The ballad-burden trick, now known too well,
    Am turned to scorn, and grown contemptible—
A too transparent artifice to pass.

"What a cheap dodge I am !   The cats who dart
    Tin-kettled through the streets in wild surprise
    Assail judicious ears not otherwise ;
And yet no critics praise the urchin's ' art,'
Who to the wretched creature's caudal part
    Its foolish empty-jingling ' burden ' ties."

Vers de Société

[*Imitation—Austin Dobson*]

THERE pay it James ! 'tis cheaply earned
    My conscience ! how one's cabman charges !
But never mind, so I'm returned
    Safe to my native street of Clarges.
I've just an hour for one cigar
    (What style these Reinas have, and what ash !)
One hour to watch the evening star
    With just one Curaçao-and-potash.

HENRY DUFF TRAILL

Ah me ! that face beneath the leaves
    And blossoms of its piquant bonnet !
Who would have thought that forty thieves
    Of years had laid their fingers on it !
Could you have managed to enchant
    At Lord's to-day old lovers simple,
Had Robber Time not played gallant,
    And spared you every youthful dimple !

That robber bold like courtier Claude
    Who danced the gay coranto jesting,
By your bright beauty charmed and awed,
    Has bowed and passed you unmolesting.
No feet of many wintered crows
    Have traced about your eyes a wrinkle ;
Your sunny hair has thawed the snows
    That other heads with silver sprinkle.

I wonder if that pair of gloves
    I won of you you'll ever pay me !
I wonder if our early loves
    Were wise or foolish, Cousin Amy ?
I wonder if our childish tiff
    Now seems to you, like me, a blunder !
I wonder if you wonder if
    I ever wonder if you wonder !

I wonder if you think it bliss
    Once more to be the fashion's leader !
I wonder if the trick of this
    Escapes the unsuspecting reader !

And as for him who does or can
    Delight in it, I wonder whether
He knows that almost any man
    Could reel it off by yards together !

I wonder if—— What's that ? A knock ?
    Is that you, James ? Eh ? What ? God bless me !
How time has flown ! It's eight o'clock,
    And here's my fellow come to dress me.
Be quick, or I shall be the guest
    Whom Lady Mary never pardons.
I trust you, James, to do your best
    To save the soup at Grosvenor Gardens.

The Modern Poet's Song

[Imitation—Swinburne]

WHERE hast thou been since battlemented Troy
    Rose like a dream to thy loud-stricken lyre ?
Why dost thou walk the common earth no more ?
Nor lead on high Parnass the Muses' choir
    As when thy Hellas rang from shore to shore
With harpings loud and hymns of holy joy ?
Well may we for thy gracious presence long :
    The fashion of the day is classic myth
    And he must liberally deal therewith
Who fain would sing the modern poet's song.

HENRY DUFF TRAILL

Shake from thy brow the hyacinthine locks
 That hide its ivory splendours !   Let thine eyes
Flash forth as blue-white lightnings lubricate,
 Spread sudden day through purple midnight skies
  Or scarlet shafts of dawn illuminate
 The grey and umber of the sleeping rocks !
O colours and O shades of every hue,
 Plain or in combination, faint or strong,
Red green and yellow, black and white and blue,
 How ye assist the modern poet's song !

Far darting Phoibos, lofty Loxias
 (Since thou the glad Greek greeting well mayst hear
  That hailed thee erst in Delos the Divine),
 If our late lays have leave to reach thine ear,
Meek, myrtle bearing, give us grace to pass
 Through the white worshippers towards thy shrine.
O apt alliteration ! how a throng
  Of self-repeating vowels and consonants,
  How lines of labials, strings or sibilants,
Make music in the modern poet's song !

I will compare thee to a fowler wight,
 'Snaring the soul with magic-woven words
  Of wondrous music and divinest art ;
Or haply I may liken, heard aright,
 Thy wingèd strains themselves to captured birds,
  Fast in the meshes of the human heart.
For men and things resemble what we please,
 Such arbitrary powers to bards belong ;
And, in default of genuine similes,
 Conceits will serve the modern poet's song.

HENRY DUFF TRAILL

Come thou, our lord; the heart within us dies,
    And, faint, as in a breathless land and bare,
      We take no profit of our piteous day.
    Give us to look upon thee, O most fair;
Appear, O sweet desire of all men's eyes,
      Eer this dread cup of life shall pass away!
For vague appeals which we interpret not,
    And moody murmurs at unstated wrong,
And aspirations for we say not what,
    Largely compose the modern poet's song.

Come thou, and I my stanzas will illume
      With all the hues that in the rainbow meet,
    Alliterate all letters that there are;
Out-do all rivals in mysterious gloom,
    Fetch metaphors like magi from afar,
      Lit by no star of meaning, to thy feet.
For these and similar poetic tricks
    Are highly praised our master's school among.
O Swinburne! and O water! how ye mix
    To constitute the modern poet's song.

PUNCH

THROUGH the courtesy of Messrs. Bradbury and Agnew we have been able to include several other parodies which have appeared in this classic journal of wit and humour, but these have been included under the names of their respective authors. This parody appeared when Oscar Wilde was the darling of the hour, and æsthetic culture was the popular craze. It is really a double travesty, for it ridicules the weak sentiment of Wilde's earlier writings, and at the same time meaningless rhymed effect of Swinburne—at his worst.

A Maudle-in Ballad

[Imitation of the School of Swinburne]

MY lank limp lily, my long lithe lily,
  My languid lily-love, fragile and thin,
With dank leaves dangling and flower-flap chilly,
That shines like the skin of a Highland gilly!
  Mottled and moist as a cold toad's skin!
    Lustrous and leper-white, splendid and splay!
Art thou not utter? and wholly akin
To my own wan soul and my own wan chin,
  And my own wan nose-tip, liked to sway
The peacock's feather, *sweeter than sin*,
  That I bought for a halfpenny, yesterday!

PUNCH

My long lithe lily, my languid lily,
  My lank limp lily-love, how shall I win!—
Woo thee to wink at me?   Silver lily,
How shall I sing to thee, softly, or shrilly?
    What shall I weave for thee—which shall I spin—
      Rondel, or rondeau, or virelay?
    Shall I bee-like buzz, with my face thrust in
    Thy choice, chaste chalice, or choose me a tin
      Trumpet, or touchingly, tenderly play
    On the weird bird-whistle, *sweeter than sin*,
      That I bought for a halfpenny, yesterday?

My languid lily, my lank limp lily,
  My long lithe lily-love, men may grin—
Say that I'm soft and supremely silly—
What care I, while you whisper stilly;
    What care I, while you smile?   Not a pin!
      While you smile, while you whisper—'Tis sweet
        to decay!
    I have watered with chlorodine tears of chagrin,
    The churchyard would I have planted thee in
      Upside down, in an intense way
    In a round red flowerpot, *sweeter than sin*,
      That I bought for a halfpenny, yesterday.

ANONYMOUS

Goosey

[Parody—W. Wordsworth]

HE dwelt in miry sodden ways,
    And differed from the dove,
A bird that poets never praise
    And only gourmets love.

They "made much of him," till he'd grown
    Prodigious to the eye,
Till his one liver—his alone
    Would fill a Strasbourg pie.

He should have lived on diet low,
    And kept his figure slim.
He gorged on all they gave,—and, oh!
    The difference to him!

ANONYMOUS

An Unexpected Pleasure

[*Parody—Christina Rossetti*]

MY heart is like one asked to dine
    Whose evening dress is up the spout ;
My heart is like a man would be
    Whose raging tooth is half pulled out.
My heart is like a howling swell
    Who boggles on his upper C ;
My heart is madder than all these—
    My wife's mamma has come to tea.

Raise me a bump upon my crown,
    Bang it till green in purple dies ;
Feed me on bombs and fulminates,
    And turncocks of a medium size.
Work me a suit in crimson apes
    And sky-blue beetles on the spree ;
Because the mother of my wife
    Has come—and means to stay with me.

ANONYMOUS

Ye Clerke of ye Wethere

[*Imitation—Chaucer*]

A CLERKE ther was, a puissant wight was hee,
  Who of ye wethere hadde ye maisterie;
Alway it was his mirthe and his solace—
To put eche seson's wethere oute of place.

Whanne that Aprille shoures wer our desyre,
He gad us Julye sonnes as hotte as fyre;
But sith ye summere togges we donned agayne,
Eftsoons ye wethere chaunged to colde and rayne.

Wo was that pilgrimme who fared forth a-foote,
Without one gyngham that him list uppe-putte;
And gif no mackyntosches eke had hee,
A parlous state that wight befelle—pardie!

We wist not gif it nexte ben colde or hotte,
Cogswounds! ye barde a grewsome colde hath gotte!
Certes, that clerke's ane mightie man withalle,
Let non dou him offence, lest ille befalle.

ANONYMOUS

Omar for Housewives

[*Parody—Omar Khayyám*]

To-MORROW a new Cook will come, you say,
To substitute the Cook of yesterday?
But shall the summer day that brings the rose,
Take Barbara and Mary Jane away?

I sometimes think that never burns the Bread
So black as when the tea is boiling red;
That every cabbage plant the garden wears
Knows more than any human Cabbage-head.

And this new maid who looks so fresh and green,
On whom with all my woes I fain would lean;
Ah, lean upon her lightly, for who knows
How soon she will get up and quit the scene?

Ah? my new handmaid! fill the pan that clears
To-day of unwashed dishes, stacked in tiers.
To-morrow? Why, to-morrow I may be
Myself obliged to wash them—and for years!

Whether we roll in gold or have to pinch,
Whether the heart despair or merely flinch,
The window panes grow speckier hour by hour,
The parlour dust is thickening inch by inch.

ANONYMOUS

Well I remember, watching on a day
Sue handling china in a heartless way
    Till one white teacup raised a broken rim
And murmured, " Gently, Susan, gently pray ! "

A box of biscuits underneath a Bough,
A can of beans, a bag of salt, and thou
    Burned out and singing in the wilderness.
Ah, wilderness were Paradise enow !

So when the Angel of the muddy drink,
Called coffee, throws the grounds into the sink,
    And, taking her departure, leaves you there
Alone to clean things up, you must not shrink ;

But make the best of so-called ' Help ' my friend,
Until we too into the dust descend.
    Take up the work where hirelings left it off,
Sans Hope, sans Help, sans Dishcloth—and sans end.

Contemporary Parodists

WILFRID BLAIR

In a little book which appeared in 1910 there are to be found many poems dealing with University life, of which the greater number are clever parodies on living poets. The book is entitled "Poets on the Isis," and the parodist is Wilfrid Blair, who is one of the ablest exponents of the younger school of twentieth-century parody. It has been difficult to choose an example of his work which would demonstrate his varied skill in both the technique and the spirit of parody; but perhaps "The Noyes of Battle" is his most characteristic production.

The Noyes of Battle

(Concluding fragment of "Drake, an English Epic.")

(After A. N., late of Exeter College.)

[*Parody—Alfred Noyes*]

Drake Plunders a Galleon.

MEANWHILE the wind had changed and Francis Drake
Put down the helm, and drave against the seas.
Once more the wind changed and the simple seaman,
Full-fraught with weather-wisdom, once again
Put down the helm, and so drave on, until
The everlasting and omnipotent
Dawn, through the splendid gloom and golden clouds,
Broke : and a great golden, gilded galleon

WILFRID BLAIR

In raggy piles of gloom and shaggy splendour
Rose up against them, clouded with the dawn.
Plushed, plumed and purpled on th' imperious poop,
Crusty with cramoisy, the Spaniards stood.
Being strangely rash, and really rather rude,
They quite refused surrender, till Drake cried
"I am El Draque!"—At once they recognised
The name, tho' spoken with a Devon burr.
Down came their flag at once upon the deck
As when a fragment of the ceiling falls.
Doom-fraught, fear-fraught, and fraught with other
    things,
They yielded to the Dragon, who disgorged
The gorgeous galleon, wallowing with wealth
Of world-wide, whacking empires, and straightway towed
It to the blooming blue of Torbay.

Drake attacks the Fleet.
                              What
Tremendous thunder burst triumphantly?
Is it—*El Draque?*   El Draque it is! (not 'arf!)
The Dragon of the Apocalypse is here
With Michael and his angels hand in glove.
Vexed by the violent volleys, th' Invincible Fleet
Staggers and surges, stampedes, struggles and swerves,
Whirled wildly down to hell like Lucifer
In that stupendous Salamis (which means
They cut their sticks and did a bunk).

WILFRID BLAIR

Drake holds a Council.

                             At last
Drake flew his signal. (It was night again:
The wind had changed: The helm had been put down.)
Then in tremendous council closely clustered
Howard, Hawkins, Frobisher, to whom Drake seemed
A tower of doom, unswervingly implacable—
Implacably unswerving doom to Spain—
Inevitably unconquerable doom.—
Clad with the night, hosed with the sheeny sea,
And buttoned up with many myriad stars,
Shoving his iron face to Howard's so close
That one might see he had not shaved himself,—
A face tempered like steel with wrought-iron lips,—
He stretched his iron-clad arm, and hissed to Howard
Such awful simple wisdom—weather-fraught,
Beastly monotonous with unconquerable
Passion, that Howard softly sibilated
And Hawkins slapped his grimly gaskined leg.
All stared upon that mighty simple seaman
Drawing his plans in mighty sweeping strokes
(As of Sir Jessop stepping out to drive).
He seemed to them a rock of adamant,
A god of battle, hell-ris'n, our ocean king
A granite crag, a Cæsar-summoning soul,
Irrevocably omnipotential.

Drake ends the business.

So things went on until the end of things,
When, blasting, blanching, bursting all their bulk,

WILFRID BLAIR

Drake drave the sea-fraught Spaniards to the North
In golden clouds of grimly-clouded gold.
Then, the wind changing, helm down, thundering over
The rolling triumph of the major sea,
Drake swept to the South—F. Drake, whose ocean fame
Shall ever more wash the world with thunder, and
With a towel of ragged splendour lightning-torn
Dry up.

Drake turns in.

　　So with instructions to the wheel
Drake went below and had a glass of grog.

SAMUEL D. CHARLES

The following parody lately appeared in *The Westminster Gazette*, and it is by courtesy of the author of the poem and the editor of the journal that it appears here. It is a very faithful caricature of the method and mannerisms of the author of "The Everlasting Mercy," although of course in its very nature of parody it loses that vitality and earnestness which characterise the original. At the same time many of John Masefield's phrasings are happily caught, notably—

> "There was a fog came on the winder
> With all the breath she left be'ind 'er."

The Everlasting Plumber

[*Parody—John Masefield*]

FROM '81 to '84
    I played with putty on the floor.
I left the kitchen taps to run,
I turned the passage gases on.
My dad 'e made a precious row.
O Lord, I am so sorry now.

In '96 my father said
That boy of ours were better dead.
He's thirsty, dirty, greedy, lazy,
He will not work, he drives me crazy.
He's not a helpful lad like some are,
He's only good to be a plumber.
I'll turn him out, I'll make him plumb—
That was the year the big frost come.

SAMUEL D. CHARLES

A plumber's road to getting profit
Is making work and keeping of it.
Is playing Man before the Fall,
Is pulling down great chunks of wall.
Is cutting pipes in various places,
Is wasting time and leaving traces.
He deals with women more than men
Through having of him in agen.
They leave his dinner on the 'ob.
My stars! it is a easy job.

That awful time, that crool December,
Which oldish 'orses can remember,
The year the waves broke all the shipping
And those fat gentlemen kep' slipping,
I crossed the road, I'd had a drop,
When Mrs. Kipps flew in the shop.
O, will you hurry, can you come?
Hold steady, I'm a-coming, mum.

The pipes is busted.
Busted where?
And flood the stairs.
O dear, O dear.
There was a fog came on the winder
With all the breath she left be'ind 'er.

I put a lot down in the bill
For running all up 'Ampstead 'Ill
With 'eavy tools, which isn't easy,
Although it was a thor, not freezy.
O Lor! my 'eart sank when I seed 'em,
I'd chose 'em wrong, I shouldn't need 'em.
I felt so faint, to rest my parcel
I 'ad to turn in Jack Straw's Carsel.

EDMUND B. V. CHRISTIAN

Mr. Christian is another member of the legal profession who has sought relaxation and won appreciation in the world of letters. His two best-known books are "The Lays of a Limb of the Law" (1889) and "At the Sign of the Wicket" (1894). Specimens of parodies from both these volumes have been selected to represent their author in this anthology.

Frost v. Knight

[Parody—Tennyson]

I

" HE loves me—nay, he loves me not ! "
  She tore the petals two by two
 From off the stem and idly threw
Them from her, 'plaining of her lot.

She stood by the untrodden ways
  Where they in other times had met ;
 With cheek and eyelash all unwet
She mused of love and other days.

She watched the fading autumn leaf,
  The sky was grey, the wind a-cold ;
 Her heart grew with the season old,
And nursed an angry, tearless grief.

EDMUND B. V. CHRISTIAN

"My love," she said, "is turned to hate,
  My love that should have crowned his life ;
  He lightly wooed me for his wife,
And now he seeks a richer mate."

II

"Stands not the woman higher than
  The dog that follows at his heel ?
  Shall she before her tyrant kneel
Whom Nature equalled with the man ?

"He took my love, nor recked the cost,
  My heart was warm to him, my Knight ;
  He took away the warmth and light,
And left me an unchanging Frost.

"I know him now. I never knew
  Till now how false his suit could be.
  He says he ne'er will wed with me,
And shall I not for vengeance sue ?

"But when ? 'Twas when his father died
  He vowed that he with me would wed ;
  I would his father now were dead,
But still he treads the hither side.

"And must I wait the uncertain day
  He passes from our moaning shore ?
  Or may I sue the son before ?
Counsel's opinion is, I may.

EDMUND B. V. CHRISTIAN

"Already he derides me : 'Lo!
    Thy path and mine shall never meet.'
    He makes my bitter wrong complete.
The writ is ready : let it go!'"

III

"We rate too highly, says the sage
    Who knew our little nature's strife,
    The power of love, whereto our life
Is less beholden than the stage.

"Perchance our spirits, from the flaw,
    The taint of earthly mould, made free,
    Shall know how great our love may be ;
For great is Love, yet greater Law.

"Love did the wrong the law redressed,
    I take the gold the jury gave ;
    No more the love he vowed I crave,
The gold I have, methinks, is best.

"This truth the student shall recall,
    Who reads of Angelina Frost,
    'TIS better to have loved and lost
Than never to have loved at all.'"

EDMUND B. V. CHRISTIAN

Of his Old Age

[*Parody—Andrew Lang*]

WHEN I am very old, at evening
　　I'll sit and smoke beside the fire and say,
Reading these scores : Ah, well, I had my day
When I was young ; I made the Oval ring,
And heard the judges say : "His play's the thing."
　　There was the rot that once I helped to stay,
　　Here is the century I chanced to play—
That was an innings worth remembering.

I shall be stiff, and stout, perchance, and staid,
A veteran, for younger batsmen laid
　　Aside, with eyesight dim, a grandsire grey ;
Shall be, but ah ! the sad years are not yet.
Come ! to the wickets once again we'll get,
　　And score our hundreds while 'tis called to-day !

"And yet Afraid to Strike"

[*Parody—Milton*]

THORNTON, thou shouldst be playing at this hour ;
　　Cricket has need of thee.　Her tallest men
Are patient potterers at the sticks, and when
"Off-theories" are bowled, that half thy dower
Of pluck had sent swift to the ropes, they cower

Or draw back silent.   We are nerveless men!
When in her joyous playing fields again
Shall England boast a batsman of thy power?
Thou hadst a drive majestically free!
  The ball soared to the skies, descending far
  Beyond the fieldsman's reach, without the ground.
Return! or teach thy followers to be
  As Stoddart, Marchant, and O'Brien are,
  Strong to attack as in defending sound!

Sonnet

[Parody—W. Wordsworth]

"SCORN not the cricket-sonnet on the ground
    Scant measures do not with great themes agree,
  Since Shakespeare's heart unlocked 'with this small key'
Perchance it may be not unworthy found
To make the glories of The Game resound,
  To laud the patient skill of Shrewsbury
  Or sing the praise of matchless W. G.,[1]
Our chief of men, through every land renowned.
"The bat is as the sonnet is, but small.
  Yet with it batsmen, a stout-hearted band,
Waged ceaseless, changing conflict with the ball
  Till Grace arose; and in his mighty hand
The thing became a sceptre, which he wields
  Unchallenged yet, Lord of the playing fields."

[1] William Grace.

ANTHONY C. DEANE

The Vicar of Great Malvern has taken the care and cure of minds as well as the care and cure of souls into his consideration, and to such good purpose, that since the publication of his first book, "Frivolous Verses" in 1892, slender but brilliant volumes of the lighter verse have from time to time appeared amongst his serious works.

The latter include "St. Columba" (1905), a poem which gained the Seatonian Prize at Cambridge, "New Testament Studies," and "A Treatise on the Reformation." In 1901 appeared "New Rhymes for Old and Other Verses," a volume chiefly devoted to parody, from which we have been generously allowed to make a selection.

Jack and Jill

[Imitation—Rudyard Kipling]

HERE is the tale—and you must make the most of it!
Here is the rhyme—ah, listen and attend!
Backwards—forwards—read it all and boast of it
If you are anything the wiser at the end!

Now Jack looked up—it was time to sup, and the bucket
was yet to fill,
And Jack looked round for a space and frowned, then
beckoned his sister Jill,
And twice he pulled his sister's hair, and thrice he smote
her side;
"Ha' done, ha' done with your impudent fun—ha' done
with your games!" she cried;

ANTHONY C. DEANE

"You have made mud pies of a marvellous size—finger
  and face are black,
You have trodden the Way of the Mire and Clay—now
  up and wash you, Jack!
Or else, or ever we reach our home, there waiteth an angry
  dame—
Well you know the weight of her blow—the supperless
  open shame!
Wash, if you will, on yonder hill—wash, if you will, at
  the spring,—
Or keep your dirt, to your certain hurt, and an imminent
  walloping!"

"You must wash—you must scrub—you must scrape!"
  growled Jack, "you must traffic with cans and pails,
Nor keep the spoil of the good brown soil in the rim of
  your finger-nails!
The morning path you must tread to your bath—you
  must wash ere the night descends,
And all for the cause of conventional laws and the soap-
  makers' dividends!
But if 'tis sooth that our meal in truth depends on our
  washing, Jill,
By the sacred light of our appetite—haste—haste to the
  top of the hill!"

They have trodden the Way of the Mire and Clay, they
  have toiled and travelled far,
They have climbed to the brow of the hill-top now,
  where the bubbling fountains are,
They have taken the bucket and filled it up—yea, filled it
  up to the brim;

But Jack he sneered at his sister Jill, and Jill she jeered
    at him :

" What, blown already ! " Jack cried out (and his was a
    biting mirth !)

" You boast indeed of your wonderful speed—but what is
    the boasting worth ?

Now, if you can run as the antelope runs, and if you can
    turn like a hare,

Come, race me, Jill, to the foot of the hill—and prove
    your boasting fair ! "

" Race ? What is a race " (and a mocking face had Jill
    as she spoke the word)

" Unless for a prize the runner tries ? The truth indeed
    ye heard,

For I can run as the antelope runs, and I can turn like the
    hare :

The first one down wins half-a-crown—and I will race
    you there ! "

" Yea, if for the lesson that you will learn (the lesson of
    humbled pride)

The price you fix at two-and-six, it shall not be denied ;

Come, take your stand at my right hand, for here is the
    mark we toe :

Now, are you ready, and are you steady ? Gird up your
    petticoats ! Go ! "

And Jill she ran like a winging bolt, a bolt from the bow
    released,

But Jack like a stream of the lightning gleam, with its
    pathway duly greased ;

He ran down hill in front of Jill like a summer lightning
flash—
Till he suddenly tripped on a stone, or slipped, and fell to
the earth with a crash.
Then straight did rise on his wondering eyes the
constellations fair,
Arcturus and the Pleiades, the Greater and Lesser Bear,
The swirling rain of a comet's train he saw, as he swiftly
fell—
And Jill came tumbling after him with a loud triumphant
yell:
"You have won, you have won, the race is done! And
as for the wager laid—
You have fallen down with a broken crown—the half-
crown debt is paid!"

They have taken Jack to the room at the back where the
family medicines are,
And he lies in bed with a broken head in a halo of vinegar;
While, in that Jill had laughed her fill as her brother fell
to earth,
She has felt the sting of a walloping—she hath paid the
price of her mirth!

Here is the tale—and now you have the whole of it,
Here is the story—well and wisely planned,
Beauty—Duty—these make up the soul of it—
But, ah, my little readers, will you mark and understand?

ANTHONY C. DEANE

Humpty-Dumpty

[*Imitation— W. E. Henley*]

CALM and implacable,
  Eying disdainfully the world beneath,
Sat Humpty-Dumpty on his mural eminence
In solemn state :
And I relate his story
In verse unfettered by the bothering restrictions of rhyme
  or metre,
In verse (or "rhythm," as I prefer to call it)
Which, consequently, is far from difficult to write.

He sat.   And at his feet
The world passed on—the surging crowd
Of men and women, passionate, turgid, dense,
Keenly alert, lethargic, or obese.
(Those two lines scan !)

Among the rest
He noted Jones ; Jones with his Roman nose,
His eyebrows—the left one streaked with a dash of gray—
And yellow boots.
Not that Jones
Has anything in particular to do with the story ;
But a descriptive phrase
Like the above shows that the writer is
A Master of Realism.

ANTHONY C. DEANE

Let us proceed.   Suddenly from his seat
Did Humpty-Dumpty slip.   Vainly he clutched
The impalpable air.   · Down and down,
Right to the foot of the wall,
Right on to the horribly hard pavement that ran beneath
    it,
Humpty-Dumpty, the unfortunate Humpty-Dumpty,
Fell.

And him, alas! no equine agency,
Him no power of regal battalions—
Resourceful, eager, strenuous—
Could ever restore to the lofty eminence
Which once was his.
Still he lies on the very identical
Spot where he fell—lies, as I said, on the ground,
Shamefully and conspicuously abased!

Three Blind Mice

[*Imitation—Wm. Watson*]

THREE mice—three sightless mice—averse from
        strife,
    Peaceful descendants of the Armenian race,
    Intent on finding some secluded place
Wherein to pass their inoffensive life;
How little dreamt they of that farmer's wife—
    The Porte's malicious minion—giving chase,
    And in a moment—ah, the foul disgrace!—
Shearing their tails off with a carving-knife!

ANTHONY C. DEANE

And oh, my unemotional countrymen,
    Who choose to dally and to temporise
When once before with vitriolic pen
    I told the tale of Turkish infamies,
Once more I call to vengeance—now, as then,
    Shouting the magic word "Atrocities!"

An Ode

[Imitation—Alfred Austin]

I SING a song of sixpence, and of rye
    A pocketful—recalling, sad to state,
The niggardly emoluments which I
    Receive as Laureate!

Also I sing of blackbirds—in the mart
    At four-a-penny. Thus, in other words,
The sixpence which I mentioned at the start
    Purchased two dozen birds.

So four-and-twenty birds were deftly hid—
    Or shall we say, were skilfully concealed?—
Within the pie-dish. When they raised the lid,
    What melody forth pealed!

Now I like four-and-twenty blackbirds sing,
    With all their sweetness, all their rapture keen;
And isn't this a pretty little thing
    To set before the Queen?

ANTHONY C. DEANE

The money-counting monarch—sordid man!—
    His wife, who robbed the little busy bees,
I disregard.   In fact a poet can
    But pity folks like these.

The maid was in the garden.   Happy maid!
    Her choice entitles her to rank above
Master and Mistress.   Gladly she surveyed
    The Garden That I Love!

—Where grow my daffodils, anemones,
    Tulips, auriculas, chrysanthemums,
Cabbages, asparagus, sweet peas,
    With apples, pears, and plums—

(That's a parenthesis.   The very name
    Of "garden" really carries one astray!)
But suddenly a feathered ruffian came,
    And stole her nose away.

Eight stanzas finished! So my Court costume
    I lay aside : the Laureate, I suppose,
Has done his part ; the man may now resume
    His journalistic prose.

Bo-Peep

[*Imitation—Andrew Lang*]

UNHAPPY is Bo-Peep,
        Her tears profusely flow,
Because her precious sheep

Have wandered to and fro,
Have chosen far to go,
For " pastures new " inclined,
    (See *Lycidas*)—and lo.!
Their tails are still behind!

How catch them while asleep ?
    (I think Gaboriau
For machinations deep
    Beats Conan Doyle & Co.)
    But none a hint bestow
Save this, on how to find
    The flock she misses so—
" Their tails are still behind " !

This simple faith to keep
    Will mitigate her woe,
She is not Ivan, to leap
    To arms against the foe
    Or conjugate τύπτω ;
Nay, peacefully resigned
    She waits, till time shall show
Their tails are still behind.

    Bo-Peep, rejoice ! Although
Your sheep appear unkind,
    Rejoice at least to know
Their tails are still behind.

O. HENRY

1867–1910

Mr. William Sidney Porter is one of the most genuine humorous writers of America, but he is little known to readers on this side of the Atlantic. Whatever may be the cause of his slight recognition here, it is certainly not due to his inferiority as a writer, for his work is full of literary charm and is provokingly funny. But the fact that so little of his work has appeared in England may account for this neglect, for at present only three of his books have been published here. These are "Cabbages and Kings" (1904), "Roads of Destiny," and "Options" (1909). It is from this last work that the parody included here is taken. It is more than the usual parody, for, funny as it is, it has a pathetic interest which makes it a work of art. It is at the same time a very apt travesty of the work of James Whitcomb Riley, another American, and a poet of no mean power.

Options

(Now here's a thing that's bound to get next to you. It's an original poem by James Whitcomb Riley. ; . . I'll read you the last two stanzas.)

> " PA lays around 'n' loafs all day
>   'N' reads and makes us leave him be.
> He lets me do just like I please,
>   'N when I'm bad he laughs at me,
> 'N' when I holler loud 'n' say
>   Bad words 'n' then begin to tease

329

O. HENRY

The cat 'n' pa just smiles, ma's mad
  'N' gives me Jesse crost her knees.
I always wondered why that wuz—
    I guess it's cause
    Pa never does.

"'N' after all the lights are out
  I'm sorry 'bout it; so I creep
Out of my trundle bed to ma's
  'N' say I love her a whole heap.
'N' kiss her, 'n' I hug her tight.
  'N' it's too dark to see her eyes.
But every time I do I know
  She cries 'n' cries 'n' cries 'n' cries.
I always wondered why that wuz—
    I guess it's cause
    Pa never does."

MARY KENDALL

THERE are few more charming lyrical writers than Miss Kendall. All her work is touched with a grace that makes it distinctive, whether it be that written in her more serious moments or when she breaks out into quiet satirical humour. Certainly she is one of our literature's few women humorists, and for that reason "Education's Martyr" is all the more valuable. As a parody it is absolutely saturate with Wordsworth style and phraseology, although its form does not so closely follow the original. It is taken from "Dreams to Sell," published in 1887, the forerunner of another volume of verse, "Songs from Dreamland" (1894). Miss Kendall has besides written many volumes of prose stories, including "From a Garret," "Such is Life," "White Poppies."

Education's Martyr

[*Parody—Wm. Wordsworth*]

HE loved peculiar plants and rare—
    For any plant he did not care
That he had seen before ;
Primroses by the river's brim
Dicotyledons were to him,
    And they were nothing more.

The mighty cliffs we bade him scan,
He banned them for Laurentian,
    With sad, dejected mien.
"Than all this bleak Azoic rock,"
He said, "I'd sooner have a block—
    Ah me ! of Pleistocene ! "

MARY KENDALL

His eyes were bent upon the sand,
He owned the *scenery* was grand,
   In a reproachful voice.
But if a centipede he found
He'd fall before it on the ground
   And worship and rejoice!

We spoke of poets dead and gone,
Of that Maeonian who shone
   O'er Hellas like a star:
We talked about the King of Men,—
"Observe," he said, "the force of κεν,
   And note the use of γαρ!"

Yes, all that has been or may be,
Slates, beauties, battles, land and sea,
   The matin-song of larks,
With glacier, earthquake, avalanche,
To him were each a separate "branch,"
   And stuff for scoring marks!

Ah! happier he who does not know
The power that makes the planets go,
   The slaves of Kepler's laws,
Who finds not glands in joy or grief,
Nor, in the blossom or the leaf,
   Seeks for the secret cause.

RHODE KNIGHT

THE author who has hidden his personality under the title of
Rhode Knight has made a particular study of Parody, and has himself practised the art to no little purpose. It is with his kind
consent that the following parodies are included in this volume.

A Man's Requirements

[*Parody—E. B. Browning*]

FEED me, Love, with all thine art,
  See, I'm shrinking,—thinner ;
Feed me in the weakest part,
  Feed me well at dinner.

Feed me like a hungry youth,
  Long and lank and slender,
With the mutton of the South,
  Succulent and tender.

Feed me with thy pigeon pies,
  Made for picnic jaunting,
Taking care to see they rise,—
  Is't Beeton thou art wanting ?

Feed me with their crusts, that fall
  Flake-like, and as fleeting ;
Feed me with stuffed hearts, that all
  Neighbours now are eating.

RHODE KNIGHT

Feed me when I feel worn out,
   Freely—open handed ;
Feed me with no loitering foot,—
   Dost thou understand it ?

Feed me with things choice, and learn
   That when faint I need thee ;
Feed me when I home return,
   When I murmur, *Feed me !*

Feed me with a dainty sole,
   When for dinner sighing ;
Feed me with a raspberry roll,
   When with hunger dying.

Feed me with delicious pears,
   When my wealth has crowned thee ;
Feed me, heeding all my prayers,
   From the dishes round thee.

Feed me just as nurses do
   For the growing baby ;
Feed me daily, fasts eschew,—
   There's a dear wee lady !

Feed me, feed me, feed me, Dear !
   And thy kindness crowning,
I will read thee, read thee, Dear,
   Rhymes by Mrs. Browning !

RHODE KNIGHT

The Ballad of the Matinee Hat

[*Parody—Austin Dobson*]

WICKER-SKIN, intricate, slight,
    Glowing like gardens at Kew,
Flowers in a riot of white,
    Rose-pink, mauve, yellow and blue;
    Mark all the dainty *frou-frou!*
Fixture as wide as a mat.
    Size that would well cover two,—
This is the Matinee Hat!

See how they writhe at the sight,
    Longing that they could see through,
Maidens as buttercups bright,
    Beauties with heads all askew,
    Chaperones, debutants, a few
Baronets, Dukes, who say—"Drat!"
    Eager the stage but to view,—
This is the Matinee Hat!

Ah, but 'tis far from polite
    Spoiling folk's joy, it is true!
Manners, we state, are not right:
    What can great managers do?
    What if their patrons withdrew?

RHODE KNIGHT

You from whose brains emerged *that*,
   Make something smaller's your cue,—
"This is the Matinee Hat!"

ENVOY

What were the secrets it knew?
   Weaving what plots where it sat?
—But what was the Matinee, too?
   This was the Matinee Hat!

E. G. V. KNOX

As "Evoe" Mr. Knox is well known to readers of *Punch*, where some happily conceived verses on the topic of the day are nearly always to be found. A selection of his poems has recently been published under the title of the "Brazen Lyre," and from these the following examples have been taken. Mr. Knox is the son of the Bishop of Manchester, and has only recently married Miss Hicks, the daughter of the Bishop of Lincoln.

Redford[1] Musagelis

[*After Matthew Arnold*]

NOT here, my good fellow,
  Are plays meet for you,
But where Aldwych[2] is hoisting
  Its pomp to the blue;

Or where moon-smitten millions
  Unceasingly crowd
At the entrance of Daly's[3]—
  Go there and be proud.

---

[1] George Alexander Redford has only lately retired from the post of Examiner of Plays, i.e. Censor.

[2] The Gaiety Theatre, situated at the junction of Aldwych and the Strand, and devoted to the production of musical comedy.

[3] Daly's Theatre, also devoted to the production of musical comedy, situated in Cranbourne Street.

E. G. V. KNOX

To the seats on the house-top
    The multitude flock ;
They are fighting their hunger
    With peppermint rock.

On the *fauteuil* beneath sits
    The blue-blooded swell ;
He has robed him and dined him
    Remarkably well.

What gowns are these coming ?
    What hats, and by whom ?
What skirt-trains outsweeping
    The vacuum broom ?

What sweet-breathing music
    Unchastened by Time ?
What hosen illumed by
    The light of the lime ?

'Tis Edwardes[1] presenting
    His loveliest dream !
They all were stupendous,
    But this is the cream !

Lo, here is the drama
    Your wits understand ;
The Muse you have fostered
    And foist on our land !

[1] George Edwardes is chairman and managing director of the
Gaiety Theatre Company, and manager of Daly's Theatre.

The choruses chirrup
  And pass to the wings;
The wags entertain us
  And somebody sings.

What strife do they tell of?
  What passions expound?
Why, earth and the motive
  That makes her go round.

First show they the flirting
  Of flappers and then
The rest of existence,
  The childhood of men;

The dance in its daring,
  The Corybant's wreath;
The time-honoured chestnut
  The Stars and their teeth.

Upon Julia's Clothes

[Parody—Herrick]

WHENAS in furs my Julia goes,
  Of slaughtered vermin goodness knows,
What tails depend upon her clothes!

Next, when I cast my eyes and see
The living whelp she lugs to tea,
Oh, how their likeness taketh me!

CHOLMONDELEY PENNELL

"Puck on Pegasus" was published in 1861, and the popularity
which this volume of light verse attained was such as to induce the
author to bring out "Pegasus Re-saddled" in 1877. But Mr.
Cholmondeley Pennell was not by profession a writer, for he entered
the public service in 1853, was for some time engaged in Egyptian
affairs, and later was appointed an Inspector of Fisheries. In his
society verse this author is particularly successful in mingling that
groat's worth of deeper thought with the million of wit and sparkle
and lyrical faculty which gives to it a real and lasting charm. The
"Fight for the Championship" is an account, in Macaulay's style, of
the boxing contest between Tom Sayers, who was an Englishman,
and John Heenan, an American, which resulted in a draw, and
established a record by reason of the length and brutal nature
of the encounter. This poem and "The Song of In-the-Water"
have been taken, with the author's permission, from "Puck on
Pegasus."

Song of In-the-Water

[Parody—Longfellow]

WHEN the summer night descended
 Sleepy on the White Witch water;
Came a lithe and lovely maiden,
Gazing on the silent water—
Gazing on the shining river—
With her azure eyes and tender!
On the river, glancing forward,
Till the laughing waves sprang upward,

CHOLMONDELEY PENNELL

Dancing in her smile of sunshine,
Curling ev'ry dimpled ripple
As they sprang into the starlight;
As they clasp'd her charmed reflection
   Glowing to their silver bosoms!
And they whisper'd, "Fairest, fairest,
   Rest upon our crystal bosoms!"

And she straightway "did according":—

Down into the water stept she,
   Down into the tranquil river,
Like a red deer in the sunset—
Like a ripe leaf in the autumn!
   Ever from her lips of coral,
From her lips like roses snow-fill'd,
   Came a soft and dreamy murmur,
   Softer than the breath of summer,
   Softer than the murm'ring river!
Sighs that melted as the snows melt,
   Silently and sweetly melted;
Words that mingled with the crisping
   Foam upon the billow resting.

From the forest shade primeval,
Piggey-Wiggey look'd out at her;
   He the very Youthful Porker—
   He the Everlasting Grunter—
Gazed upon her there and wondered!
   With his nose out, rokey-pokey—
   And his tail up, curley-wurley—
Wonder'd what on earth the row meant,
Wonder'd what the girl was up to—
What the deuce her little game was?

341

And she floated down the river,
  Like a water-tight Ophelia,
FOR HER CRINOLINE SUSTAINED HER ! !

The Fight for the Championship

[Told by an ancient gladiator to his great-grandmother]

[*Parody—T. B. Macaulay*]

LARGE Heenan of Benicia
    By ninety-nine gods he swore
That the bright Belt of England
    Should grace her sons no more.
By ninety-nine he swore it,
    And named the " fisting " day.—
" East and west and south and north,"
Said Richard Mayne,[1] "ride forth, ride forth,
    And summon mine array."

" Ride forth by heathy Hampshire
    Of ' chalk-stream-studded dells,'
And wake the beaks of Eversley
    Where gallant Kingsley[2] dwells ;
Spur fast through Berkshire spinneys,
    The Broad Hog's Back bestride,
And if the White Horse is scoured,
    Mount up amain and ride :
Spur, spur, I say, thro' England
    As the Giaour once spurred thro' Greece,
Tho' Sayers were six, he cuts his sticks
    And Dickon keeps the peace."

[1] The Chief Inspector of Police at that time.
[2] The Reverend Charles Kingsley, poet and novelist.

CHOLMONDELEY PENNELL

Fast, fast through town and hamlet
    The Smart Detectives flew—
East and west and south and north
    They watched the long day thro';
West and north—east and south
    The word went flashing by,
Look out for Sayers and Heenan.
    Policemen—mind your eye!

Sir Richard's bold moss-troopers
    Looked out uncommon keen,
From park and plain and prairie,
    From heath and upland green;
From Essex' fens and fallows,
    From Hampshire—dale and down—
From Sussex' hundred leagues of sand,
To Shropshire's fat and flowery land,
And Cheshire's wild and wasted strand,
    And Yorkshire's heather brown;—
And so, of course, the fight came off
    A dozen miles from Town.

Then first stept out big Heenan,
    Unmatched for breadth and length;
And in his chest it might be guessed
    He had unpleasant strength.
And to him went the Sayers
    That looked both small and thin,
But well each practised eye could read
The "Lion and the Bull-dog" breed,
And from each fearless stander-by
Rang out that genuine British cry,
    "Go in, my boy—*and win.*"

And he went in—and smote him
  Through mouthpiece and through cheek;
And Heenan smote him back again
  Into the ensuing week:
Full seven days thence he smote him
  With one prodigious crack,
And th' undaunted Champion straight
Discerned that he was five feet eight
  When flat upon his back:
Whilst a great shout of laughter
  Rose from the Yankee pack.

As from the flash the bullet
  Out sprang the Champion then
And dealt the huge Benician
  A vast thump on the chin;
And thrice and four times sternly
  Drove in the shatt'ring blow;
And thrice and four times wavered
  The Herculean foe;
And his great arms swung wildly
  Like ship-masts to and fro.

And now no sound of laughter
  Was heard from either side,
Whilst feint, and draw, and rally,
  The cautious Bruisers tried;
And long they sparred and countered
  Till Heenan sped a thrust
So fierce and quick, it swept away
Th' opposing guard like sapling spray—
And for the second time that day
  The Champion bit the dust.

CHOLMONDELEY PENNELL

Short time lay English Sayers
   Upon the earth at length,
Short time his Yankee foeman
   Might triumph in his strength ;
Sheer from the ground he smote him
   And his soul went with the blow—
Such blow no other hand could dash—
Such blow no other arm could smash—
   The giant tottered low ;
And for a space they sponged his face
   And thought the eye would go.

Time's up !—again they battle,
   Again the strokes fly free,
But Sayers' right arm—that arm of pride—
Now dangles pow'rless by his side,
   Plain for all eyes to see ;
And thro' that long and desperate shock—
Two mortal hours by the clock—
By sheer indomitable pluck
   With his *left hand* fought he !

With his left hand he fought him
   Though he was sore in pain,—
Full twenty times hurled backward
   Still pressing on again !
With his left hand he fought him,
   Till each could fight no more ;
Till Sayers could scarcely strike a blow,
Till Heenan could not see his foe—
Such fighting England never knew
   Upon her soil before !

CHOLMONDELEY PENNELL

They gave him of the standard
  Gold coin of the realm,
As much as one stout guardsman
  Could carry in his helm ;
They made him an ovation
  On the Exchange hard by,
And they may slap their pockets
  In witness if I lie.

And every soul in England
  Was glad, both high and low,
And books were voted snobbish,
  And " gloves " were all the go ;
And each man told the story,
  Whilst ladies' hearts would melt,
How Sayers, the British Champion
  Did battle for the Belt.

And still, when Yankees swagger
  Th' almighty " Stars and Stripes,"
And put eternal bunkum
  Into their neighbours' pipes—
With joke and gibe and banter
  Long shall the tale be told
How stout Tom Sayers kept the Belt
  And Yankee Doodle sold.

MOSTYN T. PIGOTT

MR. MOSTYN PIGOTT has published several books of humour. One of the first was a collection of burlesque stories republished from *The Isis* under the title of "Two on a Tour," and contained some particularly amusing skits on the modern novel. This was followed up in 1893 by "Common Room Carols," a volume dedicated entirely to humorous verse, from which "Punts" and "The Boy on One Roller Skate" have been taken; while in 1896 he published another book of similar verse entitled "The Songs of a Session," but in this case the themes were political. From it comes "You're young, Kaiser William," a protest called forth by one of the less tactful speeches of the German Emperor. Finally, appeared the "Joseph Jingle Book," a series of poems, many in the form of parody, which dealt with the political crisis in which England was at that time involved, and which were reprinted from *The World*.

Punts

[Imitation—Kipling]

WHAT makes canoe-ists' hearts to quake?
  What makes them lose their hair?
It isn't that they're huddled up with little room to
  spare;
  It's the everlasting dodging all the everlasting day
  Of the vacillating punter on his vacillating way.
O the punt, O the punt, O the vacillating punt!
With its silly way of navigating broadside up the Cher.;
We pack it full of cushions with a parasol in front,
And when it's under way it goes all slantindicular!

MOSTYN T. PIGOTT

What makes the sculler swear so hard with words of
    wrath and sin,
When the sweet and soothing summer-eve draws
    gradually in ?
It's not the chance of being late for supper or for
    Hall ;
It's the vacillating punter with his silly sideway crawl.
O the punt, O the punt, O the harum-scarum punt !
Colliding with the river-bank and sticking in the mud !
You shove out madly with the pole and get its nose in front,
And then against the other bank it rushes with a thud.

The dingey knows a thing or two, the cockle's rather
    fou,
The Thames-skiff isn't larky, the Canader's—a canoe ;
But the vacillating pee-wy-unt, when all is said and
    done,
Is a serpent and a switch-back and a moving-van in
    one.
O the punt, O the punt, O the idiotic punt !
The humpy-bumpy imbecile encumbering the ground,
It'll block up all the river, and 'll never go in front,
And when we get it off it starts cavorting round and round !

'Twill twist and twirl and gloom and glance—'twill
    slip and slide and spread ;
You can't regain control of it when once it gets its
    head ;
It's game to spin the whole day through, and drift
    the whole night long,
And when it comes to muddy ground it sticks there
    pretty strong.

O the punt, O the punt, O the sticky, tricky punt!
Its long side blocks the narrow stream, and no one can
get through;
Canoes are blocked to rear of us and lots of boats in front;
It's a jamb all up the Cherwell but it isn't jam for you!

So when the afternoon is past, our gratitude is large;
We manage to conduct the brute to Mr. Talboys'
barge,
And when we take the cushions out and all our woes
are past,
We thank our lucky stars that we are safely back at
last.
O the punt, O the punt, O the gloomy roomy punt!
We vow that for the future from all punting we'll abstain;
So we leave it far behind us and we give a cheerful grunt—
But we come again to-morrow and we hire the thing again!

The Boy on One Roller-Skate

[Parody—Tennyson]

I COME with whistlings shrill and loud,
I make a sudden sally,
And sparkle out among the crowd
To bicker down the alley.

The crowded streets I hurry down
With antics like a midge's,
By gas-lit shops, around the town,
And over all the bridges

MOSTYN T. PIGOTT

I wind about, and in and out,
    At people's coat-tails hauling,
That there may be without a doubt
    No danger of my falling.

And if I slip I hold on well
    And so escape a cropper ;
And here and there I grasp a " swell,"
    And here and there a " copper."

I steal by p'liceman, peer, and page,
    I slide by paper-sellers,
I move old gentlemen to rage
    And upset their umbrellas.

I slip, I slide, I gloom, I glance,
    I chill men to their marrows ;
I make the swarth Italians prance
    Who "boss" the ice-cream barrows.

In Pimlico I'm found, and Bow,
    In Holborn, by the river ;
For men may come and men may go,
    But I go on for ever.

I chatter over asphalt ways,
    I clatter o'er the pavement,
And am, so far from getting praise,
    Sworn at for my behavement.

At all my curves the people fret,
    I turn them green and yellow ;
I make a dead determined set
    At parties old and mellow.

I chatter, chatter, as I flow
    Just like a babbling river;
For men may come and men may go,
    But I go on for ever.

I bump against the gay young blood
    Who " quite regardless " dresses,
I spatter him with London mud
    That spots, and spoils, and messes.

And out again I curve and flow,
    Meand'ring like a river;
For men may come and men may go,
    But I go on for ever.

You are Young, Kaiser William

[Parody—Southey]

" YOU are young, Kaiser William," the old man ex-
        claimed,
    " And your wisdom-teeth barely are through,
And yet by your deeds the whole world is inflamed—
    Do you think this is proper of you? "
" As a baby I doted on playing with fire,"
    Replied the irascible prince,
" And though I was spanked by my excellent sire,
    I've been doing the same ever since."

" You are young," said the Sage, " and your juvenile legs
    Are not what one would call fully grown;
Yet you point out to Grandmamma how to suck eggs—
    Why adopt this preposterous tone? "

MOSTYN T. PIGOTT

"As a child," said the youth, "I perceived that my head
    Wouldn't ever allow me to learn,
So I made up my mind to start teaching instead,
    And I've taught everybody in turn."

"You are young," said the Sage, "as I mentioned just now,
    Yet with relatives over the sea
You have recently kicked up a terrible row—
    Do you think that such things ought to be?"
"In my yacht," said the youth, "I will oftentimes range,
    And at Cowes I have gybed once or twice.
So I made up my mind that by way of a change
    To gibe at a Bull would be nice."

"You are young," said the Seer, "but the Post you ignore,
    And have got an extravagant trick
Of using up telegraph-forms by the score—
    Why are you so painfully quick?"
"As a child," replied William, "they taught me to write
    An entirely illegible scrawl;
But a wire which the Post Office people indite
    Can be read without trouble by all."

"You are young," said the Sage, "but you cling to the view
    That the whole of the world must be yours;
Now show how the Transvaal's connected with you,
    And what business you have with the Boers?"
"I am tired of your questions and sick of your din,"
    Answered William: "obey my behest—
Be off! or I'll treat you as one of my kin,
    And order your instant arrest!"

SIR FREDERICK POLLOCK

THE greater part of the Right Hon. Sir Frederick Pollock's writings has been on matters of law, but in 1877 he published a little book of parodies entitled "Leading Cases Done into English," which with other matter was re-issued in 1892 as "Leading Cases Done into English, and Other Diversions." The idea of presenting lawsuits in humour guise and in the form of parody is cleverly conceived and as cleverly executed. The Parodies are some of the cleverest and wittiest in the English language, and amongst them is the famous travesty of Browning—"Scott versus Shepherd, or Any Pleader to Any Student," which the author's kind permission enables us to include in this anthology.

In the "Ode on the Death of a College Cat" it must be noted that the author has parodied not so much the exact poem of Gray as the style of verse prevalent at that period.

Lines on the Death of a College Cat

[*Imitation—Gray*]

THE Junior Fellow's vows were said ;
    Among his co-mates and their Head
His place was fairly set.
Of welcome from friends old and new
Full dues he had, and more than due ;
    What could be lacking yet ?

One said, "The Senior Fellow's vote !"
The Senior Fellow, black of coat,
    Save where his front was white,

Arose and sniffed the stranger's shoes
With critic nose, as ancients use
　　To judge mankind aright.

I—for 'twas I who tell the tale—
Conscious of fortune's trembling scale,
　　Awaited the decree ;
But Tom had judged : " He loves our race,"
And, as to his ancestral place,
　　He leapt upon my knee.

Thenceforth in common-room and hall
A *verus socius* known to all
　　I came and went and sat,
Far from cross fate's or envy's reach ;
For none a title could impeach
　　Accepted by the cat.

Whilst statutes changed, and freshmen came,
His gait, his wisdom were the same,
　　His age no more than mellow ;
Yet nothing mortal may defy
The march of *Anno Domini*,
　　Not e'en the Senior Fellow.

Beneath our linden shade he lies ;
Mere eld hath softly closed his eyes
　　With late and honoured end.
He seems, while catless we confer,
To join with faint Elysian purr,
　　A tutelary friend.

SIR FREDERICK POLLOCK

Scott v. *Shepherd*

(2 *Sm. L. C.* 480)

Any Pleader to Any Student

[*Imitation—R. Browning*]

NOW, you're my pupil!
  On the good ancient plan I shall do what I can
For *your* hundred guineas to give *my* law's blue pill
(Let high jurisprudence which thinks me and you dense
Set posse of cooks to stir new Roman soup ill) :
First volume of Smith shall give you the pith
Of leading decision that shows the division
Of action *on case* from plain action of *trespass*
Where to count in assault law benignantly says " Pass ! "

Facts o' case first.   At Milborne Port
Was fair-day, October the twenty and eight,
And folk in the market like fowls in a crate ;
Shepherd, one of your town-fool sort
(From Solomon's time they call it sport,
Right to help holiday, just make fun louder),
Lights me a squib up of paper and powder
(Find if you can the law-Latin for't)
And chucks it, to give their trading a rouse,
Full i' the midst o' the market-house.

SIR FREDERICK POLLOCK

It happed to fall on a stall where Yates
Sold gingerbread and gilded cates
(Small damage if *they* should burn or fly all);
To save himself and said gingerbread loss,
One Willis doth toss the thing across
To stall of one Ryal, who straight on espial
Of danger to *his* wares, of selfsame worth,
Casts it in market-house farther forth,
And by two mesne tossings thus it got
To burst i' the face of plaintiff Scott.
And now 'gainst Shepherd, for loss of eye
Question is, whether *trespass* shall lie.

Think Eastertide past, off crowds and packs town
Where De Grey, Chief Justice, and Nares and Black-
   stone
And Gould his brethren are set in banc
In a court full of serjeants stout or lank,
With judgment to give this doubt an end
(Layman hints wonder to counsellor friend,
If *express colour* be visible pigment,
And what's by black patch a-top serjeant's wig meant).
Nares leads off, opines with confidence
Trespass well lies and there's no pretence
But who gave squib mischievous faculty
Shall answer its utmost consequence
(*Qui facit per alium facit per se*) :
Squib-throwing a nuisance by statute, too!

SIR FREDERICK POLLOCK

Blackstone, more cautious, takes other view,
Since 'tis not all one throw, but an impetus new
Is given to squib by Ryal and Willis,
When *vis* first *impressa* thereon spent and still is ;
In fine, would have justice set mouth firm, not sound awry,
But teach forms of action to know each his boundary.
Gould holds with Nares :—If De Grey pairs ?
That were, odzooks, equipoise, *dignus vindice*
Nodus !   But—"I too on same side faith pin, d'ye see,"
So De Grey spake—"For, as I take
It, the consequences all flowed of course
From Shepherd's original wrongful force :
Seen rightly, in this case difference *nil* is
In squib's new diversion by Ryal and Willis,
Whom (against Brother Blackstone, I'm free to confess
   it) I
Account not free agents, since merest necessity
Bade cast off live squib to save selves and wares."
For such reasons, concurs with Gould and Nares.
Ergo, "*Postea* to the plaintiff."
Next, digest learned editor's notes,
Mark the refinements, preceptor acquaint if
You've duly mastered cases Smith quotes—
Eh ?—No !   What says book here ?   As I'm alive,
"Distinctions, had place in principal case,
Since fifty-two make less ado,
And in fact by Judicature Act,
After November seventy-five,
Last stumps of pleading by final weeding
Are grubbed up and thrown adown wind to perdition :
So, note's omitted in present edition ! "

SIR FREDERICK POLLOCK

Well—liquor's out, why look more at old bottle?
Gulp down with gusto, you that are young,
These new Rules' ferment tastes ill in *my* throttle,
Since Justice, *in nubibus* no more on high sitter,
Descends to speak laymen's vulgar tongue.
So be it! *Explicit—parum feliciter.*

ARTHUR T. QUILLER-COUCH

EITHER in his own individuality or as "Q," Sir Arthur Quiller-Couch is too well known to need a lengthy introduction to our readers. He added lustre to a splendid college career by early winning for himself a lasting renown in literature. Many are the books which bear his name and which his readers have long ago learnt to be grateful for. Amongst them are "From a Cornish Window" (1906), and "Green Bays" (1893), two delightful books which together have furnished the following poems.

Measure for Measure

[Parody—Omar Khayyám]

WAKE! for the closed Pavilion doors have kept
    Their silence while the white-eyed Kaffir slept,
        And wailed the Nightingale with "Jug-jug-
        jug!"
Whereat, for empty cup, the White Rose wept.

Enter with me where yonder door hangs out
Its Red Triangle to a world of drought,
        Inviting to the Palace of the Djinn,
Where Death, Aladdin, waits as Chuckerout.

Methought, last night, that one in suit of woe
Stood by the Tavern door and whispered, "Lo,
        The Pledge departed, what avails the Cup?
Then take the Pledge, and let the Wine-cup go."

But I : " For every thirsty soul that drains
This Anodyne of Thought its rim contains—
    Free-will the *can*, Necessity the *must*,
Pour off the *must*, and, see, the *can* remains.

"Then, pot or glass, why label it ' With Care ' ?
Or why your Sheepskin with my Gourd compare ?
    Lo ! here the Bar and I the only Judge :—
O, Dog that bit me, I exact an hair !"

We are the Sum of things, who jot our score
With Cæsar's clay behind the Tavern door :
    And Alexander's armies—where are they,
But gone to Pot—that Pot you push for more ?

And this same Jug I empty, could it speak,
Might whisper that itself had been a Beak
    And dealt me Fourteen Days " without the Op."—
Your Worship, see, my lip is on your cheek.

Yourself condemned to three score years and ten,
Say, did you judge the ways of other men ?
    Why, now, sir, you are hourly filled with wine,
And has the clay more license now than then ?

Life is a draught, good sirs ; its brevity
Gives you and me our measures, and thereby
    Has docked your virtue to a tankard's span,
And left of my criterion—a Cri' !

ARTHUR T. QUILLER-COUCH

De Tea Fabula

[*Parody—Bret Harte*]

PLAIN LANGUAGE FROM TRUTHFUL JAMES[1]

DO I sleep? Do I dream?
　　Am I hoaxed by a scout?
Are things what they seem,
　　Or is Sophists about?
Is our τὸ τί ἦν εἶναι a failure, or is Robert Browning
　　played out?

Which expressions like these
　　May be fairly applied
By a party who sees
　　A Society skied
Upon tea that the Warden of Keble had biled with
　　legitimate pride.

'Twas November the third,
　　And I says to Bill Nye,
" Which it's true what I've heard:
　　If you're, so to speak, fly,
There's a chance of some tea and cheap culture, the sort
　　recommended as High."

[1] The Oxford Browning Society expired at Keble the week before
this was written.—Author's note.

361

Which I mentioned its name
  And he ups and remarks :
" If dress-coats is the game
  And pow-wow in the Parks,
Then I'm nuts on Sordello and Hohensteil-Schwangan and
 similar Snarks."

  Now the pride of Bill Nye
    Cannot well be express'd ;
  For he wore a white tie
    And a cut-away vest :
Says I : " Solomon's lilies ain't in it, and they was reputed
 well dress'd."

  But not far did we wend,
    When we saw Pippa pass
  On the arm of a friend
    —Doctor Furnivall 'twas,
And he wore in his hat two half-tickets for London,
 return, second-class.

  " Well," I thought, " this is odd."
    But we came pretty quick
  To a sort of a quad
    That was all of red brick,
And I says to the porter, —" R. Browning : free passes ;
 and kindly look slick."

  But says he, dripping tears
    In his check handkerchief,
  " That symposium's career's
    Been regrettably brief,
For it went all its pile upon crumpets and busted on gun-
 powder-leaf ! "

Then we tucked up the sleeves
　　Of our shirts (that were biled),
Which the reader perceives
　　That our feelings were riled,
And we went for that man till his mother had doubted
　　the traits of her child.

Which emotions like these
　　Must be freely indulged
By a party who sees
　　A Society bulged
On a reef the existence of which its prospectus had never
　　divulged.

But I ask,—Do I dream?
　　Has it gone up the spout;
Are things what they seem,
　　Or is Sophists about?
Is our τὸ τί ἦν εἶναι a failure, or is Robert Browning
　　played out?

Behold! I am not one of those that goes to Lectures

[Imitation—Walt Whitman]

BEHOLD! I am not one that goes to Lectures or to
　　the pow-wow of Professors.
The elementary laws never apologise; neither do I
　　apologise.

ARTHUR T. QUILLER-COUCH

I find letters from the Dean dropped on my table—and every one is signed by the Dean's name—

And I leave them where they are; for I know that as long as I stay up

Others will punctually come for ever and ever.

I am one who goes to the river,

I sit in the boat and think of "life" and of "time"

How life is much, but time is more: and the beginning is everything,

But the end is something.

I loll in the Parks, I go to the wicket, I swipe.

I see twenty-two young men from Foster's watching me, and the trousers of the twenty-two young men.

I see Balliol men—*en masse* watching me.—The Hottentot that loves his mother, the untutored Bedowee, the Cave-man, that wears only his certificate of baptism, and the shaggy Sioux that hangs his testamur with his scalps.

I see the Don who ploughed me in Rudiments watching me—and the wife of the Don who ploughed me in Rudiments watching me.

I see the rapport of the wicket-keeper and umpire.

I cannot see that I am out.

Oh! you Umpires!

I am not one who greatly cares for experience, soap, bull-dogs, cautions, majorities, or a graduated Income-tax,

The certainty of space, punctuation, sexes, institutions, copiousness, degrees, committees, delicatesse, or the fetters of rhym—

For none of these do I care: but least for the fetters of rhyme.

ARTHUR T. QUILLER-COUCH

Myself only I sing. Me Impeturbe! Me Prononcé!
Me progressive and the depths of me progressive,
    And the βάθος, *Anglicé* bathos
Of me chaunting to the Public the song of Simple Enumeration.

The New Ballad of Sir Patrick Spens

[Parody—Old Border Ballad]

THE King sits in Dumferline toun
        Drinking the blude-red wine :
"O wha will rear me an equilateral triangle
        Upon a given straight line ? "

O up and spake an eldern knight
        Sat at the King's right knee—
"Of a' the clerks by Granta side
        Sir Patrick bears the gree.

" 'Tis he was taught by the Tod-huntère
        Tho' not at the tod-hunting ;
Yet gif that he be given a line
        He'll do as brave a thing."

Our King has written a braid letter
        To Cambrigge or thereby
And there it found Sir Patrick Spens
        Evaluating π.

He hadna warked his quotient
        A point but barely three,
There stepped to him a little foot-page
        And louted on his knee.

365

The first word that Sir Patrick read
    "*Plus* × " was a' he said :
The neist word that Sir Patrick read
    'Twas "*plus* expenses paid."

The last word that Sir Patrick read
    The tear blinded his e'e :
"The pound I most admire is not
    In Scottish currencie."

Stately stepped he east the wa',
    And stately stepped he north ;
He fetched a compass frae his ha'
    And stood beside the Forth.

Then gurly grew the waves o' Forth
    And gurlier by-and-bye—
"O never yet was sic a storm
    Yet it isna sic as I ! "

Syne he had crossed the Firth o' Forth
    Untill Dumferline toun
And tho' he came with a kittle wame
    Fu' low he louted down.

"A line, a line, a gude straight line,
    O King, purvey me quick !
And see it be of thilka kind
    That's neither braid nor thick."

"Nor thick nor braid ? " King Jamie said,
    " I'll eat my gude hatband
If arra line as ye define
    Be found in our Scotland."

Tho' there be nane in a' thy rule
    It sall be ruled by me " ;
And lichtly with his little pencil
    He's ruled the line A B.

Stately stepped he east the wa',
    And stately stepped he west ;
" Ye touch the button," Sir Patrick said,
    " And I sall do the rest."

And he has set his compass foot
    Untill the centre A,
From A to B he's stretched it oot—
    " Ye Scottish carles, give way ! "

Syne he has moved his compass foot
    Untill the centre B,
From B to A he's stretched it oot,
    And drawn it viz-a-vee.

The ane circle was B C D,
    And A C E the tither.
" I rede ye well, " Sir Patrick said,
    " They interseck ilk ither.

" See here, and where they interseck—
    To wit with yon point C—
Ye'll just obsairve that I conneck
    The twa points A and B.

" And there ye have a little triangle
    As bonny as e'er was seen ;
The whilk is not isosceles,
    Nor yet it is scalene."

" The proof! the proof!" King Jamie cried :
   " The how and eke the why!"
Sir Patrick laughed within his beard—
   " 'Tis *ex hypothesi*—

" When I ligg'd in my mither's wame
   I learn'd it frae my mither,
That things was equal to the same
   Was equal ane to t'ither.

" Sith in the circle first I drew
   The lines B A, B C,
Be radii true, I wit to you
   The baith maun equal be.

" Likewise and in the second circle
   Whilk I drew widdershins
It is nae skaith the radii baith
   A B, A C, be twins.

" And sith of three a pair agree
   That ilk suld equal ane,
By certes they maun equal be
   Ilk unto ilk by-lane."

" Now by my faith!" King Jamie saith,
   " What *plane* geometrie!
If only Potts had written in Scots,
   How loocid Potts would be!"

" Now, wow's my life!" saith Jamie the King,
   And the Scots lords said the same,
For but it was that envious knicht
   Sir Hughie o' the Graeme.

"Flim-flam, flim-flam!" and "Ho-indeed?"
    Quod Hughie o' the Graeme;
"'Tis I could better upon my heid
    This prabblin prablem-game."

Sir Patrick Spens was nothing laith
    When as he heard "flim-flam,"
But syne he's ta'en a silken claith
    And wiped his diagram.

"Gif my small feat may better'd be,
    Sir Hew, by thy big head,
What I hae done with an A B C
    Do thou with X Y Z."

Then sairly sairly swore Sir Hew,
    And loudly laucht the King;
But Sir Patrick tuk the pipes and blew,
    And *played* that eldritch thing!

He's play'd it reel, he's play'd it jig,
    And the baith alternative;
And he's danced Sir Hew to the Asses' Brigg,
    That's Proposetion Five.

And there they've met and there they've fet,
    Forenenst the Asses' Brigg,
And waefu,' waefu' was the fate
    That gar'd them there to ligg.

For there Sir Patrick's slain Sir Hew
    And Sir Hew, Sir Patrick Spens.
Now was not that a fine to-do
    For Euclid's Elemen's?

ARTHUR T. QUILLER-COUCH

But let us sing Long live the King !
　　And his foes the Deil attend 'em :
For he has gotten his little triangle,
　　Quod erat faciendum !

A Letter

ADDRESSED during the Summer Term of 1888, by Mr. Algernon
Dexter, Scholar of —— College, Oxford, to his cousin, Miss Kitty
Tremayne, at —— Vicarage, Devonshire.

[*Imitation —W. M. Praed*]

Dear Kitty,
　　At length the term's ending ;
　　　　I'm in for my Schools in a week ;
　　And the time that at present I'm spending
　　　　On you should be spent upon Greek.
　　But I'm fairly well read in my Plato,
　　　　I'm thoroughly red in the eyes
　　And I've almost forgotten the way to
　　　　Be healthy and wealthy and wise.
　　So "the best of all ways "—why repeat you
　　　　The verse at 2.30 a.m.,
　　When I'm stealing an hour to entreat you
　　　　Dear Kitty to come to Commem. ?

　　Oh, Come !　You shall rustle in satin
　　　　Through halls where examiners trod :
　　Your laughter shall triumph o'er Latin
　　　　In lecture-room, garden, and quad.
　　They stand in the silent Sheldonian—
　　　　Our orators, waiting—for you,

Their style guaranteed Ciceronian,
    Their subject—" The Ladies in Blue."
The Vice sits arrayed in his scarlet :
      He's pale but they say he dissem-
        bles by calling his Beadle a " varlet "
Whenever he thinks of Commem.

There are dances, flirtations at Nuneham
    Flower-shows, the procession of Eights :
There's a list stretching *usque ad Lunam*
    Of concerts and lunches and fêtes :
There's the Newdigate all about Gordon,
    —So sweet, and they say it will scan :
You shall flirt with a Proctor, a Warden
    Shall run for your shawl and your fan.
They are sportive as gods broken loose from
    Olympus and yet very em-
inent men.   There are plenty to choose from,
    You'll find if you come to Commem.

I know your excuses : Red Sorrel
    Has stumbled and broken her knees ;
Aunt Phoebe thinks waltzing immoral ;
    And, " Algy you are such a tease ;
It's nonsense, of course, but she *is* strict "
    And little Dick Hodge has the croup,
And there's no one to visit your " district "
    Or make Mother Tettleby's soup.
Let them cease for a se'nnight to plague you :
    Oh, leave them to manage *pro tem.*,
With their croup and their soups and their ague,
    Dear Kitty and come to Commem.

ARTHUR T. QUILLER-COUCH

Don't tell me Papa has lumbago
    That you haven't a frock fit to wear,
That the curate " has notions and may go
    To lengths if there's nobody there,"
That the Squire has " said things " to the Vicar,
    And the Vicar " had words " with the Squire,
That the Organist's taken to liquor,
    And leaves you to manage the choir :
For Papa must be cured, and the curate
    Coerced, and your gown is a gem ;
And the moral is—Don't be obdurate,
    Dear Kitty, but come to Commem.

" My gown ? Though, no doubt, sir, you're clever,
    You'd better leave fashions alone.
Do you think that a frock lasts for ever ? "
    Dear Kitty, I'll grant you have grown ;
But I thought of my " scene " with McVittie
    That night when he trod on your train
At the Bachelors' Ball.   " 'Twas a pity,"
    You said, but I knew 'twas Champagne.
And your gown was enough to compel me
    To fall down and worship its hem—
(Are " hems " wearing ? If not, you shall tell me,
    What is, when you come to Commem.)

Have you thought, since that night, of the Grotto ?
    Of the words whispered under the palms,
While the minutes flew by and forgot to
    Remind us of Aunt and her qualms ?
Of the stairs of the old *Journalisten ?*
    Of the rose that I begged from your hair ?

ARTHUR T. QUILLER-COUCH

When you turned and I saw something glisten—
 Dear Kitty, don't frown ; it was there.
But that idiot Delane in the middle
 Bounced in with " Our dance, I —ahem ! "
And—the Rose you may find in my Liddell
 And Scott when you come to Commem.

Then Kitty, let " yes " be the answer.
 We'll dance at the 'Varsity Ball,
And the morning shall find you a dancer
 In Christ Church or Trinity Hall.
And perhaps, when the elders are yawning
 And rafters grow pale overhead
With the day, there shall come with its dawning
 Some thought of that sentence unsaid,
Be it this, be it that—" I forget or
 Was joking "—whatever the fem-
inine fib, you'll have made me your debtor
 And come,—you will come ? to Commem.

OWEN SEAMAN

No book dealing with literary humour would be complete without some specimens of the art of Mr. Owen Seaman. As the editor of *Punch* he is well known, and many are the readers of that journal whose first anxiety is to find out a certain space, usually entirely insignificant, occupied with several stanzas of verse signed O. S. And if their search is successful they are sure of their reward, for beauty of diction and great-hearted fun, or pathos, as the case may be, have never failed the pen that wrote them. Mr. Seaman has written besides many volumes of verse mostly of a humorous nature. These include "With Double Pipe" (1888), "Horace at Cambridge" (1894), "The Battle of the Bays" (1896), "In Cap and Bells" (1899), "A Harvest of Chaff" (1904), and "Salvage," published in 1908. From this rich storehouse of parody we have, with the author's permission, made the following selection.

A Nocturne at Danieli's

[*Parody—R. Browning*]

CARO *mio*, *Pulcinello*, kindly hear my wail of woe
    Lifted from a noble structure,—late Palazzo Dandolo.

This is Venice you will gather, which is full of precious
    "stones,"
Tintorettos, picture-postcards, and remains of Doges' bones.

Not of these I am complaining; they are mostly seen by
    day,
And they only try your patience in an inoffensive way.

374

But at night when over Lido rises Dian (that's the
    Moon),
And the vicious *vaporetti* cease to vex the still lagoon ;

When the final *trovatore*, singing something old and
    cheap,
Hurls his *tremolo crescendo* full against my beauty sleep ;

When I hear the Riva's loungers in debate beneath my
    bower
Summing up (about 1.30) certain questions of the hour ;

Then across my nervous system falls the shrill mosquito's
    boom
And it's " O, to be in England," where the may is on
    the bloom.

I admit the power of Music to inflate the savage breast—
There are songs devoid of language which are quite
    among the best ;

But the present orchestration with its poignant Oboe part,
Is, in my obscure opinion, barely fit to rank with Art.

Will it solace me to-morrow, being bit in either eye,
To be told that this is nothing to the season in July ?

Shall I go for help to Ruskin ? Would it ease my
    pimply brow
If I found the doges suffered much as I am suffering
    now ?

If identical probosces pinked the lovers who were bored
By the sentimental tinkling of Galuppi's clavichord?

That's from Browning (Robert Browning)—I have left
    his works at home,
And the poem I allude to isn't in the Tauchnitz tome.

But if memory serves me rightly, he was very much
    concerned
At the thought that in the sequel Venice reaped what
    Venice earned.

Was he thinking of mosquitoes? Did he mean *their*
    poisoned crop?
Was it through ammonia tincture "that the kissing had
    to stop"?

As for later loves—for Venice never quite mislaid her
    spell—
Madame Sand and dear de Musset occupied my own hotel!

On the very floor below me, I have heard the patron say,
They were put in No. 13 (No. 36 to-day).

But they parted—"*elle et lui*" did—and it now occurs
    to me
That mosquitoes came between them in this "kingdom by
    the sea."

Poor dead lovers, and such brains, too! What am I that
    I should swear
When the creatures munch my forehead, taking more
    than I can spare?

Should I live to meet the morning, should the climate
    readjust
Any reparable fragments left upon my outer crust,

Why, at least I still am extant, and a dog that sees the sun
Has the pull of Danieli's den of " lions," dead and done.

Courage ! I will keep my vigil on the balcony till day
Like a knight in full pyjamas who would rather run away.

Courage ! let me ope the casement, let the shutters be
    withdrawn ;
Let Sirocco, breathing on me, check a tendency to yawn.
There's the sea ! and—*Ecco l'alba !* Ha ! (in other
    words) the Dawn !

A Birthday Ode to Mr. Alfred Austin

[*Parody—A. Austin*]

I

THE early bird got up and whet his beak ;
    The early worm arose, an easy prey ;
This happened any morning in the week,
        Much as to-day.

II

The moke uplift for joy his hinder hoof ;
    Shivered the fancy poodle, freshly shorn ;
The prodigal upon the attic roof
        Mewed to the morn.

377

III

His virile note the cock profusely blew ;
    The beetle trotted down the kitchen tong ;
The early bird above alluded to
        Was going strong.

IV

All this of course refers to England's isle,
    But things were going on across the deep ;
In Egypt—take a case—the crocodile
        Was sound asleep

V

Buzzed the Hymettian bee ; sat up in bed
    The foreign oyster sipping local drains ;
The impious cassowary lay like lead
        On Afric's plains.

VI

A-nutting went the nimble chimpanzee ;—
    And what, you ask me, am I driving at ?
Wait on : in less than twenty minutes we
        Shall come to that.

VII

The bulbous crowfoot drained his dewy cup ;
    The saxifrage enjoyed a morning crawl ;
The ampelopsis slowly sidled up
        The garden wall.

VIII

Her petals wide the periwinkle flung ;
  Blue gentian winked upon unweanéd lambs ;
And there was quite a pleasant stir among
    The cryptogams.

IX

May was the month alike in croft and wild
  When—here, in fact, begins the actual tale—
When forth withal there came an infant child,
    A healthy male.

X

Marred was his ruby countenance, as when
  A blushing peony is moist with rain ;
And first he strenuously kicked, and then
    He kicked again.

XI

They put the bays upon his barren crest,
  Laid on his lap a lexicon of rhyme,
Saying—" You shall with luck attain the quest
    In course of time."

XII

Stolid he gazed, as one that may not know
  The meaning of a presage—or is bored ;
But when he loosed his lips it was as though
    The sea that roared.

XIII

That dreadful summons to a higher place
  He would not, if he could, have spurned away;
But, being a babe, he had, in any case,
      Nothing to say.

XIV

So they continued—" Yes, on you shall fall
  The laurels; you shall clamber by and bye
Where Southey sits, where lately sat withal
      The Poet Pye.

XV

"As yet you are not equal to the task;
  A sense of euphony you still must lack;
Nor could you do your duty by the cask
      Of yearly sack.

XVI

"Just now, withal (that's twice we've said ' withal ')
  The place is filled by someone sitting there;
Yet poets pass; he, too, will leave his stall
      And go elsewhere.

XVII

"Meanwhile, to trust you with a pointed pen,
  Dear babe, would manifestly be absurd;
Besides all well-conducted little men
      Are seen, not heard.

OWEN SEAMAN

XVIII

"First, how to tutor your prehensile mind
   Shall be the object of our deep concern;
We'll teach you grammar; *grammar, you will find,*
     Takes years to learn.

XIX

"'Twixt—mark the pretty word—'twixt boy and man
   You shall collate from every source that's known
A blended style; which may be better than
     One of your own.

XX

"Your classic mould shall be completely mixed
   Of Rome's robustness and the grace of Greece;
And you shall be a Tory, planted 'twixt
     Plenty and peace.

XXI

"And lo! we call you Alfred! Kinglihood
   Lies in the name of Him, the Good and Great!
You may not rise to greatness; O be good
     At any rate!"

XXII

Eight happy summers passed and Southey too,
   And one that had the pull in point of age
Walked in; for Alfred still was struggling through
     The grammar-stage.

OWEN SEAMAN

XXIII

When William followed out in Robert's wake,
   An alien Alfred filled the vacant spot,
Possibly by some clerical mistake,
      Possibly not.

XXIV

Our friend had then achieved but fifteen years,
   Nor yet against him was there aught to quote ;
For he had uttered in the nation's ears
      Not half a note.

XXV

Adult, no more he dreamed the laurel-wreath,
   But wandered, being credentialled to the Bar,
There where the Northern Circuit wheels beneath
      The polar star.

XXVI

One day, asleep in Court, Apollo's crown
   All in a briefless moment his he saw ;
Then cast his interloping wig adown
      And dropped the Law.

XXVII

Henceforth with loyal pen he laboured for
   His England (situated on the main) ;
Wrote in the tragic, or satiric, or
      Some other vein.

OWEN SEAMAN

XXVIII

At forty-one he let his feelings go :—
   " If he, that other Alfred, ever die,
And I am not appointed, I will know
     The reason why ! "

XXIX

Some sixteen further autumns bound their sheaves ;
   With hope deferred wild battle he had waged,
And written books.   At last the laurel-leaves
     Were disengaged.

XXX

Felicitations, bursting through his bowers,
   Came on him hoeing roots.   With mild surprise,
" Leave me alone," he said, " among my flowers
     To botanise."

XXXI

The Prime Elector, Man of Many Days,
   Though Allan's[1] Muse adorned the Liberal side,
Seizing the swift occasion, left the bays
     Unoccupied.

XXXII

The Peer that followed, having some regard
   For humour hitherto accounted sin,
Produced a knighthood for the blameless bard
     Of proud Penbryn.

[1] Radical member for Gateshead.

OWEN SEAMAN

XXXIII

At length a callous Tory Chief arose,
　　Master of caustic jest and cynic gibe,
Looked round the Carlton Club and lightly chose
　　　　Its leading scribe.

XXXIV

And so with heaving heart and happy tears
　　Our patient Alfred took the tardy spoil,
Though spent with sixty venerable years
　　　　Of virtuous toil.

XXXV

And ever, when marsh-marigolds are cheap
　　And new potatoes crown the death of May,
If memory serve us, we propose to keep
　　　　His natal day.

The Yellow Shin-Pads

[Parody—William Morris]

A PAIR of leggings, largest size,
　　I wore to-day with bloomer guise,
And won the local Hockey Prize.
　　　　Hah! Hah! les belles jaunes jambières!

Your hands had tied them on for me,
Fair Lord, and righteous referee,
Above my crushers, daintily.
　　　　Hah! Hah! les belles jaunes jambières!

However hard Miss Jones might hit,
Though on my legs the missile lit
I felt it not one little bit.

> *Hah! Hah! les belles jaunes jambières!*

And when my stick in fragments flew,
Bringing to earth their only Blue,
I smiled aloud and looked at you.

> *Hah! Hah! les belles jaunes jambières!*

But ere her ribs had ceased to shake
I took another stick and brake
Her livid thumb for my Love's sake.

> *Hah! Hah! les belles jaunes jambières!*

I reached the goal; in ruthless wise
I caught the warder 'twixt the eyes
And so achieved to equalise.

> *Hah! Hah! les belles jaunes jambières!*

Much heated, I began to think
That I should prematurely sink
For need of just another drink.

> *Hah! Hah! les belles jaunes jambières!*

And then I thought of your dear knee
Bent as you bound my pads for me
Above my crushers daintily.

> *Hah! Hah! les belles jaunes jambières!*

2 C

OWEN SEAMAN

Whew ! how the meeting sticks went whack !
Yea, o'er the field I heard the crack
Of stitches giving down the back.

Hah ! Hah ! les belles jaunes jambières !

One minute still !   My teeth were set ;
I and the stout custodian met ;
The ball (and she) went through the net !

Hah ! Hah ! les belles jaunes jambières !

My golden hair was getting loose
Yet fell I out on that excuse ?
Not so : I dribbled like the deuce.

Hah ! Hah ! les belles jaunes jambières !

And when the half-fought fight was stayed
I scorned the lemon's feeble aid
And quaffed a gin-and-gingerade.

Hah ! Hah ! les belles jaunes jambières !

Then like a fiery steed in stall
I scarce could wait the whistler's call,
But chafed to be upon the ball.

Hah ! Hah ! les belles jaunes jambières !

Miss Brown (of Bucks) against me drew ;
She wore a skirt of purple hue ;
Our score was one and theirs was two.

Hah ! Hah ! les belles jaunes jambières !

OWEN SEAMAN

Red-cheeked I charged this bounding half,
And as I hooked her by the calf
I heard your low elusive laugh.

Hah! Hah! les belles jaunes jambières!

And as with face profusely hot
(*Les belles! les belles!*) I faltered not
But reached and took the challenge-pot,

Hah! Hah! les belles jaunes jambières!

I say again your supple knee
Bent as you bound my pads for me,
My yellow shin-pads, daintily.

Hah! Hah! les belles jaunes jambières!

HORATIO SMITH

Mr. Horatio Smith is another member of the legal profession who is well known in the world of letters. His more serious work includes the editing of a number of treatises on the law; but it is to his volumes of lighter verse that we owe the following parodies. He first published a book of poems in 1860, and from that time onward until the fifth series of "Interludes" appeared in 1910 he has at intervals brought to the press small but delightful volumes of his collected essays and poems. "At the Cock Tavern" and "An Attempt to Remember the 'Grandmother's Apology,'" appeared in the first series of "Interludes," and the parodies of William Watson and Shakespeare in the 1890 edition of this author's "Poems."

They and We

[Imitation—W. Watson]

WITH stormy joy the elephant
 Will bolt a thousand buns;
The cassowary grim and gaunt
 Will swallow stones by tons;
Man only, after dining out,
 By intermittent throes,
Either in fingers finds the gout
 Or finds it in his toes.

HORATIO SMITH

The Curate to his Slippers

[Parody—Shakespeare]

TAKE, oh take those boots away,
        That so nearly are outworn;
And those shoes remove, I pray—
        Pumps that but induce the corn!
But my slippers bring again,
                Bring again;
Works of love, but worked in vain,
                Worked in vain!

An Attempt to Remember the " Grandmother's Apology "

[Parody—Tennyson]

AND Willie, my eldest born, is gone, you say, little
        Anne?
Ruddy and white, and strong on his legs, he looks like a
        man;
He was only fourscore years, quite young, when he died;
I ought to have gone before, but must wait for time and
        tide.

So Harry's wife has written; she was always an awful fool,
And Charlie was always drunk, which made our families
cool;
For Willie was walking with Jenny when the moon
came up the dale,
And whit, whit, whit, in the bush beside me chirrupt the
nightingale.

Jenny I know had tripped, and she knew that I knew of
it well.
She began to slander me.   I knew, but I wouldn't tell!
And she to be slandering me, the impertinent, base little
liar;
But the tongue is a fire, as you know my dear, the tongue
is a fire.

And the parson made it his text last week; and he said
likewise,
That a lie which is half a truth is ever the blackest of lies;
That a downright hearty good falsehood doesn't so very
much matter,
But a lie which is half a truth is worse than one which is
fatter.

Then Willie and Jenny turned in the sweet moonshine,
And he said to me through his tears, "Let your good
name be mine,
And what do I care for Jane?"   She was never over-
wise,
Never the wife for Willie; thank God that I keep my
eyes.

"Marry you, Willie!" said I, and I thought my heart
would break,
"But a man cannot marry his grandmother, so there must
be some mistake."
But he turned and clasped me in his arms and answered,
"No, love, no,
Seventy years ago, my darling, seventy years ago!"

So Willie and I were wedded, though clearly against the
law,
And the ringers rang with a will, and Willie's gloves were
straw ;
But the first that ever I bare was dead before it was born—
For Willie I cannot weep, life is flower and thorn.

Pattering over the boards, my Annie, an Annie like you,
Pattering over the boards, and Charlie and Harry too,
Pattering over the boards of our beautiful little cot,
And I'm not exactly certain whether they died or not.

And yet I know of a truth, there is none of them left
alive,
For Willie went at eighty, and Harry at ninety-five ?
And Charlie at threescore years, aye ! or more than that
I'll be sworn,
And that very remarkable infant that died before it was
born.

So Willie has gone, my beauty, the eldest that bears the
name,
It's a soothing thought—"In a hundred years 'twill be
all the same."

"Here's a leg for a babe of a week," says doctor, in some
 surprise,
But fetch me my glasses, Annie, I'm thankful I keep
 my eyes.

At the " Cock " Tavern

[*Parody—Lovelace*]

CHAMPAGNE doth not a Luncheon make
 Nor caviare a meal ;
Men gluttonous and rich may take
 These till they make them ill.
If I've potatoes to my chop,
 And after that have cheese,
Angels in Pond and Spiers's shop
 Serve no such luxuries.

APPENDIX

Specimens from the poets and the original poems parodied in the foregoing selection.

MATTHEW ARNOLD
1822–1888

Not here, O Apollo !
Are haunts meet for thee.
But where Helicon breaks down
In cliff to the sea.

The Song of Callicles.

See E. V. Knox.—*Redford Musagelis*, p. 337.

ELIZABETH BARRETT BROWNING
1806–1861

Love me, Sweet, with all thine art
Feeling, thinking, seeing ;
Love me in the lightest part,
Love me in full being.

A Man's Requirements.

See Rhode Knight—*A Man's Requirements*, p. 333.

ROBERT BROWNING
1812–1889

O Galuppi Baldassaro, you are very hard to please.

A Toccata of Galuppi.

Several imitations of this author have been given in this book which are sufficiently distinctive to suggest certain typical poems. The imitations of Sir Frederick Pollock and Calverley deserve

APPENDIX

comparison with *Fra Lippo Lippi* in " *Men and Women.*" Bayard
Taylor in " *Mutatis Mutandis*" is very close to Browning's
" *Mesmerism*" ; and J. K. Stephen in " *Of R. B.*" has approached
very nearly the style and diction of " *A Light Woman.*"

See Owen Seaman—*A Nocturne at Danieli's*, p. 374.

BORDER BALLADS

THE King sits in Dumferline toune,
  Drinking the blude-reid wine :
O quhar will I get guid sailor,
  To sail this schip of mine ?

Up and spak an eldern knicht,
  Sat at the king's richt kne :
Sir Patrick Spence is the best sailor
  That sails upon the se.

The Ballad of Sir Patrick Spens.

See A. T. Quiller-Couch—*The New Ballad of Sir Patrick Spens*, p. 365.

WILLIAM CULLEN BRYANT

1794–1878

THE Summer day is closed—the sun is set,
Well have they done their office those bright hours,
The latest of whose train goes softly out
In the red West.   The green blade of the ground
Has risen and herbs have cropped it : the young twig
Has spread its plaited tissues to the sun ;
Flowers of the garden and the waste have blown
And withered : . . .
                    And as I lean
Amid the thickening darkness lamps are lit. . . .

An Evening Revery (from an unfinished poem).

See Oliver Wendell Holmes—*Evening.—By a Tailor*, p. 215.

APPENDIX

ROBERT BURNS

1759–1796

Is there for honest poverty,
    That hangs his head, and a' that !
The coward slave, we pass him by,
    And dare be poor for a' that.
For a' that, and a' that ;
    Our toils obscure, and a' that ;
The rank is but the guinea-stamp,
    The man's the gowd for a' that.

Song.

See Shirley Brooks—*More Luck to Honest Poverty,* p. 182.

THOMAS CAMPBELL

1777–1844

.   .

A CHIEFTAIN to the Highlands bound
    Cries, " Boatman, do not tarry !
And I'll give thee a silver pound,
    To row us o'er the ferry."

.   .

" Come back, come back !" He cried in grief,
    Across the stormy water :
" And I'll forgive yon Highland Chief,
    My daughter !—Oh my daughter !"

Lord Ullin's Daughter.

See Oliver Wendell Holmes—*The September Gale,* p. 217.

APPENDIX

WILLIAM COWPER
1731–1800

THE twentieth year is well nigh past
Since first our sky was overcast ;
Ah ! would that this might be our last !
$\qquad$ My Mary !

.   .   .   .

But well thou play'dst the housewife's part.
And all thy threads with magic art
Have wound themselves about this heart,
$\qquad$ My Mary !

To Mary.[1]

See Lord Byron—*To Mr. Murray*, p. 7.

AUSTIN DOBSON

CHICKEN-SKIN, delicate, white,
 Painted by Carlo Vanloo, etc.

Ballade on The Pompadour's Fan.

See Rhode Knight—*The Ballade of the Matinée Hat*, p. 335.

SIR POET, ere you crossed the lawn
 (If it was wrong to watch you, pardon,)
Behind this weeping birch withdrawn,
 I watched you saunter round the garden.
I saw you bend beside the phlox,
 Pluck, as you passed, a sprig of myrtle,
Review my well-ranged hollyhocks,
 Smile at the fountain's slender spurtle.

A Garden Idyll.

See Henry Duff Traill—*Vers de Société*.

[1] It is possible that Miss Ann Taylor derived her inspiration of her celebrated poem " *My Mother* " from these verses of Cowper, and that Byron had the more sentimental and popular lines in his mind when he wrote his parody. On the other hand, " *My Murray* " is a closer approximation to " *My Mary* " than the later poem.

APPENDIX

JOHN DRYDEN

1631-1700

Sublime on radiant spires he rode
When he to fair Olympia prest,
And while he sought her snowy breast,
Then round her slender waist he curl'd,
And stamp'd an image of himself, a sovereign of the world.
—The listening crowd admire the lofty sound ;
A present deity ; they shout around :
A present deity ! the vaulted roofs rebound :
With ravish'd ears
The monarch hears,
Assumes the god ;
Affects to nod
And seems to shake the spheres.

Alexander s Feast.

See The Rolliad, p. 92.

THOMAS GRAY

1716-1771

I

'Twas on a lofty vase's side,
Where China's gayest art had dyed
The azure flowers that blow,
Demurest of the tabby kind
The pensive Selima, reclined,
Gazed on the lake below.

On a Favourite College Cat, drowned in a Tub of Gold Fishes.

See Sir Frederick Pollock's *Ode on the Death of a College Cat,* p. 353.

1 It should be noted, however, that this author has parodied the style of eighteenth-century versification and has rather taken his subject from Gray's poem.

APPENDIX

II

YE distant spires, ye antique towers
   That crown the watery glade,
Where grateful Science still adores
   Her Henry's holy shade ;
And ye, that from the stately brow
Of Windsor's heights th' expanse below
   Of grove, of lawn, of mead survey,
Whose turf, whose shade, whose flowers among
Wanders the hoary Thames along
   His silver-winding way :

Ode on a Distant Prospect of Eton College.

See **Thomas Hood** (the Elder)—*Ode on a Distant Prospect of Clapham Academy*, p.48.
   Also **James Kenneth Stephen**—*Retrospect of Eton College*, p. 268.

III

THE curfew tolls the knell of parting day,
The lowing herd wind slowly o'er the lea,
The ploughman homeward plods his weary way,
And leaves the world to darkness and to me.

Elegy written in a Country Churchyard.

See **Horace Smith**—*Evening*, p. 123.

FRANCIS BRET HARTE

1839–1902

WHICH I wish to remark,—
   And my language is plain,—
That for ways that are dark
   And for tricks that are vain,
The heathen Chinee is peculiar.
   Which the same I would rise to explain.

Plain Language from Truthful James.

See *The Shotover Papers*—*Truthful James Again*, p. 261.
Also **Arthur Clement Hilton**—*The Heathen Pass-ee*, p. 243.

APPENDIX

W. E. HENLEY

1849–1903

Scherzando.

Down through the ancient Strand
The spirit of October, mild and boon
And sauntering, takes her way
This golden end of afternoon,
As though the corn stood yellow in all the land,
And the ripe apples dropped to the harvest-moon.

London Voluntaries, iii.

See Anthony C. Deane—*Humpty-Dumpty*, p. 324.

ROBERT HERRICK

1591–1674

Whenas in silk my Julia goes,
With what a sweet contentment flows
The liquefaction of her clothes.

See E. V. Knox—*Julia's Clothes,* p. 339.

JEAN INGELOW

1820–1897

An empty sky, a world of heather,
   Purple of foxglove, yellow of broom ;
We two among them wading together
   Shaking out honey, treading perfume.

Crowds of bees are giddy with clover,
   Crowds of grasshoppers skip at our feet,
Crowds of larks at their matins hang over,
   Thanking the Lord for a life so sweet.

Divided.

See Bayard Taylor—*The Shrimp-Gatherers,* p. 275.

APPENDIX

JOHN KEATS

1795–1821

THOU still unravish'd bride of quietness,
  Thou foster-child of silence and slow time,
Sylvan historian, who canst thus express
  A flowery tale more sweetly than our rhyme :
What leaf-fringed legend haunts about thy shape
  Of deities or mortals, or of both,
    In Tempé or the dales of Arcady ?
What men or gods are these ?   What maidens loth ?
  What mad pursuit ?   What struggle to escape ?
    What pipes and timbrels ?   What wild ecstasy ?

Ode on a Grecian Urn.

See Bayard Taylor—*Ode to a Jar of Pickles*, p. 278.

RUDYARD KIPLING

HEH !   Walk her round.   Heave, ah heave her short again !
Over, snatch her over, there, and hold her on the pawl ;
Loose all sail and brace your yards aback and full—
Ready jib to pay her off and heave short all !

Anchor Song from *Many Inventions.*

See Anthony C. Deane—*Jack and Jill*, p. 320.

THE 'eathen in 'is blindness bows down to wood an' stone ;
'E don't obey no orders unless they is 'is own ;
'E keeps 'is side-arms awful : 'e leaves 'em all about,
An' then comes up the regiment an' pokes the 'eathen out.

All along o' dirtiness, all along o' mess,
All along o' doing things rather-more-or-less,

APPENDIX

All along of abby-nay kul, an' hazar-ho,
Mind you keep your rifle an' yourself just so.

The 'Eathen.

See Mostyn T. Pigott—*Punts*, p. 347.

Both these quotations from Mr. Kipling's poems are intended to
illustrate the style of the author, for both these parodists have
reproduced the mannerisms of their original rather than the type of
his poetry.

CHARLES LAMB

1775–1834

.   .   .   .

PAST midnight this poor Maid hath spun,
And yet the work is not half done,
Which must supply from earnings scant
A feeble bed-rid parent's want.
Her sleep-charged eyes exemption ask,
And Holy hands take up the task :
Unseen the rock and spindle ply,
And do her earthly drudgery.
Sleep, saintly poor one, sleep, sleep on ;
And, waking, find thy labours done.

.   .   .   .

Gardener bright from Eden's bower,
Tend with care that lily-flower,
To its leaves and roots infuse
Heaven's sunshine, Heaven's dews.
'Tis a type, and 'tis a pledge,
Of a crowning privilege.

Angel Help.

See Charles Lamb—*Nonsense Verses*, p. 58.

APPENDIX

HENRY WADSWORTH LONGFELLOW

1807–1882

I

Speak ! speak ! thou fearful guest !
Who, with thy hollow breast
Still in rude armour drest,
        Comest to daunt me !
Wrapt not in Eastern balms,
But with thy fleshless palms
Stretched as if asking alms,
        Why dost thou haunt me ?

The Skeleton in Armour.

See Charles Stuart Calverley—*Ode to Tobacco*, p. 194.

II

Should you ask me, whence these legends ?
Whence these stories and traditions,
With the odours of the forest,
With the dew and damp of meadows,
With the curling smoke of wigwams,
With the rushing of great rivers,
With their frequent repetitions,
With their wild reverberations,
As of thunder in the mountains ?
    I should answer, I should tell you,
" From the forests and the prairies,
From the great lakes of the Northland,
From the land of the Ojibways,
From the land of the Dacotahs,
From the mountains, moors and fenlands,
Where the heron, the Shuh-shuh-gah,
Feeds among the reeds and rushes."

Hiawatha.

See Shirley Brooks—*Hiawatha*, p. 178.

APPENDIX

III

THE shades of night were falling fast,
As through an Alpine village passed
A youth who bore, 'mid snow and ice,
A banner with the strange device
　　　　Excelsior.

See Chas. G. Leland—*Top-side Galow*, p. 235.　　　　*Excelsior.*

RICHARD LOVELACE

1618–1658

STONE walls do not a prison make,
　　Nor iron bars a cage ;
Minds innocent and quiet take
　　That for an hermitage ;
If I have freedom in my love
　　And in my soul am free,
Angels alone, that soar above,
　　Enjoy such liberty.

To Althea from Prison.

See Horatio Smith—*At the " Cock " Tavern*, p. 392.

JOHN MILTON

1608–1674

HENCE, loathéd Melancholy,
　　Of Cerberus and blackest Midnight born,
In Stygian cave forlorn,
　　'Mongst horrid shapes, and shrieks, and sights unholy,
Find out some uncouth cell,
　　Where brooding Darkness spreads his jealous wings,
　　And the night-raven sings ;
　　There under ebon shades, and low-brow'd rocks
　As ragged as thy locks,
　　In dark Cimmerian desert ever dwell.

See Horace Twiss—*Fashion*, p. 146.　　　　*L'Allegro.*

APPENDIX

THOMAS MOORE
1780–1852

I

WHEN he who adores thee has left but the name
    Of his fault and his sorrows behind,
Oh ! say wilt thou weep, when they darken the fame
    Of a life that for thee was resign'd ?
Yes, weep, and however my foes may condemn,
    Thy tears shall efface their decree ;
For, Heaven can witness, though guilty to them,
    I have been but too faithful to thee.

Pro Patri Moria.

See William Maginn—*To a Bottle of Old Port*, p. 73.

II

LESBIA hath a beaming eye,
    But no one knows for whom it beameth ;
Right and left its arrows fly,
    But what they aim at no one dreameth.
Sweeter 'tis to gaze upon
    My Nora's lid that seldom rises ;
Few its looks, but every one
    Like unexpected light surprises.
O my Nora Creina, dear,
    My gentle, bashful Nora Creina,
        Beauty lies
        In many eyes,
But love in yours, my Nora Creina !

See Charles Dickens—*New Song*, p. 213.

THERE is not in the wide world a valley so sweet,
    As that vale in whose bosom the bright waters meet ;
Oh ! the last ray of feeling and life must depart,
    Ere the bloom of that valley shall fade from my heart.

The Meeting of the Waters.

See Phoebe Cary—*There's a Bower of Bean-Vines*, p. 209.

APPENDIX

ALFRED NOYES

So on a misty grey December morn
Five ships put out from calm old Plymouth Sound ;
Five little ships, the largest not so large
As many a coasting yacht or fishing trawl
To-day ; yet these must brave uncharted seas
Of unimagined terrors, haunted glooms,
And shadowy horrors of an unknown world
Wild as primæval chaos.   In the first,
The *Golden Hynde*, a ship of eighteen guns,
Drake sailed : John Wynter, a queen's captain, next
Brought out the *Elizabeth*, a stout new ship of sixteen guns.

Drake, an English Epic, Book ii.

See Wilfrid Blair—*The Noyes of Battle*, p. 309.

AMBROSE PHILIPS

1679–1743

Timely blossom, Infant fair,
Fondling of a happy pair,
Every morn and every night
Their solicitous delight,
Sleeping, waking, still at ease,
Pleasing, without skill to please ;
Little gossip, blithe and hale,
Tattling many a broken tale,
Singing many a tuneless song,
Lavish of a heedless tongue ;
Simple maiden, void of art,
Babbling out the very heart.

To Charlotte Pulteney.

See Henry Carey—*Namby-Pamby*, p. 10.

APPENDIX

EDGAR ALLAN POE

1809–1849

I

IT was many a year ago,
   In a kingdom by the sea,
That a maiden there lived whom you may know
   By the name of Annabel Lee ;
And this maiden she lived with no other thought
   Than to love and be loved by me.

                     Annabel Lee.

See Robert F. Murray—*Andrew M'Crie*, p. 257.

II

ONCE upon a midnight dreary, while I pondered, weak and weary,
Over many a quaint and curious volume of forgotten lore,—
While I nodded, nearly napping, suddenly there came a tapping,
As of some one gently rapping, rapping at my chamber door.
" 'Tis some visitor," I muttered, " tapping at my chamber door,—
      Only this and nothing more."

                     The Raven.

See Robert Brough—*The Vulture*, p. 161.
Also Henry S. Leigh—*Châteaux d'Espagne*, p. 232.

III

THE skies they were ashen and sober ;
   The leaves they were crisped and sere,—
   The leaves they were withering and sere ;—
It was night in the lonesome October
   Of my most immemorial year ;
It was hard by the dim lake of Auber,
   In the misty mid region of Weir,—
It was down by the dank tarn of Auber,
   In the ghoul-haunted woodland of Weir.

                     Ulalume.

See Bret Harte—*The Willows*, p. 173.
Also Bayard Taylor—*The Promissory Note*, p. 286.

APPENDIX

JAMES WHITCOMB RILEY

"O, HENRY, Afrite-Chef of all delight !
Of all delectables conglomerate
That stay the starved brain and rejuvenate
The Mental Man : the æsthetic appetite—
So long enhungered that the 'inards' fight
And growl gutwise—its pangs thou dost abate
And all so amiably alleviate,
Joy pats its belly as a hobo might,
Who haply hath obtained a cherry pie
With no burnt crust nor no seeds in it,
Nothin' but crisp crust, and thickness of it,
And squashing-juicy, an' jes' mighty nigh
To dratted drippin'—sweet for human needs,
But for the sosh o' milk that goes with it."

See O. Henry—*Options*, p. 329.

DANTE GABRIEL ROSSETTI

1828–1882

WITHIN the window's heaped recess
    The light was counterchanged
In blent reflexes manifold
From perfume-caskets of wrought gold
    And gems the bride's hair could not hold.

See Bayard Taylor—*Cimabuella*, p. 281.   *The Bride's Prelude.*

"WHY did you melt your waxen man,
                Sister Helen ?
To-day is the third since you began."
"The time was long, yet the time ran,
                Little brother."
        (O Mother, Mary Mother,
Three days to-day, between Hell and Heaven !)
See H. D. Traill—*After Dilettante Concetti*, p. 293.   *Sister Helen.*

APPENDIX

NICHOLAS ROWE
1674–1718

DESPAIRING beside a clear stream,
  A shepherd forsaken was laid ;
And while a false nymph was his theme,
  A willow supported his head :
The wind that blew over the plain,
  To his sighs with a sigh did reply,
And the brook, in return for his pain,
  Ran mournfully murmuring by.

Colin's Complaint.

See George Canning's *The Elderly Gentleman*, p. 14.

WILLIAM SHAKESPEARE
1564–1616

TAKE, O take those lips away
  That so sweetly were forsworn,
And those eyes, the break of day,
  Lights that do mislead the morn :
  But my kisses bring again,
        Bring again—
  Seals of love, but seal'd in vain,
        Seal'd in vain !

Frustra.

See Horatio Smith — *The Curate to his Slippers*, p. 389.

ALL the world's a stage,
And all the men and women merely players ;
They have their exits and their entrances ;
And one man in his time plays many parts,
His acts being seven ages.

As You Like It.

See Horace Twiss — *The Patriot's Progress*, p. 146.

APPENDIX

Oberon. That very time I saw (but thou could'st not),
Flying between the cold moon and the earth,
Cupid all armed : a certain aim he took
At a fair vestal thronèd by the west ;
And loosed his love-shaft smartly from his bow,
As it should pierce a hundred thousand hearts :
But I might see young Cupid's fiery shaft
Quench'd in the chaste beams of the watery moon,
And the imperial votaress passed on,
In maiden meditation, fancy-free !

Midsummer Night's Dream, Act ii. Sc. ii.

See Phoebe Cary. Parody—*Shakespeare*, p. 208

ROBERT SOUTHEY

1774–1843

For thirty years secluded from mankind
Here Marten lingereth.   Often have these walls
Echoed his footsteps as with even tread
He paced around his prison ; not to him
Did Nature's fair varieties exist,
He never saw the sun's delightful beams,
Save when through yon high bars he poured a sad
And broken splendour.   Dost thou ask his crime ?
HE HAD REBELLED AGAINST THE KING, AND SAT
IN JUDGEMENT ON HIM ; for his ardent mind
Shap'd goodliest plans of liberty on earth
And peace and liberty.   Wild dreams ! but such
As Plato loved ; such as with holy zeal
Our Milton worshippèd.   Blessed hopes !   Awhile
From men withheld, even to the latter day
When Christ shall come and all things be fulfilled.

*Inscription for the apartment in Chepstow Castle where
Henry Marten, the regicide, was imprisoned.*

See George Canning's Sonnet on *Mrs. Brownrigg*, p. 17.

APPENDIX

Weary way-wanderer, languid and sick at heart,
Travelling painfully over the rugged road ;
Wild-visaged wanderer !   Ah ! for thy heavy chance !

Dactylics.

See George Canning's *The Soldier's Wife.*

Cold was the night wind ; drifting fast the snow fell ;
Wide were the downs, and shelterless and naked ;
When a poor wanderer struggled on her journey,
Weary and way-sore.

.   .   .   .   .

Then on the snow she laid her down to rest her ;
She heard a horseman : " Pity me ! " she groaned out,
Loud was the wind, unheard was her complaining ;
On went the horseman.

See George Canning's *The Friend of Humanity and the Knife-Grinder.*
Also Lewis Carroll—*You're old, Father William.*
Also Mostyn T. Pigott—*You're young, Kaiser William.*

EDMUND SPENSER

Circa 1552–1599

A gentle knight was pricking on the plain,
Ycladd in mightie armes and silver shielde,
Wherein old dints of deepe woundes did remaine,
The cruel markes of many a bloody fielde ;
Yet armes till that time did he never wield :
His angry steede did chide his foming bitt,
As much disdayning to the curbe to yield :
Full iolly knight he seemed and faire did sitt,
As one for knightly giusts and fierce encounters fitt

See John Keats—*A Portrait,* p. 56.
Also Bret Harte—*North Beach,* p. 176.

APPENDIX

ALGERNON CHARLES SWINBURNE
1837–1909

I

If you were queen of pleasures,
    And I were king of pain,
We'd hunt down love together,
Pluck out his flying-feather,
And teach his feet a measure
    And find his mouth a rein ;
If you were queen of pleasure,
    And I were king of pain.

A Match.

See Thomas Hood (the Younger)—*A Catch.*

Cold eyelids that hide like a jewel
    Hard eyes that grow soft for an hour :
The heavy white limbs and the cruel
    Red mouth like a venomous flower ;
When these are gone by with their glories,
    What shall rest of thee then, what remain,
        O mystic and sombre Dolores
            Our Lady of Pain ?

Dolores.

See Arthur Clement Hilton—*Octopus.*

Ere frost-flower and snow-blossom faded and fell
    and the splendour of winter had passed out of sight,
The ways of the woodlands were fairer and stranger
    than dreams that fulfil us in sleep with delight ;
The breath of the mouths of the winds had hardened
    on tree-tops and branches that glittered and swayed,
Such wonders and glories of blossom-like snow or of
    frost that out-lightens all flowers till it fade.

March.   An Ode (1887).

See Algernon Charles Swinburne—*Nephelidia*, p. 271.

411

APPENDIX

ALFRED, LORD TENNYSON

1809–1892

I

Below the thunders of the upper deep ;
Far, far beneath in the abysmal sea,
His ancient, dreamless, uninvaded sleep
The Kraken sleepeth : faintest sunlights flee
About his shadowy sides : above him swell
Huge sponges of millennial growth and height ;
And far away into the sickly light,
From many a wondrous grot and secret cell
Unnumber'd and enormous polypi
Winnow with giant arms the slumbering green.
There hath he lain for ages and will lie
Battening upon huge seaworms in his sleep,
Until the latter fire shall heat the deep,
Then once by man and angels to be seen,
In roaring he shall rise and on the surface die.

The Kraken.

See D. G. Rossetti—*MacCracken,* p. 259.

II

And Willy, my eldest-born, is gone, you say, little Anne ?
Ruddy and white, and strong on his legs, he looks like a man.
And Willy's wife has written : she never was over-wise,
Never the wife for Willy ; he wouldn't take my advice.

The Grandmother.

See Horatio Smith—*An Attempt to Remember the " Grandmother's Apology,"* p. 389.

III

Nightingales warbled without,
Within was weeping for thee :
Shadows of three dead men

APPENDIX

Walk'd in the walks with me,
Shadows of three dead men and thou wast one of the three.

In the Garden at Swainston.

See *Shotover Papers—In the Schools at Oxford*, p. 262.

IV

I HELD it truth with him who sings
  To one clear harp in divers tones,
  That men may rise on stepping stones
Of their dead selves to higher things.

In Memoriam.

See E. B. V. Christian—*Frost v. Knight*, p. 315.

V

I COME from haunts of coot and hern,
  I make a sudden sally,
And sparkle out among the fern,
  To bicker down the valley.

The Brook.

See Mostyn T. Pigott—*The Boy on One Roller-Skate*, p. 349.

VI

THEN I remember'd one myself had made,
What time I watch'd the swallow winging south
From mine own land, part made long since and part
Now while I sang, and maidenlike as far
As I could ape their treble, did I sing.
"O Swallow, swallow, flying, flying South,
Fly to her, and fall upon her gilded eaves,
And tell her, tell her, what I tell to thee."

The Princess.

See R. F. Murray—*A Tennysonian Fragment*, p. 255.

413

APPENDIX

VII

So all day long the noise of battle roll'd
Among the mountains by the winter sea;
Until King Arthur's table, man by man,
Had fallen in Lyonesse about their Lord
King Arthur: then because his wound was deep,
The bold Sir Belvedere uplifted him,
Sir Belvedere, the last of all the knights,
And bore him to a chapel nigh the field,
A broken chancel with a broken cross,
That stood on a dark strait of barren land.

Morte d'Arthur.

See **W. E. Aytoun**—*La Mort d'Arthur*, p. 156.

VIII

THE rain had fallen, the Poet arose,
   He passed by the town and out of the street,
A light wind blew from the gates of the sun,
   And waves of shadow went over the wheat.

The Poet's Song.

See **R. F. Murray**—*The Poet's Hat.*

IX

HE clasps the crag with crooked hands;
Close to the sun in lonely lands,
Ring'd with the azure world, he stands.

The wrinkled sea beneath him crawls,
He watches from his mountain walls,
And like a thunderbolt he falls.

The Eagle.

See *Shotover Papers*—*Horae Tennysonianae*, p. 264.

APPENDIX

x

In her ear he whispers gaily,
  "If my heart by signs can tell,
Maiden, I have watch'd thee daily,
  And I think thou lov'st me well."

The Lord of Burleigh.

See F. Locker-Lampson—*The Unfortunate Miss Bailey*, p. 251.

W. M. THACKERAY

1811–1863

Know ye the willow tree
  Whose grey leaves quiver,
Whispering gloomily
  To yon pale river?
Lady, at even-tide
  Wander not near it,
They say its branches hide
  A sad lost spirit.

Once to the willow tree
  A maid came fearful,
Pale seemed her cheek to be,
  Her blue eye tearful;
Soon as she saw the tree
  Her step moved fleeter,
No one was there,—ah me!
  No one to meet her.

   .   .   .

Shrill blew the morning breeze
  Biting and cold,
Bleak peers the grey dawn
  Over the wold;
Bleak over moor and stream

415

APPENDIX

Looks the grey dawn,
Grey, with dishevelled hair,
Still stands the willow tree—
THE MAID IS GONE !

Domine, Domine !
Sing we a litany,
Sing for poor maiden hearts broken and weary ;
Domine, Domine !
Sing we a litany,
Wail we and weep we a wild Miserere !

See **W. M.** Thackeray—*The Willow Tree*, p. 288.

The whole original poem has been given to show how the author has aimed at a parody of the sense of the original, and has allowed the metre to suggest rather than imitate the original.

MARTIN FARQUHAR TUPPER

1810–1889

A MINDFUL man, but hearted like a child
Lived near my dwelling ; he was frank and glad,
(Tho' some deep sorrows might have made him sad.)
But, to say sooth, his cheerfulness beguil'd
The way of life so well that trouble's power
Was half unheeded, like a passing shower,
For he did good, with all the good he had :
Still as he went he sang, hoping the best,
And restless energy claimed every hour,
And with a buoyant spirit he was blest :
And Independence, and outspoken Truth,
And courage, ev'n alone to stand and fight,
Had lived and moved in him from earliest Youth
With purity, and zeal, and love of light.

Three Hundred Sonnets.

See Shirley Brooks—*Sonnet CCCI*, p. 181.

416

APPENDIX

WILLIAM WATSON

WITH stormy joy, from height on height
  The thundering torrents leap,
The mountain tops, with still delight
  Their great inaction keep.

They and We.

See Horatio Smith—*They and We*, p. 388.

ARAB, Egyptian, English—by the sword
Cloven or pierced with spears, or bullet-mown—
In equal fate they sleep ; their dust is grown
A portion of the fiery sands abhorred. . . .

Gordon.

See Anthony C. Deane—*Three Blind Mice*, p. 325.

ISAAC WATTS

1674–1748

I

How doth the little busy bee
  Improve each shining hour,
And gather honey all the day
  From every opening flower !

Song xx.

See Lewis Carroll—*How Doth the Little Crocodile*, p. 198.

II

'TIS the voice of the sluggard ; I heard him complain,
" You have waked me too soon, I must slumber again."

The Sluggard.

See Lewis Carroll—*'Tis the Voice of the Lobster*, p. 198.

APPENDIX

WALT WHITMAN

1819–1892

I THINK I could turn and live with animals, they are so placid and
  self-contained ;
I stand and look at them sometimes half the day long.
They do not sweat and whine about their condition ;
They do not lie awake in the dark and weep for their sins ;

. . . . .

Not one is respectable or industrious over the whole earth.

The Brutes.

See A. T. Quiller-Couch—*Behold ! I am not one of those that goes to
Lectures,* p. 363.

JOHN GREENLEAF WHITTIER

1807–1892

MAUD MÜLLER, on a summer's day,
Raked the meadow sweet with hay.

Beneath her torn hat glowed the wealth
Of simple beauty and rustic health.

Singing, she wrought, and her merry glee
The mock-bird echoed from his tree.

See Bret Harte—*Mrs. Judge Jenkins,* p. 170.

GEORGE WITHER

1588–1667

SHALL I, wasting in despair,
Die because a woman's fair !
Or my cheeks make pale with care
'Cause another's rosy are ?

APPENDIX

Be she fairer than the day
Or the flowery meads in May—
If she be not so to me
What care I how fair she be ?

The Manly Heart.

See Ben Jonson—*Answer to Mr. Wither's song, " Shall I, wasting
in despair ? "* p. 53.
Also Walter Raleigh—*Another answer to Wither,* p. 89.

WILLIAM WORDSWORTH

1770–1850

I

There's something in a flying horse,
There's something in a huge balloon ;
But through the clouds I'll never float
Until I have a little Boat,
Shaped like the crescent-moon.

Peter Bell.

See John Hamilton Reynolds—*Peter Bell,* p. 101.
Also Percy Bysshe Shelley—*Peter Bell the Third,* p. 143.
Also Thomas Hood (the Elder)—*Ode to Mr. Graham,* p. 44.
Also Mary Kendall—*Education's Martyr,* p. 331.

II

Milton ! thou should'st be living at this hour :
England hath need of thee : she is a fen
Of stagnant waters : altar, sword, and pen,
Fireside, the heroic wealth of hall and bower,

Have forfeited their ancient English dower
Of inward happiness.   We are selfish men :
Oh ! raise us up, return to us again ;
And give us manners, virtue, freedom, power.

Thy soul was like a Star, and dwelt apart :
Thou hadst a voice whose sound was like the sea,
Pure as the naked heavens, majestic, free ;

419

APPENDIX

So didst thou travel on life's common way
In cheerful godliness ; and yet thy heart
The lowliest duties on herself did lay.

See E. B. V. Christian—*Thornton, thou shouldst be playing at this hour*, p. 318.

III

Two Voices are there ; one is of the Sea,
One of the Mountains ; each a mighty voice :
In both from age to age thou didst rejoice,
They were thy chosen music, Liberty !

There came a tyrant, and with holy glee
Thou fought'st against him,—but hast vainly striven :
Thou from thy Alpine holds at length art driven,
Where not a torrent murmurs heard by thee.

—Of one deep bliss thine ear hath been bereft ;
Then cleave, O cleave to that which still is left—
For, high-soul'd Maid, what sorrow would it be

That Mountain floods should thunder as before,
And Ocean bellow from his rocky shore,
And neither awful Voice be heard by Thee !

England and Switzerland, 1802.
See J. K. Stephen—*A Sonnet*, p. 266.

IV

. . . . A simple Child
That lightly draws its breath,
And feels its life in every limb,
What should it know of Death ?

I met a little Cottage Girl :
She was eight years old she said ;
Her hair was thick with many a curl
That clustered round her head.

We are Seven.

See Henry S. Leigh—*Only Seven*, p. 228.

APPENDIX

V

SHE dwelt among the untrodden ways
    Beside the springs of Dove ;
A maid whom there were none to praise,
    And very few to love.

Lucy II.

See Anonymous—*Goosey.*
See Phoebe Cary—*Jacob*, p. 207.

VI

THE Cock is crowing,
The stream is flowing,
The small birds twitter,
The lake doth glitter,
The green field sleeps in the sun ;
The oldest and youngest
Are at work with the strongest ;
The cattle are grazing,
Their heads never raising ;
There are forty feeding like one !

*Written in March while resting on the bridge at the
foot of Brother's Water.*

See John Keats—*On Oxford*, p. 57.

VII

A SLUMBER did my spirit seal ;
    I had no human fears :
She seem'd a thing that could not feel
    The touch of earthly years.

No motion has she now, no force ;
    She neither hears nor sees ;
Roll'd round in earth's diurnal course
    With rocks, and stones, and trees.

Lucy V.

See Phoebe Cary—*The Wife*, p. 208.

APPENDIX

Scorn not the Sonnet ; Critic, you have frowned,
Mindless of its just honours ; with this key
Shakespeare unlocked his heart ; the melody
Of this small lute gave ease to Petrarch's wound ;
A thousand times this pipe did Tasso sound ;
With it Camöens soothed an exile's grief ;
The Sonnet glittered a gay myrtle leaf
Amid the cypress with which Dante crowned
His visionary brow ; a glow-worm lamp,
It cheered mild Spenser, called from Faery-land,
To struggle through dark ways ; and, when a damp
Fell round the path of Milton, in his hand
The Thing became a trumpet, whence he blew
Soul-animating strains—alas, too few !

See E. B. V. Christian—*Scorn not the Cricket-Sonnet,* p. 319.

SONG

I'M afloat ! I'm afloat ! on the fierce rolling tide—
The ocean's my home, and my bark is my bride ;
Up, up, with my flag, let it wave o'er the sea—
I'm afloat ! I'm afloat ! and the Rover is free !
I fear not the monarch, I heed not the law—
I've a compass to steer by, a dagger to draw ;
And ne'er as a coward or slave will I kneel,
While my guns carry shot or my belt bears a steel !
Quick, quick, trim her sails, let the sheets kiss the wind,
And I'll warrant we'll soon leave the sea-gulls behind !
Up, up, with my flag, let it wave o'er the sea—
I'm afloat ! I'm afloat ! and the Rover is free !

See Robert B. Brough—*I'm a Shrimp,* p. 167.